FORGOTTEN WORLDS

"From China's incongruous Caucasian mummies and Egypt's Great Sphinx to a lost Germanic civilization and extraterrestrial influences, *Forgotten Worlds* presents a panoramic view of Atlantis, as broad as it is comprehensive. As such, Patrick Chouinard offers us previously unconsidered, even startling possibilities for Plato's perennial kingdom."

FRANK JOSEPH,
AUTHOR OF *ATLANTIS AND 2012* AND
ADVANCED CIVILIZATIONS OF PREHISTORIC AMERICA

FORGOTTEN WORLDS

From Atlantis to the X-Woman of Siberia and the Hobbits of Flores

PATRICK CHOUINARD

Bear & Company

Rochester, Vermont • Toronto, Canada

Bear & Company
One Park Street
Rochester, Vermont 05767
www.BearandCompanyBooks.com

Text stock is SFI certified

Bear & Company is a division of Inner Traditions International

Library of Congress Cataloging-in-Publication Data

Chouinard, Patrick.
   Forgotten worlds : from Atlantis to the X-woman of Siberia and the hobbits of
flores / Patrick Chouinard.
      p. cm.
   Summary: "An examination of the mythological, historical, and archaeological
evidence for lost civilizations throughout the world"—Provided by publisher.
   Includes bibliographical references and index.
   ISBN 978-1-59143-138-1 — ISBN 978-1-59143-892-2 (e-book)
   1. Civilization, Ancient. 2. Extinct cities. 3. Lost continents. 4. Antiquities. 5.
Geographical myths. 6. Atlantis (Legendary place) 7. Curiosities and wonders. I.
Title.
   CB311.C546 2012
   930—dc23
                                                                2011052438

Printed and bound in the United States by Lake Book Manufacturing, Inc.
The text paper is SFI certified. The Sustainable Forestry Initiative® program
promotes sustainable forest management.

10 9 8 7 6 5 4 3 2 1

Text design and layout by Jack Nichols
This book was typeset in Garamond Premier Pro with Gill Sans and Tiepolo used
as display typefaces.

To send correspondence to the author of this book, mail a first-class letter to the
author c/o Inner Traditions • Bear & Company, One Park Street, Rochester, VT
05767, and we will forward the communication.

This book is dedicated to the memory of my mother,

Nancy Jo Chouinard.

I miss you, Mom . . .

Contents

Foreword

ROBERT M. SCHOCH, PH.D.

Patrick Chouinard's book *Forgotten Worlds* is about Atlantis. Or to put it more explicitly, it is about the search not just for the physical location of Atlantis, but also for the meaning of Atlantis. Why another book on Atlantis? Because the very concept of Atlantis is so rich and complex that, despite the extensive literature on the topic, the subject begs for more insight, more analysis, and Chouinard has been studying Atlantology for more than two decades. Ever since Plato's account of Atlantis was written in the fourth century BCE, the topic has continually expanded. It has been interpreted and reinterpreted, again and again, to cover virtually anything and everything related to our predecessors and possible progenitors that is deemed poorly understood yet very ancient, very mysterious, and apparently very advanced (whether technologically advanced or psychomentally advanced, applying a variation of the term utilized by the great Russian ethnographer S. M. Shirokogoroff to describe this important, but often overlooked, aspect of culture).

Atlantis has become a catchall for the idea of a lost legacy from the very distant past, an advanced society that existed thousands of years before civilized life as conventionally understood is supposed to have first arisen. According to mainstream archaeologists and historians, the origins of civilization date back a mere five thousand to six thousand years, but by Plato's estimation Atlantis was catastrophically destroyed about 11,600 years ago. That is, the destruction of Atlantis coincides more or less with the end of the last ice age as understood by modern geologists. For many authors and Atlantologists, Atlantis represents the primordial high civilization, a culture that may have been global in extent, a society that sowed the seeds of all later civilizations. It is also possible that more than one "Atlantis" existed, or as Chouinard aptly refers to them, more than one "forgotten world" existed. Besides Atlantis per se, we have the related ideas of Lemuria, Mu, and Eden (to name just a few about which you will read in *Forgotten Worlds*).

Where was Atlantis located, in time and in space? This is a central question posed by Atlantologists and extensively explored in Chouinard's book. Perhaps not surprisingly, one researcher or another has placed Atlantis in virtually every imaginable location on Earth, from one pole to the other, on every continent, and in every sea and ocean. But the speculation is not bounded by the physical confines of our planet! Perhaps Atlantis was actually a UFO, and the Atlanteans were representatives of a population of technologically sophisticated extraterrestrial organisms who visited planet Earth in the distant past and jump-started, if you will, human civilization. Maybe Atlantis was located on Mars. Or could it be found on a planet other than Earth or Mars, perhaps even in a different solar system or galaxy? Or was Atlantis not a physical place at all? Could it be a state of mind, represented by a race of beings with far greater mental abilities—perhaps full-fledged psychic powers—that allow them to dispense with the technological trappings that are generally seen as the hallmarks of the "progress" and "advanced civilization" of the present day?

What about the temporal placement of Atlantis? Many Atlantologists begin with the assumption, based on Plato's account, that Atlantis existed around twelve thousand years ago, give or take a few millennia. However, some Atlantologists (generally those with a classical archaeological training and a "conventional" academic stance) equate Atlantis with the destruction of Minoan Crete by the eruption of a volcano on the island of Thera (also known as Santorini) a mere 3,500 or so years ago. Others of the mainstream school have linked Atlantis with the Corinthian city-state of Helike, destroyed by an earthquake during Plato's lifetime. On the opposite end of the temporal spectrum are those who contend that the Atlanteans were the Neanderthals or other prehistoric peoples dating back tens of thousands of years, or perhaps even a hundred thousand years or more. The diversity of opinion on Atlantis could not be greater—thus the never-ending need for further exploration of this most pivotal subject.

Although I was familiar with Plato's account of Atlantis as early as my late preteens, when I first read it in translation, it was decades before I came to consider the story seriously. I was personally forced to confront Atlantis in 1990 when I began my work on redating the Great Sphinx of Egypt (which is reviewed in *Forgotten Worlds;* see also my books *Voyages of the Pyramid Builders,* 2003, and *Pyramid Quest,* 2005). Based on my analysis of the geological data, I concluded that the oldest portions of the Great Sphinx originated thousands of years earlier than the 2500 BCE date generally accepted for the statue by modern classical Egyptologists and historians. Indeed, the Great Sphinx is a relic from a time thousands of years prior to the widely recognized advent of civilization. I suddenly found myself in the thick of the debate over Atlantis.

As a trained academic, having earned my doctorate in geology and geophysics from Yale University, I initially wanted nothing to do with Atlantis. The concept of Atlantis smacked of "New Age woo-woo," channeling and other psychic nonsense, pseudoscience, and pseudohistory. Atlantis, in my opinion at that time, was not something that a respectable scholar took seriously. Indeed, I was so concerned over the possibility that I might be associated with the "pyramidiots" who plague the study of ancient Egypt (many of the pyramidiots link the Egyptian pyramids to the survivors of the destruction of Atlantis), for a couple of years I refused to even utter or write the word *Atlantis.* Instead, in casual conversation I simply referred to the "A-word." Since then I have had a change of heart, or some might say I have "seen the light." I came to consider Atlantis (at least at some level) a topic worthy of serious research. Indeed, by the late 1990s I was actively writing about Atlantis (see the chapter titled "Looking for the Lost Cities" in my book *Voices of the Rocks,* 1999), adding my own speculations to the voluminous literature.

I am still not sure about the when, where, and what of Atlantis. I am convinced, however, that within the Atlantis myth are incorporated ancient and enduring mysteries in the deepest and most profound sense, as well as reflections of us in the modern age and clues about what the future may hold. Thus it is with good reason that the inquiry continues. I encourage you, the reader, to join the search for "forgotten worlds." From the fantastical and far-fetched to the fruitful if perhaps speculative, it is an enticing quest that, before you know it, may just draw you in to the ranks of the full-fledged Atlantologists.

ROBERT M. SCHOCH, PH.D., has been a full-time faculty member at the College of General Studies at Boston University since 1984. In 1983 he earned his Ph.D. in geology and geophysics at Yale University. Robert Schoch is the author or coauthor of both technical and popular books, including the trilogy with R. A. McNally of *Voices of the Rocks: A Scientist Looks at Catastrophes and Ancient Civilizations* (1999), *Voyages of the Pyramid Builders: The True Origins of the Pyramids from Lost Egypt to Ancient America* (2003), and *Pyramid Quest: Secrets of the Great Pyramid and the Dawn of Civilization* (2005). He is also the author of *Forgotten Civilization: The Role of Solar Outbursts in Our Past and Future* and *The Parapsychology Revolution: A Concise Anthology of Paranormal and Psychical Research.* His works have been translated into numerous languages and distributed around the world.

Acknowledgments

Special thanks to Robert Schoch for introducing me to the fascinating community of alternative scholars and independent researchers, and for always inspiring and encouraging me, no matter what. I would also like to dedicate this book to the memory of Jake Walsh, forever devoted to the movement; to Frank Joseph for grooming me and helping me get this book published; and to Wayne May for believing in my ability as a writer and being the first, together with Frank, to recognize my talents and publish my early works. I am pleased that I had the opportunity to work closely with Mike Capps, my business associate and webmaster. His talents are of vital importance to me and the movement. I would like to extend special acknowledgment to the late Pat Lambert. She was my high school instructor in the late 1980s and an ongoing supporter. She will be missed. Also, thanks to Sister Mary Louis, Sister Dola Rita, and Sister Rose Marie for their love and support when I was a troubled six-year-old. Thanks to my friends Bradley Eugene Mastry, Linda Mastry, Timothy Balogh, Michael Lynch, Catherine Quindiagan, and Robert L. Smith for being there for me. I would also like to express my gratitude to my special friend Debbie, whose support is limitless.

TIME LINE OF PIVOTAL EVENTS DISCUSSED IN THIS BOOK

6 billion BCE	The solar system is born
650 million BCE	The Huronian Glaciation, the worldwide ice age, reaches its zenith
530 million BCE	The Cambrian Explosion
65 million BCE	A massive asteroid impacts Earth, ending the reign of dinosaurs
3.7 million BCE	Upright walking hominids evolve in the Caucasus
900,000 BCE	First northern Europeans evolve
58,000 BCE	Anomalous artifacts dating to this time found in Colorado suggest very early habitation of the New World
50,000 BCE	The time of Ra; the Osirian Empire emerges; Neanderthals and the X-Woman become extinct; hobbits evolve on Flores Island, Indonesia
27,000 BCE	Tiahuanaco is constructed (according to Edmund Kiss)
16,000 BCE	The Jomon rule Japan
12,000 BCE	Göbekli Tepe is under construction
9600 BCE	Construction on Göbekli Tepe ceases and Atlantis is destroyed; the Sphinx is built as a monument to Atlantis
8000 BCE	Yonaguni and Lemuria are submerged
3500 BCE	Post-cataclysmic Sumer emerges as the first civilization of the new age
3300 BCE	The Scorpion Inscription, the earliest hieroglyphics, are first used
2055 BCE	The Egyptian Middle Kingdom is formed
1900 BCE	Possible reign of Cecrops I
373 BCE	The lost civilization of Helike is destroyed by a tsunami
712 CE	The Konjiki, a Japanese epic, is composed
1882	Percival Lowell observes canals on Mars
1898	*War of the Worlds* is published
1976	The Face on Mars is discovered

Beyond History—Understanding the New Time Line

It has long been assumed that civilization began no earlier than around 3500 BCE along the banks of the Tigris and Euphrates Rivers in what is now present-day Iraq. It was here, and only here, so the official story goes, that the world witnessed the first stirrings of urbanism, an invention that could be called the granite foundation of civilization. The area's inhabitants also developed a complex social infrastructure and a written language. Through diffusion this primal civilization spread throughout Eurasia, only to be surpassed thousands of years later by the cultures it had nurtured. For most of archaeology's brief history, this has been the prevailing model of human social development.

However, since the early 1990s numerous discoveries have expanded our knowledge of the past, prompting new definitions of what it means to be human. By the turn of the twenty-first century hundreds of books and articles supporting the notion of a once noble race raising humankind through its infancy and into evolutionary adulthood had been published. Among them is an account of the Great Library of Alexandria in Egypt, an edifice of the ancient world that knows no equal. Built by the Ptolemaic dynasty in the third century BCE, it remained a major center of investigation and learning for six centuries, until a Christian mob burned it to the ground in the third century CE. Hidden within its burned-out ruins were fragments of an old card catalog. One of the charred papyrus scrolls made mention of a book written by the Babylonian priest Berossus. The title of this lost book was *The True History of Mankind over the Last 100,000 Years*.

The discovery of this ancient manuscript, or at least the record of it, hinted at a fascinating possibility (Childress 1995, pp. 1–6). Berossus estimated the time between the creation of the world and the great flood at 432,000 years, more than two hundred times longer than the Old Testament account. Frustratingly enough, we will never know all the secrets contained in Berossus's lost history (Sagan 1980, p. 20). However, the very existence of such an ancient document compels modern scholars to re-examine the true origins and age of humanity. Ultimately, Berossus's rediscovered history implies that human civilization could be far older than previously believed.

This idea of immense human antiquity is consistent with some of the traditional or mythological accounts of a past human civilization. Such narratives are abundant in the various Sanskrit texts of India. These texts describe a lost culture known as the Rama Empire, featuring the Seven Rishi Cities, a system of ancient metropolises to which Harappa, a city associated with the Indus Valley Civilization, belonged.

Many myths and legends describe a time when Earth was ruled by the gods, not only the Hindu Rama but also the Egyptian Osiris and the Greek Poseidon. In Egypt the legends say the gods eventually delegated their duties to another race, known as the "Companions of Horus." It was said that the later rulers and pharaohs of Egypt drew their strength from this race of benefactors. Similarly, the Australian and Native American peoples had visions of a glorious past under the stewardship of powerful beings. Yet these are but a few of hundreds of traditional accounts from cultures all across the globe that speak of a lost civilization that existed eleven thousand to thirteen thousand years ago, which was destroyed in a flood or some other major cataclysm. Perhaps foremost among these are accounts of the lost civilization of Atlantis.

Numerous theories are dedicated to Atlantis. The author and explorer David Hatcher Childress correctly observes that more books have been written about Atlantis than any other subject (Clotworthy 2011). This Atlantean theme resonates with a larger audience today than ever before. It seems to strike some primal chord deep within our psyche. We know that we came from somewhere else.

The popularity of Atlantis is largely due to the writings of the Greek philosopher Plato. In two of his famous dialogues, the *Timaeus* and the *Critias,* he describes its culture and geography, its military exploits, and its relations with foreign powers. Finally, he concludes his account with the destruction of Atlantis in 9600 BCE.

There were those, even in ancient times, who questioned the validity of Plato's claims. His gifted pupil Aristotle doubted his teacher's sincerity regarding the account. He wrote that he had never heard any mention of Atlantis prior to its appearance in Plato's dialogues. Aristotle was highly regarded; the Roman natural philosopher Pliny referred to him as "a man of supreme eminence in every branch of science" (King 2005, p. 108). His status among ancient scholars makes him a valuable witness.

After the time of Plato, however, one finds many ancient accounts describing either Atlantis or an Atlantis-like civilization, including works by Plutarch, Diodorus of Sicily, Theopompus, and even the first-century Romanized Jewish historian Josephus. Furthermore, a notation on maps of Antillia that were originally sketched by the fifteenth-century cartographer Andrea Biancaa show what appears to be a continent in the Atlantic more than a decade before Columbus was even born (Jueneman 1987).

Had Atlantis been solely the brainchild of Plato, where then do all these other stories come from? Some may be attributable to a phenomenon first popularized in the early twentieth century—that of the Jungian archetypes, the idea of certain symbols or myths common to all cultures, that are part of a universal subconscious. This could provide a logical explanation and exclude a literal interpretation of the various stories about Atlantis. However, the mythological evidence for Atlantis is overwhelming, and most mythology bears a kernel of truth. Even if Atlantis is never found, 2,500 years of speculation and theory have provided a rich mythological backdrop for future discoveries.

Recent research indicates the presence around the globe of long-forgotten cultures and unusual genetic populations. These discoveries may help us understand the human race in an entirely different light. In recent years, for instance, Central Asia has established its importance as a site of early humanity. Many of the previously recognized advances, such as the wheel and horseback riding, which were originally attributed to the Hittites and other Near Eastern and Mediterranean cultures, have taken a backseat on the techno-evolutionary time line. Now it seems possible that ancient nomads who once thrived in what is now known as the Russian Stans together formed the wellspring of civilization.

Exploration of the Indian subcontinent has raised the possibility of sunken cities and flooded land bridges. From this research a new chronology for the emergence of human life and civilization may unfold, as well as new mechanisms for understanding how and why societies and species change over time. Great mother cities, such as those found near Caral in Peru, and anomalous finds in North America hint at very ancient settlements in the New World, some 58,000 to 48,000 BCE. We also now know that Stone Age peoples, once thought to be uncivilized brutes, apparently had a working knowledge of astronomy.

In *Technologies of the Gods,* a video produced by Atlantis Rising, David Hatcher Childress points out that mainstream science has a very linear interpretation of human development, viewing evolution as a straight and narrow path from our most primitive apelike ancestors to modern humans. According to this view, technology advanced far enough to warrant the birth of civilization in only the past six thousand years, and we are now at our most advanced and perfected state. But Childress and others maintain that history is a roller coaster. It is a series of peaks and valleys punctuated by periods of immense growth and technological development, as well as dark ages of very low technology and relative barbarism. That each culture remains unaware that another civilization preceded it is due to a phenomenon Graham Hancock calls "racial amnesia." The conclusion is that twenty-nine thousand years ago, technology, rather than being highly primitive, was actually more advanced than it is today.

In 1993 Michael A. Cremo and Richard L. Thompson published a 914-page alternative science book titled *Forbidden Archaeology.* It was the first of three books attempting to explain human prehistory from a Hindu creationist perspective. The novelty of this viewpoint is readily apparent. Until *Forbidden Archaeology,* the battlefield was divided between mainstream science and Christian fundamentalists. This book offered a third alternative: not just apologetics and logic arguments but genuine physical evidence that university academics could not deny.

Initially, Cremo says, he and his coauthor thought it would take just a few months of research and the book would be finished. They didn't anticipate that this minor project would grow into an endeavor that would take well over four years to complete. They discovered an entirely different story from what is contained in the works of many mainstream scientists and anthropologists, and they provided a wealth of evidence in favor of a greater antiquity for the human race. Among the well-documented examples are fully modern human skeletons dating back some 320 million to 280 million years (Cremo and Thompson 1993, pp. 267–79). Since the publication of *Forbidden Archaeology,* even more staggering discoveries have come to light. These include the remains of a metal vase dating back 600 million years, which was discovered in the Tyrolian Alps, and a metallic grooved sphere recovered from Ottosdal, South Africa, with an age of 2,800 million years, dating to the Precambrian Era (Gallegos 2009, p. 9).

Forbidden Archaeology claims, contrary to the teachings of modern education, that humankind did not evolve from more primitive apelike forms but rather coexisted with them. The book is rather ambiguous when referring to how humans became the intelligent and creative creatures they are today. But what is certain is that there is an alternative that neither Darwin nor the Christian Bible considered. The much awaited sequel to *Forbidden Archaeology,* a book titled *Human Devolution: A Vedic Alternative to Darwin's Theory,* proposes that each life-form, including every human, begins as a high spiritual force, and rather than evolving into increasingly advanced physical forms, the individual devolves into flesh and base matter. Thus, instead of evolving upward from the ape, we have devolved into our current physical state through a process of downward progression. At the core we are still those same illuminated beings who once radiated throughout the cosmos. We still have the same potential to work for good rather than evil. This is a very metaphysical interpretation for humankind, and at the same time a very traditional Hindu outlook.

Carl Sagan was without question one of the world's greatest doubters. To him, science provided the answers and meanings of existence, which conventional religion simply could not supply. But the Hindu religion caught his eye because of its compatibility with what mainstream science had proclaimed concerning the creation, age, and eventual end times of the universe. Sagan writes:

The Hindu religion is the only one of the world's great faiths dedicated to the idea that the Cosmos itself undergoes an immense, indeed an infinite, number of deaths and rebirths. It is the only religion in which time scales correspond to those of modern scientific cosmology. Its cycles run from our ordinary day and night to a day and night of Brahma, 8.64 billion years long, longer than the age of the Earth or the Sun and about half the time since the Big Bang. And there are much longer time scales still. (1980, p. 258)

Sagan goes on to explain:

There is the deep and appealing notion that the universe is but the dream of the god who, after a hundred Brahma years, dissolves himself into a dreamless sleep. The universe dissolves with him—until, after another Brahma century, he stirs, recomposes himself and begins again to dream the great cosmic dream. Meanwhile, elsewhere, there are an infinite number of other universes, each with its own god dreaming the cosmic dream. These great ideas are tempered by another, perhaps still greater. It is said that men may not be the dreams of the gods, but rather that the gods are the dreams of men. (p. 258)

The Hindu faith provides an ideal starting point in our search to better understand the ancient past and decode its mystical secrets. Unlike the simplistic Judeo-Christian and Muslim cosmologies, Hinduism allows no room for a simple morality play or the exaltation of a single solar deity. Rather, it offers a direct connection to the infinite and the eternal. It provides wisdom in ways no Catholic priest or Jewish rabbi ever could, unlocking the forbidden truth of the new cosmology.

Early in this century, Graham Hancock, Robert Bauval, and John Anthony West developed a series of fascinating new chronologies in which they theorized that a sophisticated maritime civilization thrived on the coastal regions of the world during the last ice age. According to an underground author and publisher of an alternative website, "This so-called Ice Age civilization may have been more advanced, especially in social structure and relations with higher intellectual/spiritual levels, than any later civilization including our present."

Graham Hancock—truly a fascinating individual whose theories deserve full explanation—believes that the ancient story of Atlantis and other sunken civilizations is a last vestige of a primordial memory of a now extinct supercivilization that reached the height of its glory approximately 10,000 BCE. For him the lost civilization was not confined to a single part of the Atlantic, nor merely the Egyptian and Greek worlds. It applied to a global network of cultures and civilizations that was wiped out by a final cataclysm at the end of the last ice age. During the ice age a massive drop in sea level occurred as the polar regions as well as much of the northern seas became locked in massive glaciers. This exposed enormous tracts of land that were later submerged when the ice melted and sea levels rose. One of the most famous of these sunken landmasses is Beringia, the land bridge between Asia and North America that, supposedly, was the path taken by the first Paleo-Indians.

To buttress his argument about the existence of these ancient civilizations, Hancock introduces a variety of well-reasoned theories and out-of-place artifacts that he believes offer compelling evidence to support his position. The first and foremost among these items is the Piri Reis map. In 1929, during work aimed at transforming the Topkapi Palace in Istanbul into a historical museum, a fragment of a sixteenth-century map was discovered. It had been drawn by a Turkish sailor named Hadji Muhiddin Piri Ibn Hadji. Fanatically loyal and battle-hardened, he was given the title of reis, or admiral, for his dedication and service to the Ottoman Empire (but even this distinction could not spare him the shame of execution for treason at the age of ninety) (Levy 2007, pp. 114–17).

Piri's notes explain that his map was based on a number of preexisting maps (including those belonging to previous voyages), a variety of Ptolemaic maps, and some Portuguese charts outlining what were then some of the most recent discoveries in the New World. The Piri Reis map features what appears to be an imaginary southern continent, which it identifies as Terra Australis Incognito, though some experts have maintained that it is merely the coast of Patagonia and Tierra del Fuego, oriented to run west–east rather than north–south (Levy 2007, pp. 114–15).

Hancock and American academic Charles Hapgood strongly disagree with those opinions. They believe that the map actually depicts part of the Antarctic coastline as it looks beneath the massive ice sheet that today completely envelops its surface. Hapgood maintains that in recent geologic time Antarctica was situated in a temperate or tropical zone, and then crustal displacement shifted it into its current position—an idea that Albert Einstein openly supported and considered quite logical and scientific. According to Hapgood's theory, presented in his books *The Earth's Shifting Crust* (1958) and *Path of the Pole* (1970), Earth's thin crust occasionally shifts or slips on the molten mantle beneath it. While there were many earlier prototypes of the theory of Earth crust displacement (ECD), Hapgood remains the pioneering theorist.

Strangely enough, the Piri Reis map perfectly matches twentieth-century maps showing the subglacial appearance of the Antarctic. How is it possible that a sixteenth-century cartographer was able to obtain such detailed information about a continent that wasn't even discovered until the nineteenth century, and even more, to depict features of the coastline that were only revealed by advanced mapping technology of the twentieth century (Levy 2007, p. 115)? To Hancock and others this seems to be fairly convincing evidence in support of Hapgood's theories, with the implication being that the Piri Reis map was based on earlier maps from a time when the southern continent was free of ice.

But that was several million years ago. Or was it? Crustal displacement could have caused the continents to shift their position abruptly, condemning the lost civilization of Hancock's vision to extinction in 9600 BCE. Quite possibly this map is also a portent of future events as we approach December 21, 2012. (We might have some extra time, however, since a slight miscalculation in the Mayan calendar has been found that might suggest that the true date of the end of our current age and the birth of the new one is December 21, 2050.)

In the final chapter of *Maps of the Ancient Sea Kings,* Charles Hapgood writes:

> The evidence presented by the ancient maps appears to suggest the existence in remote times, before the rise of any of the known cultures, of a true civilization, of a comparatively advanced sort, which either was localized in one area but had worldwide commerce, or was, in a real sense, a worldwide culture. This culture, at least in some respects, may well have been more advanced than the civilizations of Egypt, Babylonia, Greece, and Rome. (1979, p. 10)

It is the thesis of my book that a number of protocivilizations existed prior to 3200 BCE, perhaps between 10,000 and 4500 BCE. These early cultures then influenced and inspired emerging Stone Age societies. Those already at a Neolithic stage of evolution then adopted the ideas and basic technologies of the more advanced cultures. This may be how the first historical civilizations emerged. Hapgood touches upon this idea as well:

> The idea of the simple linear development of society from the culture of the Paleolithic (Old Stone Age) through the successive changes must be given up. . . . We shall assume that, some 20,000 or more years ago, while Paleolithic peoples held out in Europe, more advanced cultures existed elsewhere on the earth, and we have inherited a part of what they once possessed, passed down from people to people. (p. 20)

It is likely that our primitive ancestors witnessed the eventual disintegration of these parent cultures. This may have been the event to which Plato and other writers of similar ancient accounts alluded. Such a group of civilizations could have met their demise at the end of the last ice age with a series of floods or as the result of a comet or asteroid impact. Today little of these lost civilizations remain. In *Hamlet's Mill,* Hertha von Dechend writes, "Gradually, we are told, step by step, men produced the arts and crafts, this and that, until they emerged into the light of history. Those soporific words 'gradually' and 'step by step,' repeated incessantly, are aimed at covering an ignorance which is both vast and surprising" (Magli 2009, p. 3).

As stated earlier, this ignorance is what Graham Hancock calls racial amnesia, a complete loss of the sum total of our history, technology, conventions, and faith. This total collapse of human knowledge and society is comparable with the fall of classical civilization and Europe's descent into the Dark Ages. As Carl Sagan notes, "It was as if the entire civilization had undergone some self-inflicted brain surgery, and most of its memories, discoveries, ideas and passions were extinguished irrevocably. The loss was incalculable" (1980, p. 336).

The greatest loss was the awareness of the existence of lost civilizations. But our own knowledge of those far-off times is growing. Slowly but surely, through the work of intrepid archaeologists, we are gaining a clearer notion of what came before. I invite you to join me in exploring an ancient world of vast dimensions, both in time and space.

In this book you will find a generous sampling of varied theories and discoveries, from artifacts to mummies to traces of written language, from all parts of the world. They expand our understanding from one cradle of civilization to many—in Europe and the Americas, Central Asia and the Middle East, mid-Pacific as well as mid-Atlantic, China and India, and even extraterrestrial—with previously unimaginable time lines. We will gain insights from the glimpses of history preserved in myth and learn more about the various theories regarding the global cataclysms, from deluge to impact, that may have caused the end of these civilizations, contributing to their status as "forgotten worlds."

The first thinkers of the modern age to be concerned with the rise and fall of lost civilizations and a greater antiquity for the human race were the late-nineteenth- and early-twentieth-century mavericks who dared to challenge what, by then, was already a firmly entrenched world paradigm.

Now it is up to us, their successors, to do the same.

1

The Children of Atlantis

In those days the Atlantic was navigable; and there was an island situated in front of the straits which you call the Columns of Heracles. . . . The island was larger than Libya and Asia put together, and was the way to other islands, from the islands you might pass through the whole of the opposite continent which surrounded the true ocean; for this sea which is within the Straits of Heracles is only a harbor, having a narrow entrance, but that other is a real sea, and the surrounding land may be most truly called a continent. Now, in the island of Atlantis there was a great and wonderful empire . . .

SOLON, QUOTED IN PLATO'S *TIMAEUS*,
APPROXIMATELY 360 BCE

THE MYTH AWAKENS

In 600 BCE, Plato's ancestor, the Athenian statesman Solon, visited Egypt and had the opportunity to engage in discourse with the Egyptian priesthood. It was there that he learned of a unique connection between their two countries, even rumors that Egypt originally seeded Greek civilization.

In the *Timaeus,* we read: "This city [Sais] was founded by a goddess whose name was 'Neith' in Egyptian (according to the people there), 'Athena' in Greek" (Jowett and Harward 1952, p. 443). According to Plato's account, Solon then challenged their knowledge of ancient history and brought up "Phoroneus—the first human being" and "told the story of how Deucalion and Pyrrha survived the flood" (Rosenberg 1982, p. 56).

Solon went on to trace the lines of descent of their posterity and tried to compute their dates by calculating the number of years that had elapsed since the events of which he spoke. Their response was quick: "Ah, Solon, Solon you Greeks are forever children. You don't even know your own history" (Jowett and Harward 1952, p. 447). The elder priest told Solon that the Athenians were ignorant of their once glorious past. He explained that there were past ages of such wonder that they could scarcely be imagined. Solon then accepted their invitation to be shown the ancient records that, they claimed, would tell him the secrets of a lost civilization, more ancient and mighty than the great Corinthian city-state Helike and powerful Troy combined. They brought Solon to a nearby temple. The priests then motioned him over to one of the stone columns and pointed to the ancient text preserved in hieroglyphic form. One of the priests read the words while the older one translated into Greek (Levy 2007, p. 26).

This was the original Egyptian story on which Plato's two dialogues, the *Timaeus* and the *Critias*, were based. This sacred knowledge was then passed on to Solon's cousin Dropides. Later, Plato heard the story from his great-grandfather Critias, who was a direct descendant of Dropides. Plato then copied them down from his memory of what his great-grandfather had described.

In the *Critias* we are given a detailed description of Atlantean society and a history of how it was founded. The dialogue further explains how Atlantis evolved into a near-perfect society, only to be eventually destroyed. Plato writes about the Egyptian priests' comments concerning the Greeks:

You are really young in mind; . . . you have no knowledge hoary with age. [But] our traditions here are the oldest. . . . In our temples we have preserved from earliest times a written record of any great or splendid achievement or notable event which has come to our ears, whether it occurred in your part of the world, or here, or anywhere else; whereas with you, and others, writing and the other necessities of civilization have only just been developed when the periodic scourge of the deluge descends, and spares none but the unlettered and uncultured, so that you have to begin again like children, in complete ignorance of what has happened in our part of the world or in yours in early times. (Jowett 1952)

The priest continues his narrative, now speaking of thousands of years in the past.

There was an island opposite the strait that you call the Pillars of Hercules, an island larger than Libya and Asia combined; from it travelers could in those days reach the other islands, and from them the whole opposite continent, which surrounds what can truly be called the ocean. On this island of Atlantis has arisen a powerful and remarkable dynasty of kings. . . . Their wealth was greater than that possessed by any previous dynasty, or provided with everything they could require. Because of the extent of their power they received many imports, but for most of their needs the island itself provided. It had mineral resources from which were mined both solid materials and metals, including one metal which survives today only in name, but was then mined in quantities in a number of localities in the island, orichalc, in those days the most valuable metal except gold. There was a plentiful supply of timber for structural purposes and every kind of animal domesticated and wild, among them numerous elephants. For there was plenty of grazing for this largest and most voracious of beasts, as well as for all creatures whose habitat is marsh, swamp and river, mountain or plain. Besides all this, the earth bore freely all of the aromatic substances it bears today. . . . There were cultivated crops. . . . There were the fruits of trees. . . . All these were produced by their sacred island, then still beneath the sun, in wonderful quality and profusion. (Hancock 1992, p. 320)

But this grandiose civilization would not last forever. Its successes had already planted the seeds of its decline and eventual demise. Just as famous is the account of its destruction. Plato's first dialogue, the *Timaeus,* presents a general description of Atlantis and outlines its rulers' plans to conquer the entire known world. The heroic Athenians thwarted this blatant attempt at aggression but they stood alone in so doing; the other world powers had abandoned them. The defeat of the Atlanteans foreshadowed the disaster to come—shortly thereafter the entire continent and all its inhabitants sank beneath the waves, never to return.

The climactic end to this lost civilization can be considered its most enduring legacy in that it inspired generations of well-traveled explorers and armchair theorists to rediscover the lost city of Atlantis, if only in their imagination.

IGNATIUS DONNELLY: A NEW PERSPECTIVE

Countless scribes over the centuries have further extrapolated from and modified Plato's original story, but no single author has left a more indelible mark on the ideal of ancient Atlantis than Ignatius T. T. Donnelly. Without question, he is the founder of modern Atlantology, and Atlantis enthusiasts turn to him time and again for inspiration and insight.

Donnelly was born on November 3, 1831, in Philadelphia. He considered himself a farmer-politician, but he became the lieutenant governor of Minnesota, then a state senator, and finally a U.S. congressman.

Eventually, he was nominated for vice president under the Populist ticket, but he died shortly before the beginning of the campaign (Jueneman 1987). His political career was dwarfed, however, by his impact on world culture as a result of his theories on ancient Atlantis. Donnelly's writings established the core beliefs of the Atlantis movement, and there would probably never have been a fight against the established paradigm had it not been for him.

Noted geologist and author Robert M. Schoch was correct when asserting that Donnelly speaks to us from a nineteenth-century universe, filled with outmoded arguments and antiquated racial beliefs. Nevertheless, in many regards Donnelly maintained a progressive intellect. His first novel, *Doctor Huguet,* was an appeal for racial tolerance, and his second, *Caesar's Columns,* was a cautionary tale that predicted the rise of twentieth-century totalitarian movements (Jueneman 1987).

Despite his feelings of loyalty to Plato, Donnelly introduced new ideas and interpretations of Atlantis and inadvertently remade Atlantis in his own image. He brought it into a modern mythological context. He has either directly or indirectly influenced everyone from Madame Blavatsky to Graham Hancock.

Donnelly published his theories in 1882 in a book titled *Atlantis: The Antediluvian World.* It has become the unofficial bible of Atlantis enthusiasts. Donnelly's influence actually surpasses that of Plato in that much of what we now associate with the name *Atlantis* actually can be attributed to Donnelly, not Plato. In his book, Donnelly writes: "There once existed in the Atlantic Ocean, opposite the mouth of the Mediterranean Sea, a large island, which was the remnant of an Atlantic continent, and known to the ancient world as Atlantis. . . . The description of this island given by Plato is not, as has been long supposed, a fable, but veritable history" (1882, p. 1).

Ignatius Donnelly reenergized the mythic traditions of the lost civilization of Atlantis and, in so doing, engendered controversy about his beliefs. He was aware of Darwin's theory of natural selection and how it applied to human beings. After the famous *Origin of Species by Means of Natural Selection* (1859), Darwin wrote *The Descent of Man, and Selection in Relation to Sex* (1871), which directly linked humankind to primitive apelike ancestors, probably originating on the African continent. Donnelly thought that humans began in an entirely savage state. Only later did humanity evolve into Plato's famous Atlanteans.

Donnelly also believed that Atlantis was the original location of the true Garden of Eden. From this small common nucleus our fertile species set forth and multiplied, extending its reach to every corner of the globe. The human race thus became the dominant species on planet Earth. One might contest the idea that Donnelly revived the notion of Atlantis as a real place, more so than even Plato himself. We must remember, though, that Plato insisted from the beginning that the story of Atlantis was a true one, and one that had been handed down by the Egyptians to the ears of Solon, his ancestor.

It was Donnelly's argument, on the other hand, that all ancient civilizations originally stemmed from Atlantis, that it was the source of advanced cultures the world over, with colonies among the Maya and ancient Egyptians, and even the Irish, Chinese, and Indians. Donnelly was an ardent proponent of euhemerism—that is, the belief that the characters and events found in ancient mythology have a real, historical basis (Levy 2007, p. 66). He also linked mythological, and quite often Atlantean, references to actual cultures and civilizations. As he states in the preface of *Atlantis: The Antediluvian World,* "The gods and goddesses of the ancient Greeks, the Phoenicians, the Hindus, and the Scandinavians were simply the kings, queens, and heroes of Atlantis; and the acts attributed to them in mythology are a confused recollection of real historical events" (Donnelly 1882, pp. 1–2).

Donnelly had his shortcomings, but he likely did not intend to provoke a clash of ideas with his writings. And in spite of his controversial outlook, he maintained an awesome pull on the proponents of Atlantis. He was confident that agriculture, metallurgy, pyramid building, writing, and mathematics all originated from one primordial source: Atlantis. Moreover, Donnelly believed that the notion of nature worship, as well as that of sun worship, so prevalent throughout ancient cultures, originated there. He also described a connecting plateau, or land bridge, that linked the three continents of North America, Atlantis, and Europe.

According to Donnelly, many of the world's most ancient cultures, such as the Phoenicians, harken back to the earliest days of Atlantis. In fact it is they, the Phoenicians, whom conventional theorists sometimes identify as the prototype of the Atlantean people. The Phoenicians spread trade and commerce throughout the Mediterranean and beyond the Pillars of Hercules, reaching straight across the Atlantic in search of copper and tin. Without question they could confirm any rumors of continents or landmasses in those regions, and much of what they said was astounding. They recounted the existence of several landmasses, perhaps the New World, while others remain more mysterious. It is obvious to us now that these islands no longer exist, at least not in the same form as originally described.

This bold era of adventure and discovery was systematically halted by the crushing blow issued against the Phoenicians by the victorious Romans in what was the third and final Punic War. This silenced the growing passion for exploration and dimmed any hopes at verifying the legends and possible origins of Atlantis. There would be no chance of recovering ancient artifacts or documenting native oral traditions for at least another millennium, if not longer (Jueneman 1987).

PLATO, THE WAR, AND
THE DESTRUCTION OF ATLANTIS

Let's now examine Plato's story of Atlantis in greater detail to determine the extent of its veracity. In the *Timaeus,* Plato's great-grandfather Critias describes the lost civilization's final death throes. As explained to Solon by the Egyptians, Atlantis attempted to subjugate the ancient Greeks of Athens. This, in time, would lead not only to the defeat of the Atlanteans but also to the eventual destruction of Atlantis itself. Plato writes:

> This vast power, gathered into one, endeavored to subdue at a blow our country and yours and the whole of the region within its straits; and then, Solon, your country shone forth, in the excellence of her virtue and strength, among all mankind. She was preeminent of courage and military skill, and was the leader of the Hellenes. And when the rest fell off from her, being compelled to stand alone, after having undergone the very extremity of danger, she defeated and triumphed over the invaders, and preserved from slavery those who were not yet subjugated, and generously liberated all the rest of us who dwell within the pillars. (Jowett and Harward 1952, pp. 445–46)

This final war between Atlantis and Athens, as described by the Egyptians, produced a cataclysmic aftermath: "Afterwards there occurred violent earthquakes and floods; and in a single day and night of misfortune all your warlike men sank into the earth, and the island of Atlantis in like manner disappeared in the depths of the sea" (Jowett and Harward 1952, pp. 445–46). Plato provided even more in-depth descriptions of how and why Atlantis was destroyed. He attributed it to the anger of Zeus, the king of the Olympian gods. In the *Critias* we read that the Atlanteans upheld a standard of virtue unequaled in the ancient world. To them material needs in excess of a basic minimum were no longer necessary. But, as with all great societies, such a noble attitude could not endure. The Atlanteans became "diluted too often and too much with the mortal admixture, and their human nature got the upper hand, they then, being unable to bear their fortune, behaved unseemly, and to him who had an eye to see, grew visibly debased" (p. 446).

PLATO'S ATLANTIS: WHOSE TRUTH?*

Plato did not invent the myth of Atlantis. He merely retold a story that had been reverberating through world culture since prehistory. The mythology of his fellow Greeks and of his European and Near Eastern neighbors had long told of a deluge sent by the gods that destroyed a lost civilization, with only a handful of scattered survivors, who then rebuilt the world in their own image. Such accounts are plentiful in Celtic and Teutonic mythology and also among the noncanonical texts of the Bible, such as the Book of Enoch. However, we must remember that although the idea of Atlantis as an Ur-civilization, or primordial homeland for the human race, was a popular theme in the ancient chronicles and texts, Plato himself never endorsed the idea, and his Atlantis was relegated to a simple morality tale.

Plato emphasized that Atlantis was contemporary with Egypt, Greece, and several unidentified countries in Asia. In addition to the war the Atlanteans fought with the Athenians, many wars were also fought between Atlantis and ancient Egypt, as well as other areas of Greece. To further this point, in the *Timaeus,* Plato tells us that the Atlanteans annexed enormous territories of Europe and North Africa. There is no indication, however, that the Atlanteans used this

---

*This next section regarding Atlantis chronology is adapted from a series of e-mail exchanges between me and Atlantologist Kenneth Caroli, a profoundly conservative and authoritative individual.

opportunity to civilize these conquered territories. Until the birth of the Roman Empire the concept of nation building, or introducing civilization where it did not previously exist, was virtually unknown. Furthermore, in almost every case, both conquered and conquerors were urban and literate, with the former often older than the latter (Caroli 2011, personal communication).

As Atlantologist Kenneth Caroli admits, analyzing Plato's account can be an exceedingly complex undertaking. The majority of classical scholars today accept the notion that the story of Atlantis was merely a well-conceived allegory. However, a certain minority of classicists accept Plato's account as being based on a model like Minoan Crete or Thera, or perhaps even the Corinthian city-state of Helike, which was destroyed and submerged by an earthquake and tsunami in the fourth century BCE, when Plato was fifty. To accept either Thera or Helike as the possible basis for Atlantis requires more searching through pre-Platonic sources.

While it is only partially conclusive that Solon reported firsthand on the Egyptian account of Atlantis, which we will accept as truth in this book, Plato himself also visited the temple of Sais between 399 and 386 BCE. Plato may have been merely confirming the Atlantis story as told by his ancestor, Solon, or this coincidence could indicate something more, perhaps an indication that the story of Atlantis originated with Plato and not Solon. There are many problems with Plato's account as a literal interpretation of the facts. Few scholars in classical times believed the epic to be true. Surprisingly enough, however, there was an abundance of academic support for other more ancient accounts that fleshed out material, such as Hesiod's *Theogony* or the Bible, that Plato had skimmed over. (The oldest translations that have survived the passage of centuries date from more than a thousand years after Plato originally wrote them down.) Even though classical texts filtered into Europe from Muslim Spain (eighth through fifteenth centuries CE) and from Venetian ports unloading ancient manuscripts from Constantinople during the thirteenth century, in the Middle Ages there was a long dearth of commentary regarding Atlantis (Caroli 2011, personal communication).

A cache of manuscripts was brought to Florence in the mid-fifteenth century from Constantinople. It was then that the *Critias* was fully translated into Latin, possibly for the first time. Sadly, few if any of these manuscripts appear to have survived the "bonfire of the vanities"—the burning of thousands of priceless objects deemed to be of a sinful nature.

The tragedy for both Atlantologists and mythologists is the indiscriminate incineration of hundreds of works on classical mythology and manuscripts by pre-Christian Greek and Roman authors. Thus, all subsequent editions relied primarily on existing Latin translations from the fifteenth to sixteenth centuries. These were then copied down by Italian neo-Platonists of the late fifteenth century. As such, most modern Greek or English translations of both the *Timaeus* and the *Critias* are based on the fifteenth- to sixteenth-century Latin versions. Given this, there are considerable grounds for confusion regarding the dating, location, and other details. Exactly what the originals said is, at this point, total conjecture.

Caroli suggests that symbolic numerology and simple exaggeration may account for some of the uncertainty (Caroli 2011, personal communication). Many classical sources claimed that the Egyptians were counting the months, or a four-week cycle, as years, which the Greeks then unilaterally accepted as a full annual cycle. Such alternative chronologies were invariably linked to divine and semidivine dynasties of prehistory.

Whether true or not, this idea became especially popular among early Christian chronographers who struggled to fit the pagan figures within the framework allowed by the Bible. In the second century BCE the earliest versions of the Septuagint, the original Greek translation of the Old Testament, were finally transcribed in Alexandria. This was most notable because the older versions of the Septuagint did not distort the timeframes as the later ones did. The date for Creation in the

Septuagint mirrors that for Egypt's unification by the pharaoh Menes in approximately 3000 BCE. Similarly, the date for the great deluge coincides with the date ancient historians and archaeologists mark as the start of Egypt's Middle Kingdom, approximately 2055 BCE.

It is the comparison of Plato's apparent literal dates for Atlantis's demise with modern chronologies for Egypt and Sumer that resulted in the idea that the birth of Atlantis greatly preceded both. Caroli affirms that today's knowledge that the last ice age ended suddenly in approximately 9700–9400 BCE has heartened literalist Atlantologists. The shorter version of Manetho's prehistoric period in Egypt has the end of the divine dynasties occurring about 9900 BCE and Menes being crowned circa 5900 BCE. This could mean that Plato dated the rise of Atlantis to coincide with the epoch of Egypt's gods, which was from 35,000 to 15,000 BCE.

PERSIAN AND HINDU SOURCES

In ancient Persian lore, sometimes the events happening within mortal history were determined to have begun in the tenth millennium BCE in response to rule by the demigods. The Persians themselves would come to rule Egypt from 525 to 401 BCE, and again from 343 to 332 BCE. Sadly, the Zoroastrian sacred texts were destroyed when Alexander the Great burned Persepolis in 330 CE (assuming they'd been written down before that). All we have are reconstructions compiled in Sassanid times (which peaked from 224 to 641 CE).

Another area of interest for the budding Atlantologist working with specific dates and cosmologies is interpreting the Hindu Yugas. This can ultimately become a virtual juggling game of numbers with differing calendars and theories of the length of each epoch, which are difficult to tie to Western chronology. Where Atlantis would fit is open to conjecture, but the Theosophists set it in the Davpara Yuga, the Bronze Age that preceded the current Kali Yuga. Other interpretations have placed Atlantis as late as 700 BCE. Of course it remains an open question whether Atlantis is to be found in Hindu lore at all, despite fervent attempts by Atlantologists since the nineteenth century to find it there. Phonetic similarities between Atlantis and Atala, the Hindu version of Atlantis, may be due in large part to the relationship between Vedic and Greek languages.

CONCLUSIONS

When Plato first described Atlantis he was presenting a moral tale of a race of people who had everything—wealth, power, technological sophistication, and global admiration—but who degenerated into greed and the lust for political and military dominance. So much of what Plato said reminds us of our own culture today, which is why studying the eventual fate of Atlantis is so important. By rediscovering Atlantis we are revealing much about ourselves. As the great American science fiction writer Rod Serling once wrote:

> The tools of conquest do not necessarily come with bombs and explosions and fallout. There are weapons that are simply thoughts, attitudes, prejudices—to be found only in the minds of men. For the record, prejudices can kill and suspicion can destroy, and a thoughtless, frightened search for a scapegoat has a fallout all its own—for the children, and the children yet unborn. (Zicree 1989, p. 91)

This is the great social dilemma posed by Plato's Atlantean parable and could shed light on the real Atlantis, that which is described in countless stories passed down to us from nearly every culture on Earth. Rediscovering our Atlantean past is but the first step.

2
Sunken Ruins and the Search for Atlantis

Think of it: On the surface, there is hunger and fear. Men still exercise unjust laws. They fight and tear one another to pieces. A mere few feet beneath the waves, their reign ceases, their evil drowns. Here on the ocean floor is the only independence. Here, I am free. Imagine what would happen if they controlled machines such as this submarine boat. Far better that they think there's a monster and hunt me with harpoons . . .

CAPTAIN NEMO, IN JULES VERNE,
TWENTY THOUSAND LEAGUES UNDER THE SEA, 1870

ICE, FIRE, AND WATER:
FROM SUNKEN CITIES TO THE END OF ATLANTIS

Many myths from cultures all around the world speak of massive floods that destroyed a lost civilization. Some of the most well known to Westerners are the biblical and qur'anic flood myths involving Noah's Ark, the Greek Deucalion flood myth, and *The Epic of Gilgamesh*. In each legend a few select individuals survive the torrent to rebuild civilization and repopulate the Earth. In most mythical stories of a great flood, a god or gods are responsible for the catastrophe, often as an act of divine retribution for various sins committed by human society. In most cases such deluges are preludes to a mass extinction or the end of the world.

The Mesopotamian tradition of a great deluge and the biblical story of Noah and the Great Flood are linked to a probable flood that occurred between 3000 and 2000 BCE. A Greek version of the story, in which Deucalion and his wife, Pyrrha, are the sole surviving humans, shares much in common with the biblical account. This story begins with the king of Arcadia, Lycaon, sacrificing a boy to Zeus, who sends a flood as a punishment for this wickedness and sin. It presents a moral code by instructing the Greeks that the gods do not approve of the cannibalism and human sacrifice that they practice. The flood theme was also worked into the Greek version of the Atlantis legend. In Greek tradition the flood was a catastrophic and global event, covering all the Earth. The Earth was so devastated from this deluge that Attica, the region of Greece containing Athens, remained without a king until the rise to power of Cecrops (Gaster 1969).

Less familiar flood myths abound. In a more obscure one, the god Faro of the Bambara people of Mali held back the deluge that will someday come crashing forth to drown the present world in ultimate preparation for a new world that will arise. Faro warned the people of the coming catastrophe so that they could prepare by arming themselves with objects capable of imbuing them with eternal salvation. Iranian texts speak of the coming snows and floods that will cover the Earth at the final moments of the cosmic millennium. In response to these terrible events, Yima comes forth, gathers the best races of humanity, and descends into the Earth to await the millennial destruction. He then surfaces from his underground sanctuary and repopulates the world (Williams 1886, pp. 22–41).

The Aztec and Maya of Mesoamerica believed that the world has gone through many cycles, or eras, which the Aztec called "suns," each one ending with invasions of fire and water. The creation story of the Maya, one of the most brilliant societies known to humankind, with glories that rivaled anything in Europe or Asia, sounds remarkably close to our own Jewish and Christian story of creation: One day, as Hurakan wandered through the cosmos, he came upon a watery world with no land and no life. He called it by name, and land appeared. Then his relatives decided to make animals to populate the world. Out of wood they fashioned the first human beings. Yet they were evil, and they hurt the animals and caused misery to the Earth. The gods called forth a great flood and destroyed the evil humans. Birds descended from the skies and poked out their eyes, tore off their heads, blood squirting and gushing, and pounded their bones into dust. Then Hurakan took maize and from that made the second race of humans, from which the Maya descended. Thus we have a world of beauty, dignity, and honor and, according to this legend, only in the year 2012 will the world finally cease.

In the Sanskrit writings of India, the *Mahabharata,* a successive number of creations are identified, after which everything in existence is destroyed by the converging waters; in the aftermath, these waters form a new ocean in which the next major creation will take place (Bansal 2009, 3.188.80, 3.189.42). The cyclical periods of creation and destruction are part of a larger spiritual phenomenon known as the Hindu Yuga cycles, the current one being the Kali Yuga, which, in contrast to the previous incarnations, is one of iniquity and chaos.

There is no question that mythology plays a major role in dechipering humankind's ancient mysteries. But geology also offers significant clues. Many people believe that, based on geological evidence, prior to 650 million years ago almost the entire planet was covered in ice. Known as the snowball hypothesis, this proposes that prior to the Cambrian Explosion the planet was covered in ice and parts of it remained so until 650 million years ago. Geologists call this probable epoch in Earth's history the Huronian glaciations. Some scientists accept this hypothesis because it explains certain anomalies within the sedimentary layers. To be fair, the evidence for this primordial glaciation still remains somewhat inconclusive.

In any event, there is clear evidence that Earth has been undergoing a period of recurring ice ages for the past 2.6 million years. Some scientists even claim we are still living in an ice age, perhaps of a lesser degree, with an even more frigid epoch awaiting us in the near future. These periods of global cooling have been attributed to significant changes in the Earth's orbit around the sun. Still other experts of a more extreme persuasion have suggested volcanism, asteroidal or cometary impacts, or even crustal displacement as probable causes of the cooling (Hancock 2002, p. 57).

As Graham Hancock noted at the beginning of his epic work, *Underworld: The Mysterious Origins of Civilization,* millions of square kilometers of "useful human habitat" equivalent to all of China and Europe combined were "swallowed up by rising sea-levels at the end of the Ice Age" (2002, p. 24). Proof for this reality, Hancock insists, is all around us. Strange, anomalous structures and sunken ruins date back to a time when cities simply did not exist, according to mainstream scientists. Hancock believes it is our duty as human beings to follow up on the evidence and seek answers to these persistent incongruities.

More than a decade ago Graham Hancock traveled to Bangalore to see one of India's chief marine archaeologists, S. R. Rao. During a series of conversations Rao commented:

> You see, some people, some traditions, do say that there was a continent in the Indian Ocean, a very long time ago, more than 16,000 years ago, that got submerged. . . . Quite possible. You see, we are not doing thorough research. If we had taken more time and more funds and all that, perhaps we could find many more structures, not only that one, and then you could come to some kind of conclusion about the much earlier epoch. (p. 27)

Archaeologists and independent researchers are discovering a wealth of evidence of human history going back hundreds of thousands of years, a time frame that offers scant evidence of human civilization, according to mainstream science. These discoveries also provide clues to more recent societies. From the Mediterranean to the southern coast of Japan, cities that have been submerged for thousands of years are now coming to light. The sunken cities and underwater ruins of the world provide us an excellent opportunity to view humankind's history from an entirely new perspective, and they will ultimately shed light on some of the imaginative myths and legends that have become such a vital part of our culture.

THE ATLANTIS/TARTESSOS ENIGMA

Since Plato's original account was written down more than two thousand years ago, numerous attempts have been made to verify the existence and location of Atlantis. This quest has led to everything from placing it in Antarctica to Indonesia. Could Atlantis really exist? The possibility is too tantalizing to resist. The discovery of Atlantis would have an incalculable impact on world culture. We would have to rewrite human history, evolution, and linguistics—and the entire basis of world archaeology. Finally, those answers are now within our grasp. With the aid of satellite photography, ground-penetrating radar, and underwater technology, a genuine attempt to find the lost civilization is currently under way (ScienceDaily 2011a).

In 2009 and 2010, a dedicated team of Spanish archaeologists and geologists led by University of Hartford professor and archaeologist Richard Freund and University of South Florida geographer Philip Reeder attempted to solve this very ancient and persistent mystery. These scientists set out to explore and excavate the remnants of an ancient city that go back some four thousand years (ScienceDaily 2011a).

The focal point of the investigations was a series of ruins, possibly those of the historical Atlantis, located in Dona Ana Park in southern Spain, one of the largest swamps in mainland Europe. It offers evidence of a massive series of natural catastrophes, specifically tsunami-generated floods that could very well have submerged a city the size of Atlantis and then carried the bulk of it out to sea (ScienceDaily 2011a).

This is one line of thinking. Another posits that the mudflats of Dona Ana Park investigated by Richard Freund and his team were once an open bay. This is where Freund and other historical revisionists depart from tradition and claim that a coastal harbor, not an island in the Atlantic, was the model for Plato's Atlantis. According to Plato's account, Atlantis encompassed ten kingdoms. Among them was Gadeiros, which he placed in Iberia. Revisionists claim that the Egyptians were unfamiliar with islands, so the word Plato wrongly interpreted as "island" meant simply "shore" or "coast" (Levy 2007, pp. 30–31).

In another development in Spain, German physicist Dr. Rainer Kuhne identified what he believed to be the actual remnants of the historical Atlantis in a number of satellite photographs taken near the plain of Cadiz. The first photos, which came to his desk in the early 2000s, revealed half-hidden structures. For Kuhne, this was compelling evidence placing the legendary Atlantis directly at the site of the Bronze Age city-state of Tartessos (Levy 2007, p. 31).

This ancient city, like Atlantis, is a lost civilization. It is spoken of throughout ancient historical sources, including those of the Roman geographer Strabo, who wrote about the city extensively. In the Bible, Tartessos is known as Tarshish in the Book of Chronicles. This city was the supposed destination of Jonah in the well-known biblical account in which he was cast overboard and then swallowed by a whale (Childress 1996, p. 259). But around the second millennium BCE all mention of the city and its exact location disappeared, with only the mention that it suffered some great cataclysm similar to that described by Plato in the dialogue *Timaeus*.

In 2004 Kuhne told the BBC, "We have in the photos concentric rings just as Plato described" (Levy 2007, p. 31). Kuhne's work was inspired by the theories and writings of Atlantologist Werner Wickboldt. He affirmed that "this is the only place that seems to fit [Plato's] description" (p. 31).

Although Tartessos shares many things in common with the Atlantis of myth, they differed in scale and general function. Atlantis was said to be a military empire larger than Libya and Asia combined, while Tartessos was a powerful trading port whose network reached into Asia and across the known world. In terms of their similarities, both are said to have been situated beyond the Pillars of Hercules (the Straits of Gibraltar). Atlantis was equipped with a vast system of canals by which it dominated its empire. Tartessos too had a sizable canal network branching off from the Guadalquivir River. Atlantis was said to have ancient scrolls of law and knowledge dating back eight thousand years, while Tartessos possessed thousands of ancient manuscripts dating back to before 10,000 BCE.

This idea of Tartessos being the historical Atlantis actually predates Kuhne by almost a century. In the early 1920s Atlantologists such as Richard Hennig and Adolf Schulten joined a group of revisionists who sought to reinterpret the specific details of the Atlantis myth to correspond with real historical locations. Errors were found during the transcription and translation process, such as the discovery that Plato's dates were wrong by a factor of ten (Levy 2007, pp. 30–31). This places Plato's account not nine thousand years before the dawn of classical Greek civilization, but rather a mere nine centuries before it (approximately 1300 BCE).

To establish once and for all whether the civilization resting beneath the mudflats did indeed spawn world culture, we must obtain physical evidence, preferably a sign of material culture such as an artifact that could be dated to around the proposed time period for the Tartessos/Atlantean culture. Several ritualistic figurines dating to the early Bronze Age that displayed a mixture of Mediterranean and Near Eastern culture were in fact found in Tartessos. Richard Freund believes that these tiny images represent the smoking gun—a confirmation that the culture that precipitated the spread of civilization throughout the Old World, if not farther, sprang from this location five thousand years ago.

There is a big problem with this theory, however. Both the artifacts and the civilization have been dated to between 3000 and 2000 BCE. This is simply too young to be the primordial Ur civilization—the ancestral culture from which all others emerged. The beginnings of some of the most significant cultures in the Mediterranean and Middle East, such as Egypt and Mesopotamia, in addition to Old European cultures, the Indus Valley Civilization, China, and Caral in the New World predate this chronology by more than a thousand years.

Ken Caroli offers this observation:

Many modern Atlantologists are not really seeking Plato's island. They're looking for a culture or cultures X that predated known history and gave rise to the civilizations we know. It was a 'parent culture.' Since this implies diffusion, so in reality they are ultra-diffusionists. That sets them at odds with mainstream archaeologists and historians who largely discount diffusion as a tenet of fringe science. (Caroli 2011, personal communication)

Perhaps Atlantis was not an island at all. Perhaps it was, as the revisionists claim, a city on a coastline, something like Tartessos on the Iberian Peninsula. Tartessos, like Atlantis, was rich in natural resources and might even have been destroyed by catastrophic floods. The dates of the recovered figurines, however, suggest that Tartessos is not the ancient land that inspired the myth of Atlantis. Might further excavation at this site point toward a date of even greater antiquity?

These investigations in Spain are but two of many attempts to uncover the true location of the lost city of Atlantis. But perhaps we're missing the whole point with these pursuits. Atlantis could have been a metaphor for not just one civilization, but many—a representation of a time long ago when humans existed in a highly evolved state.

SUNKEN CITIES IN THE MEDITERRANEAN

Theories connecting the demise of Atlantis with cyclical destruction associated with the Earth's periodic ice ages seem possible given our current concept of geophysics. In his 1996 release, *Lost Cities of Atlantis, Ancient Europe and the Mediterranean,* David Hatcher Childress presents a rather inventive alternative. Hard evidence supports many of his conclusions, while others amount to nothing more than rampant speculation. In time, such claims may acquire more definitive proof.

Childress believes that twenty thousand years ago the Mediterranean was not a sea but rather a fertile river valley. Centuries later the valley was overcome by a great deluge, transforming it into a saltwater sea. According to Childress, hundreds of sunken cities remain undiscovered in the Mediterranean, their ruins resting on the bottom of the sea floor. He links the flooding of the Mediterranean with the destruction of Atlantis. This event was precipitated by an unexplained but sudden change in Earth's oceans, he says, the result of which was a massive tsunami that drowned the continent of Atlantis in thousands of feet of water and then flooded and obliterated the Mediterranean cities and much of predynastic Egypt. Ultimately this was also the cause of the legendary flooding of the early Sumerian civilization.

Archaeologists have recently discovered the ruins of Pavlopetri, a five-thousand-year-old town submerged off the southern Laconia coast of Greece. It may prove to be the inspiration for many of the pre-Platonic folk traditions describing a civilization that was submerged in prehistoric times. The earliest artifacts retrieved from the underwater site date to the Late Neolithic period, or "New Stone Age," while others found elsewhere at the site dated to the Bronze Age. Approximately 150 square meters of habitation were discovered, including various buildings and temple structures, along with ceramics dating to at least 1100 BCE, placing them in the Bronze Age—the age of Atlantis, as once suggested by Atlantologist Ken Caroli (ScienceDaily 2009).

The rest of the structural remains date to the Mycenaean period, a subset of the Bronze Age, which dates to around 1600–1000 BCE. This town was part of the civilization that launched a thousand ships in the heroic literature of Homer's epics depicting the Trojan War and the return of Odysseus. It was a major port at the time of Agamemnon and offers archaeologists deep insight into the overall workings of Mycenaean society. This unique maritime settlement was a base of operations for coordinated local and long-distance commerce (ScienceDaily 2009).

Underwater archaeologist Dr. Jon Henderson explains:

This site is unique in that we have almost the complete town plan, the main streets and domestic buildings, courtyards, rock-cut tombs and what appear to be religious buildings, clearly visible on the sea-bed. The study of archaeological material we have recovered will be extremely important in terms of revealing how maritime trade was conducted and managed in the Bronze Age. (ScienceDaily 2009)

One of the buildings was identified as a megaron—a large rect-angular hall—dating to the Early Bronze Age. Included among the 150-square-meters is what appears to be the first example of a pillar crypt ever found. Pithos, earthenware jars used to hold grain or oil, were also found at the site (ScienceDaily 2009).

Another sunken civilization that deserves discussion is the lost civilization of Helike, a Greek city-state founded during the Bronze Age, roughly about the same time that Pavlopetri was at its height (ScienceDaily 2009). In 373 BCE a cataclysmic earthquake and a lethal tsunami nearly obliterated and then submerged the once proud civili-zation of Helike. Positioned on the southwestern shore of the Gulf of Corinth, Helike was the principal member of a coalition of twelve Greek city-states known as the first Achaean League. Helike was also highly expansionistic. The city-state established colonies in both Asia Minor and southern Italy. In the Atlantis myth Plato described a Temple of Poseidon that was the holiest of shrines, according to the Atlanteans, comparable only to the Temple of Solomon. Helike, interestingly enough, built a sanctuary of Poseidon that was famous throughout the classical world (Katsonopoulou 1999, 2002).

Plato was approximately fifty-four years old when the tsunami engulfed the city of Helike. Without question, Plato must have known about the great destruction and took note of its key characteristics. The power wielded by Helike's ruler, the vast colonial ambitions, and the destruction by earthquake and flood all fit into the Atlantis story. Another link to Atlantis is the fact that the inhabitants of Helike grew sullen and morally bankrupt and defiled the Temple of Poseidon (Katsonopoulou 1999, 2002). The city's destruction was thus associated with the wrath of the mighty sea god, who punished them for their misdeeds and sacrilege.

For millennia the true location of Helike has eluded every attempt to find it, yet we have hints of its existence. Ancient Roman reports indicated that tourists could sail over the ruins, look beneath the waters, and see its broken streets and battered statuary. In 174 CE a traveler named Pausanias claimed to have visited the site and saw the fallen walls and broken ramparts of the city (Levy 2007, pp. 22–23).

The evidence is in. Was Helike the real Atlantis? This author will let *you* decide.

ANCIENT TEMPLE FOUND UNDER LAKE TITICACA

A group of international archaeologists diving in Lake Titicaca discovered the underwater ruins of an ancient stone temple flanked by a 2,600-foot-long wall. (Lake Titicaca, the world's highest lake, is located in the Andes on the border of Peru and Bolivia.) Among the artifacts retrieved from the site were small golden statues used for veneration purposes; ancient stone ceremonial heads; and a treasure-trove of other religious artifacts including talismans, small idols, pottery, tools, and even some weapons (BBC News 2000).

It became clear that the ruins did not belong to a single temple but rather signified a true underwater city. Was this yet another example of a lost human civilization dating back to a forgotten period in human existence? Local legends allude to alien contact as a catalyst for the building of this city. Are these rumors true? That ancient astronauts could be behind the building of such structures is mere speculation. What *is* certain is that the conventional view of chronology for human civilization is falling apart, piece by piece.

THE FORGOTTEN UNDERWORLD OF JAPAN

Graham Hancock explains his initial interest in prehistoric underwater archaeology in chapter 28 of *Underworld,* titled "Maps of Japan and Taiwan 13,000 Years Ago?" In the opening paragraph he writes, "It was the submerged structures of Japan that first awakened me to the possibility that an underworld in history, unrecognized by archaeologists, could lie concealed and forgotten beneath the sea" (2002). Since the book's release, Hancock has become the world's most outspoken proponent of investigating sunken ruins in an effort to learn more about possible lost civilizations.

Many anomalous structures scattered around the world bear the signature of human design. In addition to the few we have discussed, other notable ones are the sunken city beneath the Gulf of Cambay off the southwest coast of India, the ruins found off Cuba, and finally, and most important, the underwater pyramids of Yonaguni, Japan. All of these structures, except those found off Cuba, are known to have been above water within the past thirteen thousand years, during the last ice age.

In the earliest times the prehistoric inhabitants of Japan, the Jomon, developed a sophisticated material culture. The Jomon were not of typical East Asian descent; they were proto-Caucasoids, fair-skinned with prominent noses and full, light-colored beards. Many other similarities link them to other primitive people in the Americas and ancient northern Europe. Although their society was primitive by the standards of later times, they were the first culture on Earth to develop pottery, according to mainstream theorists. Examples of this technology date back to 16,000 BCE. This was a time when many of the submerged structures of Yonaguni would have been above water, and if they were in fact built by human hands, this would have been the time that their construction was under way. Some of the figurines from later in the Jomon period depict what appear to be humanoid creatures with space suits, including helmets, or even, in some cases, underwater breathing apparatuses.

Erich von Däniken noted this in a number of his books, including his most famous, *Chariots of the Gods?* His intent was to point directly to ancient aliens, but I'd rather think that in the distant past humans were more inventive than they are now and that there were civilizations deep in antiquity, perhaps of terrestrial origin, whose technology and cultural sophistication far surpassed our own. The Jomon even possessed, though cruder in construction, megalithic technology; several stone circles built by them are known to exist.

Without a doubt, Japanese culture is graced with a rich mythological heritage. In 712 CE this wealth of myth and legend culminated in the first written chronicle of Japan, known as the Kojiki. Many stories in this manuscript told of horrendous earthquakes and conflagrations. There were entire ages when the world was ruled by the gods. During this mythical age of gods and empires the Jomon were the dominant race of the Japanese islands.

The modern legacy of Japan's underwater ruins dates back to 1987. On a clear and windy spring day, divemaster Kihachiro Aratake headed out to explore. Shortly after entering the sapphire blue water of the East China Sea, he began searching for unique formations that would prove interesting. Suddenly he was confronted with an enigma. Right before him was what appeared to be a massive stone monument rising some twelve meters from the ocean floor. Aratake said when he looked at it for the very first time he thought of the pyramids of Egypt, such as the stepped pyramid of Saqqarah, or those of ancient Mesopotamia. He felt that some noble race must have built these awesome ruins, for some divine reason. He called this initial site Iseki Point, or "Monument" Point.

Aratake's initial discovery was 73 meters long, 27 meters wide, and 14 meters high (Joseph 2005, pp. 172–77). But this wasn't the only relevant discovery. Additional sites were also located from the small island of Yonaguni in the southwest to Okinawa and a considerable swath of the surrounding territories. Two of these locations were Kerama and Aguni, approximately 500 kilometers away.

Graham Hancock had an opportunity to investigate these locations early on in his scuba-diving career. As Hancock reports, for a number of years the divers at the island of Aka, in the Kerama group some 40 kilometers west of Okinawa, have talked about a series of submerged stone circles at a depth of some 30 meters. Other structures very close by show evidence of being cut and worked by human hands. The preeminent structure at Kerama is the "Central Circle." Resting at an approximate depth of 27 meters, it has a diameter of 20 meters. Other features include the "Small Center Circle" and the "Stone Circle," the latter of which has an enormous diameter of about 150 meters (2002, p. 10).

Off Aguni Island they've discovered what appear to be stone shafts built by human hands. Hancock writes:

As they are lined with small blocks, there is little doubt that these shafts are man-made. The largest and deepest has a diameter of 3 meters and reached a maximum depth (below the summit of the seamount) of about 10 meters. Others are typically 2 to 3 meters in diameter with a depth of less than 7 meters. A few are narrower and shallower. One has a subsidiary chamber cut sideways into the wall of the main shaft. (2002, p. 10)

In 1996 Ken Shindo, a local Okinawan divemaster, told Graham Hancock a fascinating story of an anomalous underwater structure near the tiny fishing community of Yonaguni, Japan, the southernmost island of the Japanese chain. Shindo explained that he had been working with Professor Masaaki Kimura, a marine seismologist of the University of the Rykyus. He outlined several basic points regarding direct human intervention in the formation of the site. These include "traces of marks that show that human beings worked the stone. There are holes made by wedge-like tools called *kusabi* in many locations" (Hancock 2002, p. 597).

The structure is continuous from under the water to land, and evidence of the use of fire is present. Stone tools are among the artifacts found underwater and on land. Some tablets with carving that appears to be letters or symbols, such as what we know as the plus mark "+" and a "V" shape, were retrieved from under the water (Hancock 2002, p. 598). These findings exist amid a cultural and mythological backdrop that seems vast, imposing, and incalculable.

Frank Joseph is a scholar and author who has studied the matter of Japanese ruins extensively. In an article published in *Atlantis Rising* magazine in 1997 titled "Japan's Underwater Ruins," he writes, "If, after all ongoing exploration here does indeed reveal more structures linking Yonaguni with Okinawa, the individual sites may be separate components of a huge city lying at the bottom of the Pacific" (2005, p. 172). Frank Joseph wholeheartedly believes in the significance of this discovery. It is possible that in time his belief in a once vast Pacific motherland will prevail. With the enormous advances in archaeology and independent research, confirmation may yet take place. However, the concept of a sophisticated civilization in the Pacific is in part a product of his hyperdiffusionism.

Joseph writes:

Okinawa's drowned structures find possible counterparts at the eastern limits of the Pacific Ocean, along Peruvian coasts. The most striking similarities occur at ancient Pachacamac, a sprawling religious city a few miles south of the modern capital at Lima. Although functioning into Inca times, as late as the sixteenth century, it pre-dated the Incas by at least 1,500 years and was the seat of South America's foremost oracle. Pilgrims visited Pachacamac from all over Tawantinsuyu, the Inca Empire, until it was sacked and desecrated by the Spaniards under Francisco Pizarro's high-spirited brother, Hernando, with 22 heavily armed conquistadors. Enough of the sun-dried, mud-brick city remains, with its sweeping staircases and broad plazas, to suggest parallels with the sunken buildings around Okinawa. Two other pre-Inca sites in the north, just outside Trujillo, likewise share some leading elements in common with the overseas, undersea structures. The so-called Temple of the Sun is a terraced pyramid built two thousand years ago by a people known as the Moche. More than 100 feet high and 684 feet long, the irregularly stepped platform of unfired adobe bricks was formerly the colossal centerpiece of a city sheltering thirty thousand inhabitants. Its resemblance to the structure found at Yonaguni is remarkable. (2005, p. 174)

Others such as my good friend Robert Schoch—although open to differing theories of civilizations that are now submerged—consider at least a few of the known examples, including Yonaguni, to be naturally formed. Regarding Yonaguni, Schoch writes:

As far as I could determine, [the monument was] composed entirely of solid "living" bedrock. No part of the monument is constructed of separate blocks of rock that have been placed into position.

This is an important point, for carved and arranged rock blocks would definitively indicate a man-made origin for the structure—yet I could find no such evidence. During my initial two dives of September 1997 I was unable to determine, even in a general way, the stone of which the Yonaguni Monument is composed. This was due to the fact that the surfaces of the rocks are covered by various organisms (algae, corals, sponges, and so forth) that obscure the actual surfaces. I believe that this coating of organic material tends to make the surfaces of the Yonaguni Monument appear more regular and homogeneous than they actually are. This, in part, enhances the impression that this must be an artificial, man-made structure. (1999)

Schoch has often suggested that such natural geologic formations could have been utilized or modified by humans during that above-water period. He says in *Voices of the Rocks:*

Possibly the choice between natural and human-made isn't simply either/or. Yonaguni Island contains a number of old tombs whose exact age is uncertain, but that are clearly very old. Curiously the architecture of the tombs is much like that of the monument. It is possible that humans were imitating the monument in designing the tombs, and it is equally possible that the monument was itself somehow modified by human hands. That is, the ancient inhabitants of the island may have partially reshaped or enhanced a natural structure to give it the form they wished, either as a structure on its own or as the foundation of a timber, mud or stone building that has since been destroyed. It is also possible that the monument served as a quarry from which blocks were cut, following the natural bedding, joint and fracture planes of the rock, then removed to construct buildings that are now long gone. (Hancock 2002, pp. 599–600)

Schoch offers compelling, practical, and engaging arguments, with a fair dose of common sense. But I don't feel we can measure structures like Yonaguni with any practical measuring systems. The ruins of Yonaguni, or whatever they are, have passed away from our normal realm of existence into the shadowy underworld of the unusual and unexplained. We must view the ruins with an open mind and must not be afraid to ask strange or absurd questions, because that devotion to curious inquiry is truly the root of all human knowledge.

CONCLUSIONS

Conclusive evidence must and will be found regarding the artificiality of anomalous underwater structures such as those found at Yonaguni and off the coast of Cuba. Furthermore, ruins such as those found near India and beneath the waters of Lake Titicaca offer further evidence for the existence of a vast underwater world containing structures stretching back to the dimmest chapters of human antiquity. Contrary to Plato's vision of the existence and destruction of Atlantis, it is becoming clear that there may in fact be more than one Atlantis—whether it be near Tartessos, Helike; or Palvoperti in Greece; Dwarka, off the coast of India; or the sunken pyramids at Rock Lake, Wisconsin. We are learning more with every discovery, and through independent research and investigation and the implementation of the latest in investigative technology we are cracking the code of the underwater worlds with regard to how they relate to our ancient past.

3
Decoding the Ancient Past

There is a thing confusedly formed,
Born before Heaven and Earth.
Silent and void
It stands alone and does not change,
Goes round and does not weary.
It is capable of being the mother of the world.
I know not its name
So I style it "The Way."
I give it the makeshift name of "The Great."
Being great, it is further described as receding,
Receding, it is described as far away,
Being far away, it is described as turning back.

LAO-TZU, *TAO TE CHING*, CHINA, ABOUT 600 BCE

There is a way on high, conspicuous in the clear heavens,
called the Milky Way, brilliant with its own brightness. By
it the gods go to the dwelling of the great Thunderer and his
royal abode. . . . Here the famous and mighty inhabitants of
heaven have their homes. This is the region which I might
make bold to call the Palatine [Way] of the Great Sky.

OVID, *METAMORPHOSES*, ROME, FIRST CENTURY CE

Since the birth of modern archaeology, sociologists, historians, scholars, and excavators alike have wondered about the evolutionary development of the first cities: where they came from, how they were built, when they first appeared, and why. Most evidence points to the first cities—at least those of the old centers of civilization (Egypt, Mesopotamia, India, and China)—originating from around 7000 to 4000 BCE. This applies only if one counts the protocities that flourished in earlier times. (True cities did not develop, according to outmoded wisdom, for another two thousand to three thousand years.)

JERICHO'S ELEVEN-THOUSAND-YEAR-OLD "COSMIC TOWER"

In 1952, at Tel Jericho in the West Bank, archaeologists made a stunning discovery: an eleven-thousand-year-old stone tower rising approximately nine meters above the walled proto-Neolithic settlement. These were the early years of Israeli archaeology, and a number of phenomenal finds marked the era as a signature period in Near Eastern studies, including the glorious Dead Sea Scrolls, which literally stood the whole of Judeo-Christianity on its head.

The tower at Jericho promised to offer the same profound insights, this time providing a key to an even earlier age. This "World's First Skyscraper" predates the development of food production and agriculture in the region (ScienceDaily 2011b).

Doctoral student Roy Liran and Dr. Ran Barkai of Tel Aviv University's Jacob M. Alkow Department of Archaeology and Near Eastern Cultures at the Lester and Sally Entin Faculty of Humanities have undertaken computer-based research with hopes of illuminating this most ancient of mysteries. Their general conclusion is that the position of the tower is coordinated with the longest day of the year (ScienceDaily 2011b).

Liran and Barkai claim that "reconstruction of the sunset revealed to us that the shadow of the hill as the sun sets on the longest day of the year falls exactly on the Jericho tower, envelops the tower and then covers the entire village. For this reason, we suggest that the tower served an earthly element connecting the residents of the site with the hills around them and with the heavenly element of the setting sun" (ScienceDaily 2011b). They theorize that the tower's construction can be attributed to the primal fears of the villagers, as well as to their profound connection to the cosmos and nature. These were the hallmark beliefs of Jericho's Stone Age population (ScienceDaily 2011b).

The tower suggests that the villagers were not merely superstitious but held much more complex religious concepts. Throughout time sun worship has been one of the oldest and most dominant forms of religion. In most cases the sun was later personified as a deity. Much speculation and commentary has been made regarding this practice. The late Carl Sagan, in *Cosmos*, had this to say:

> The Sun warms us and feeds us and permits us to see. It fecundated the Earth. It is powerful beyond human experience. Birds greet the sunrise with an audible ecstasy. Even some one-celled organisms know to swim to the light. Our ancestors worshiped the Sun, and they were far from foolish. And yet the Sun is an ordinary, even a mediocre star. If we must worship a power greater than ourselves, does it not make sense to revere the Sun and stars? (1980, p. 243)

H. G. Wells touched upon the idea of sun worship representing the foundation of cultural and religious life in *An Outline of History.* He wrote of a lost "heliolithic," or "sun-stone," civilization, a culture that thrived throughout southern Europe, North Africa, Eurasia, East Asia, Oceania, and Peru. Their highest level of development lasted from fifteen thousand to ten thousand years ago. They successfully colonized the tropical regions of the Earth and were responsible for the enormous explosion of civilization and technology in the southern latitudes, which began occurring around 8000 BCE (1920, pp. 141–42).

Tel Jericho's heritage goes far back into prehistory. It is one of the oldest sites on Earth, perhaps competing with Turkey's Göbekli Tepe on the shores of Lake Van, an ancient temple structure so old that it defies conventional wisdom and predates the destruction of Atlantis. The Tel Jericho tower was constructed featuring a steep staircase approximately one meter wide. Surrounding the tower are four-meter walls that probably enclosed the entire city, a highly fortified site for its day. Although Jericho was really only a preagricultural settlement of hunter-gatherers, it has often been identified as Earth's first city (ScienceDaily 2011b).

TWILIGHT OF THE GODS: THE LOST CIVILIZATION OF TIAHUANACO

In the 1930s German archaeologist Dr. Edmund Kiss ventured to the remote Bolivian Andes of South America to conduct research at the ancient ruins of Tiahuanaco (Von Däniken 2010, p. 21). The lost city of Tiahuanaco is often considered one of the most controversial archaeological ruins on the planet, but there is little doubt, even among skeptics, that these ancient structures predate the Inca Empire, and probably by many hundreds if not thousands of years (Childress 1986, p. 135). To Childress, what made these ruins so controversial was that they represented a reality beyond that which is taught to us in school and in history books. The sophisticated technology it took to build these great edifices suggested something greater than the mainstream model: either extraterrestrial intervention in the history of the human race, or something even more significant.

Dr. Kiss himself was no stranger to controversy. He had the misfortune of being a German archaeologist in a decade in which the only people a working scientist such as himself could turn to for financial support were the dreaded SS under Heinrich Himmler. This association was suicide once Germany was defeated in 1945 because of the stigma attached to anything even remotely affiliated with the Third Reich.

Kiss loved ancient civilizations, and when he arrived at Tiahuanaco he was awe-struck by its complexity and scale. Greeting him was a towering, rectangular monolithic gate built from a single eleven-ton andesite block. In the center of this massive arch stared a grim figure that became known as the "Weeping God" (Childress 1986, p. 137). The archway was given the illustrious title "Gateway of the Sun." It is carved with mysterious hieroglyphs and other engravings that suggest a complex solar calendar. Further study revealed that, with extraordinary precision, the gateway depicted the coming of the summer and winter solstices, the equinoxes, and the phases of the moon. The remainder of the site consisted of thousands of stone slabs that clearly had been carefully cut and transported to that location. Kiss marveled at the ancient ruins. His research led him to believe that Tiahuanaco was constructed around 27,000 BCE (Von Däniken 2010, pp. 28–31).

According to legend, Tiahuanaco was erected in a single night by the gods, while conventional references state only that Tiahuanaco was built by the "Tiahuanaco Culture." Childress explains that visitors to the site immediately notice the "stark contrast" between the stunning mountain vista of Machu Picchu and the barren, Martian-like hills of swirling dust over which the city of Tiahuanaco stands vigil. In 1864 the site was visited by E. G. Squier, an American anthropologist whose career produced two works that eventually became standard reading for all young anthropologists, *Ancient Monuments of the Mississippi Valley* and *Aboriginal Monuments of the State of New York*. He was highly impressed by the immensity of the ruins and their impressive display of engineering knowledge. He called the site the Baalbek of the New World in reference to the ruins of Baalbek in modern-day Lebanon, one of the most impressive megalithic sites in the world (1986, p. 136).

Cieza de León, an early-sixteenth-century Spanish chronicler, noted that the natives of the region told the Spaniards who arrived at the site that the Incas had found the city abandoned and desolate, in total ruins, and that the Inca believed it had been in that state for hundreds of generations (Childress 1986, p. 137).

Yet the state of the fallen structures and half-standing edifices seem to indicate that the city's demise was due to something more than just the passage of centuries. In Kiss's viewpoint, as Erich von Däniken explains in *Twilight of the Gods,* Tiahuanaco was not only tens of thousands of years older than the oldest recorded civilization, but it was destroyed by a flood—perhaps the same flood described in the Old Testament, the *Epic of Gilgamesh,* and so many other ancient accounts (2010, pp. 24–25, 60). Plato described a profoundly ancient culture that sank into the sea in a single day and night, the legendary Atlantis. Kiss undoubtedly believed in this myth, and for him the indication of a flood at Tiahuanaco twenty-nine thousand years ago gave credence to Plato's account as well as the works of his mentor, Hans Hoerbiger (Von Däniken 2010, p. 61). This revelation set the stage for future investigations into the greater antiquity of the human race.

In addition to proving an apparent link to the global flood, Kiss was also interested in the inscriptions on the Gateway of the Sun. As previously stated, he believed they comprised some type of a solar calendar. He also believed, however, that not only were these inscriptions an incredibly ancient form of dating, but they dated to before the last ice age, an assertion that irked his archaeological colleagues outside Germany (Von Däniken 2010, pp. 60–64). He wasn't alone, however, in his struggle to unlock the secrets of the forgotten time line of human civilization.

THE LOST CIVILIZATION OF CARAL

For decades the Olmec of south-central Mexico were considered the oldest civilization of the Americas. Recently, however, a number of finds place Peru at the forefront of archaeological research aimed at identifying the earliest American civilization. In 2001 archaeologists unearthed the ruins of a previously unknown civilization located approximately 193 kilometers north of Lima.

Excavations took place for more than a year and the level of sophistication of this early kingdom that was uncovered amazed scientists. Conventional archaeologists now believe that this ancient site, known as Caral, is the missing link between the earliest known civilizations of the New World and the forgotten realms of prehistory. Perhaps the most startling discovery was that this lost Peruvian civilization had achieved many glorious things and yet was a Stone Age culture—a revelation that has forever changed our understanding of Neolithic technology and engineering.

Caral was a preceramic culture. It was without pottery, and all artifacts that were found in the ruins were made of wood, bone, stone, or reeds. These relics were often found together in lavishly ornamented burial chambers fashioned from crude stone tools. This is clearly a Neolithic society, yet they knew how to use cotton to weave textiles—a craft usually not seen in the Americas and other parts of the world, including some parts of Europe and Asia, until centuries later (Chouinard 2002).

In Caral and other primitive states the chieftains and councils of earlier times gave rise to powerful, godlike emperors who inspired the building of great structures and pyramids. They commanded the labor force and armies to do their bidding. The idea of an advanced Stone Age culture supports Graham Hancock's vision of a civilization far older than many mainstream archaeologists and historians are prepared to admit (Chouinard 2002).

For nearly fifty centuries the enigmatic lost "mother city" of Caral remained untouched and unseen, hidden amid the swirling grit of Peru's Supe Valley. Its ancient walls and massive monuments were consumed by the sands and left in utter silence. Now, for the first time since it was abandoned by an advanced pre-Columbian civilization, it is once again ready to tell its story (BBC 2002).

Radiocarbon dating of reed bags found at the site places the age of the ancient city between 2627 and 2000 BCE. This makes the find as old as the pyramids of Giza and predates the Olmec civilization, once thought to be the oldest in the New World, by one thousand years. This is without question the greatest archaeological find in the history of the Americas, comparable only to the discovery of the Clovis point in the 1930s. These new revelations are reshaping our knowledge of the Americas and the rest of the world (BBC 2002).

Caral's discoverer is Ruth Shady. Although Caral was known to some small extent prior to her first visit in the early 1990s, it was Shady who first recognized that the crumbling megaliths and stone structures were formed by human hands and obviously belonged to an ancient and advanced civilization. "When I first arrived in the valley in 1994," she told the BBC, "I was overwhelmed. This place is somewhere between the seat of the gods and the home of man. It is a very strange place" (BBC 2002).

While standing amid a mound of blowing dust, Shady was amazed to see the vague outline of what appeared to be pyramids. She discovered six of them altogether. Superficially, they somewhat resemble those seen in the Mississippian culture. The main difference is that rather than a simple mound of manipulated earth piled high above the plains, these pyramids were formed with mud plaster and stone (BBC 2002). Guy Gugliotta, writing for the *Washington Post*, stated, "Unlike the celebrated Egyptian pyramids, Caral's monuments were relatively simple structures—rectangular retaining walls of fitted stones, fronted with mud plaster and filled with reed bags full of rocks carried from the Supe River" (2001).

Like their future Mayan cousins to the north, these Caral pyramids are terraced and feature steps ascending the structures, indicating that they were probably used for religious practices. They are only 18 meters high, which is not a staggering height when compared with those of Mesoamerica, but their bases are more than 152 meters wide, making these structures the largest ever to have graced the Americas.

Additional sites are scattered across the region, hinting that Caral could have been a focal point for a more complex civilization of vast proportions. According to Winifred Creamer, an archaeologist at Northern Illinois University, "Besides Caral, there also appear to be four other sites you can see from one to another. If they are contemporaneous, we are looking at thousands of people in the valley at a very early date" (Gugliotta 2001).

FORBIDDEN ARCHAEOLOGY

At Table Mountain in Tuolumne County, California, miners were digging for gold and other precious ores in 1966. At 55 meters below the surface they discovered a mortar and pestle. Unbelievably, scientists called to the site could offer no clues to their origin. Analysis of the strata revealed that they were between thirty-three million and fifty-five million years old. A formidable attempt was launched to debunk the artifacts, but it proved nearly impossible. A number of human skeletal remains dating to the same time period were also found at the site (Gallegos 2009, pp. 9–10).

Many of these anomalous discoveries have engendered controversy; they are often met with a "knowledge filter," a system that judges all new theories—not on their merits but rather on the basis of preexisting academic theories (Gallegos 2009, 11). There is little chance of a truly original and paradigm-shattering idea ever gaining widespread acceptance within mainstream scientific circles. The guardians of the establishment simply don't want to risk their reputations and careers on a competing idea, even if that idea is the correct one. Rather than acting to support a genuine search for the truth, this filter is nothing more than a political power play, the ultimate result of which is that all ideas, evidence, or speculation not officially sanctioned by the academic hierarchy are thought to be unworthy of consideration or further investigation and are consigned to the domain of "fringe science." This is a death sentence for any scientist attempting to gain broad acceptance for a new theory.

A perfect example of this chilling effect occurred in 1966. The U.S. Geological Survey sent a team of three seasoned excavators to investigate reports of anomalous finds at Hueyatlaco, a palaeo-Indian site 121 kilometers southeast of Mexico City. Among the team members was geologist and graduate student Dr. Virginia Steen-McIntyre. Although the site itself was discovered by Mexican archaeologist Juan Armenta Camacho and American archaeologist Cynthia Irwin-Williams, Virginia Steen-McIntyre is best associated with the site due to her adherence to the facts of her discovery and her determination to let the truth be known.

She unearthed sophisticated stone tools whose origins she dated to roughly two hundred thousand years ago. Despite the fact that a team from the United States Geological Survey confirmed the great antiquity of the finds, when she attempted to publish her findings she faced tremendous roadblocks. Her statements of finding an unusually ancient set of stone tools were ridiculed. It was as if she was claiming that Bigfoot lived in the White House. She was promptly fired from her position as geologist and field archaeologist and stripped of her prestige as a respected member of the academic community. Furthermore, never again was she able to get a job in her beloved field of archaeology or any legitimate position as a mainstream geologist (Gallegos 2009, p. 10).

THE RENEGADE VELIKOVSKY

Although the late, great Carl Sagan readily identified himself with what my friend John Anthony West calls the priesthood of science, he did make a heroic appeal on behalf of Polish scholar Immanuel Velikovsky, who is best known for his book *Worlds in Collision,* published in 1950. Velikovsky's theories included the idea that Venus was actually an anomaly generated in the Jovian system (Sagan 1980, pp. 90–91). Velikovsky maintained that the planet, or comet as he called it, left the gravitational influence of Jupiter and entered the inner solar system approximately 3500 BCE. During two close encounters with

Earth in 1450 BCE, the direction of Earth's rotation was altered radically (Alexander 2005, pp. 21–24).

According to Velikovsky, Earth's rotation then reverted to its original direction on its next pass through the orbit of the inner solar system. In the second and final confrontation with Earth, the comet caused substantial volcanism, floods, and even the parting of the Red Sea as described in the Book of Exodus. Following this phase of its journey it settled into its current orbit and became the planet Venus as we know it today. Mars also passed dangerously close to Earth between 776 and 687 BCE, prompting Earth's axis to oscillate by ten degrees (Alexander 2005, pp. 21–24).

According to Sagan, the academic community attempted to suppress Velikovsky's ideas and he (Sagan) condemned these actions. They didn't allow Velikovsky to speak at universities or publish his ideas in scientific journals, and they dissuaded newspapers and other media from releasing updates on his research. "Science," concluded Sagan, "is generated by and devoted to free inquiry; the idea that any hypothesis, no matter how strange, deserves to be considered on its merits. The suppression of uncomfortable ideas may be common in religion and politics, but it is not the path to knowledge; it has no place in the endeavor of science" (1980, pp. 90–91).

There are exceptions to the pattern of suppression, however. Quite recently a new theory has emerged that promises to rewrite Darwinian theory. But rather than being met with scorn and skepticism, it has attracted many adherents among conventional anthropologists and biologists, and it is now almost considered part of the mainstream scientific arena. This theory was first presented by the distinguished neurosurgeon Aaron G. Filler, M.D., Ph.D. In his recently published book *The Upright Ape: A New Origin of the Species,* Filler proposes the theory that rather than humans evolving from apes, or at least apelike hominids, it happened the other way around. He believes that apes evolved from humans from a common upright ancestor (Gallegos 2009, pp. 11–12).

In a college paper titled "Beyond History: Alternative Historical Perspective," San Jose State University student Fernando S. Gallegos commented: "Imagine the implications within our institutional views if this turned out to be true; we would have to completely restructure our whole preconceived views of our history as a human species" (2009, p. 11).

CONCLUSIONS

The nineteenth-century German philosopher Friedrich Wilhelm Nietzsche once wrote, "It is our future that lays down the law of our today." While there is some truth to this viewpoint, it is our past that defines humanity as a species and steers us forward to an uncertain but perhaps glorious future. The legacy of the pyramids, Stonehenge, ancient Greek and Roman civilization, the enigma of the Maya, the solemn ruins of Chaco Canyon in the American Southwest, ancient Chinese and Japanese civilization, the sum total of our earthly heritage—all pushes us forward to a final destiny. That future is only now starting to take shape. Through history and archaeology we can discover the reason and purpose behind it.

4

The Tower of Babel Revisited

THE BASICS OF EARLY WRITING

Traditional sources suggest that writing developed in Mesopotamia in 3500 BCE and then spread to Egypt, Elam, and the Indus Valley. As Western Europe's knowledge of the world expanded during the Age of Exploration, Europeans came into direct contact with a number of ancient cultures. Among them were the civilizations of East Asia and the Americas. Indeed, the then newly discovered writing systems of China and Mesoamerica, it was found, developed independently of western Asia. Thus, the diffusionist model of all written languages stemming from a single Mesopotamian ancestor was proved incorrect.

Without writing, the development of civilization would have been impossible. The invention of written language has given birth to a world of unparalleled technology and global communication. Such a twenty-first-century reality would be unimaginable to the primitive tribal chieftains and shamans who formed the first ancestral script.

MODERN PERCEPTIONS OF WRITING

Written language is considered one of the primary "markers" of civilization, yet writing is by no means exclusive to civilization, nor is it a prerequisite. With the publication of Charles Darwin's *Origin of Species* and the growing pseudoscience of social Darwinism, there has been a growing tendency to classify all human cultures in purely Darwinistic terms. In the mid-nineteenth and early twentieth centuries, anthropologists placed specific writing systems on an evolutionary time line. Ancient scripts, such as those of China and India, were labeled primitive and decidedly inferior, while those of the great Western tradition were considered more advanced than scripts derived from non-Western sources.

Before science supplanted religion as the primary method of understanding the world around us, many heroes, gods, and monsters were believed to be responsible for the birth of writing, as well as civilization, and early writing was often imbued with a mystical element. For instance, God's word was thought to be burned into the two stone tablets Moses brought down from Mount Sinai, known as the Ten Commandments.

In December 1998, Günter Dreyer, director of the German Archaeological Institute in Egypt, announced "new radiocarbon dates for tombs at Abydos, on the Nile about 250 miles south of Cairo. The dates indicated that some hieroglyphic inscriptions on pots, bone and ivory in the tombs were made at least as early as 3200 BCE, possibly 3400" (Wilford 1999). It was now an "open question," Dreyer said, whether writing appeared first in Egypt or Mesopotamia (Wilford 1999).

EARLIEST SCRIPT FOUND IN INDUS VALLEY?

A discovery made by archaeologists in Pakistan may help prove that Mesopotamia was not the first civilization to develop a system of writing and that the invention of a written language itself is far older than previously thought. Graham Hancock, a journalist and amateur archaeologist who has been the target of criticism from mainstream academics for his controversial theories, firmly believes that civilization as we know it is merely a vestige of a once glorious age on which many of our Atlantean myths are based. An archaeological find in Pakistan may help support his contention.

The site, known as Harappa, was the location of the ancient Indus Valley Civilization. It was settled in 3500 BCE and over the succeeding millennia grew in a vast urban sprawl that became one of the chief civilizations of ancient times. Here archaeologists uncovered an ancient piece of pottery dating back almost six thousand years, to around 3500 BCE. Etched into the surface of the pottery were various "plantlike" and "trident-shaped" symbols, according to Dr. David Whitehouse, writing for BBC News (Whitehouse 1999).

Most recently Egypt was credited as the birthplace of writing. A collection of small clay tablets engraved with an archaic form of hieroglyphics was found in 1998 in the tomb of the Scorpion King, one of the rulers of Egypt prior to the foundation of the glorious Old Kingdom. Carbon-14 dating revealed that the tablets had been inscribed around 3300 to 3200 BCE, a century or two earlier than the supposed invention of cuneiform writing by the Sumerians approximately 3100 BCE.

Archaeologists now believe that this system of writing did not develop as a natural outgrowth of a spoken language. They contend that it was invented at the command of a ruler who needed to find the best way to make records and levy taxes. A uniform system of writing would prove to be the perfect agent not only for civic leaders but also for priests wishing to put down in writing their various incantations, the descriptions of holy rites, and the stories that their faiths were based upon. It is very probable that pre-Columbian civilizations such as the Aztec and Maya employed this same rationale.

The key to understanding the Indus Valley script is to compare it with known Egyptian hieroglyphs. But unlike the Scorpion inscriptions, we have nothing that could be used to compare with the Harappan script, no common Rosetta Stone from which to unlock its mysteries. "It's a big question as to if we can call what we have found true writing," Dr. Richard Meadow of Harvard University explains, "but we have found symbols that have similarities to what became Indus script" (Whitehouse 1999). Meadow, the director of the Harappa Archaeological Research Project, said that his excavators will continue to search for more examples of this unique writing system to determine whether it is indeed a genuine form of writing and, if so, how it developed from its primitive form to the more advanced writing we see today (Whitehouse 1999).

The Harappan civilization left no linguistic descendants; their language is essentially dead, which makes the task of deciphering the script next to impossible. The Rosetta Stone was important because it contained three languages: ancient Egyptian hieroglyphs, Egyptian demotic script, and ancient Greek. Champollion, the eighteenth-century linguist who cracked the code, used the latter two languages to cross-reference the hieroglyphs, after which the ancient writing could be read at last. No such relic for the Harappan civilization is known to exist.

Whitehouse observes:

What historians know of the Harappan civilisation makes them unique. Their society did not like great differences between social classes or the display of wealth by rulers. They did not leave behind large monuments or rich graves. They appear to have been a peaceful people who displayed their art in smaller works of stone. Their society seems to have petered out. Around 1900 BC Harappa and other urban centres started to decline as people left them to move east to what is now India and the Ganges. (1999)

Whitehouse closes his article by stating that perhaps writing arose independently in three places at once between 3500 and 3100 BCE: Egypt, Mesopotamia, and Harappa. Doubtless, there is much more to this story than mainstream scientists or archaeologists are prepared to admit. The clock is constantly turning back the antiquity of civilization as new evidence is uncovered, transforming our understanding of the past. In time, more relics will be unearthed, and perhaps the visions of Graham Hancock and others will be forever validated.

A DISCOVERY IN JERUSALEM

An artifact discovered in Jerusalem promises to prove that that city was a booming urban center during the Late Bronze Age, far predating its conquest by King David. The relic is a fragment chipped off an officially inscribed clay tablet, apparently part of a now lost royal archive.

It measures 2 × 2.8 centimeters in length and width and 1 centimeter in thickness and dates back to the fourteenth century BCE. The text appears to be Akkadian in origin and written with cuneiform symbols. The fragment is believed to be a part of an archive contemporary with the Egyptian pharaoh Akhenaten. In the nineteenth century at the excavations at Amarna, in Egypt, a cache of 380 tablets was found. Evidence indicates this cache either belonged to the pharaoh himself or was part of a related archive. Some scholars believe Akhenaten to be the Egyptian ruler responsible for the invention and spread of monotheism, leading first to the Jewish and then to the Christian and Muslim faiths. This idea was first forwarded by Sigmund Freud in his book *Moses and Monotheism,* in which he claimed the Hebrews learned about monotheism through Akhenaten during the years of captivity and slavery in Egypt.

The fragment was discovered while sifting through ruins during an excavation outside the walls of Jerusalem's Old City in the summer of 2010. Professor Wayne Horowitz, a scholar of Assyriology at Hebrew University Institute of Archaeology, says that the inscription itself bears little intrinsic value, but its presence is extremely significant. The person responsible for the inscription was probably a skilled scribe working for the reigning king at that time. This shows that by the fourteenth

century BCE the inhabitants of Jerusalem already possessed a sophisticated and highly stratified society and that Jerusalem was either part of
or the focal point of an advanced culture.

This new discovery predates the Hezekiah tablet previously found in
the Shiloah water tunnel in the City of David area of Jerusalem, which
dates to the eighth-century BCE reign of King Hezekiah (ScienceDaily
2010c). This find was preceded just two years earlier, in 2008, by the
discovery of the earliest known Hebrew text in proto-Canaanite script.
It was unearthed in the same region that David supposedly slew the
giant Goliath. This is also the location of the earliest known fortified
Judean city, the Elah Fortress (Khirbet Qeiyafa). That discovery is more
than three millennia old, antedating the Dead Sea Scrolls by more than
a thousand years (ScienceDaily 2008).

THE EARLIEST WRITING FOUND IN THE AMERICAS?

In September 2006 archaeologists in Veracruz, Mexico, announced a
major discovery: a stone block inscribed with what is thought to be the
earliest writing in the New World. It is known as the Cascajal block;
certain features of it have led experts to link it to the Olmec civilization, one of the oldest New World civilizations. Some Mormon scholars
claim the block provides evidence for the Jaredite culture, a people written of in the Book of Mormon who, at the time of the Tower of Babel,
escaped by boat across the ocean and established a civilization in the
Americas. The stone has been dated to the first millennium BCE.

Carved out of serpentine, it weighs 11.79 kilograms and measures
some 36 centimeters in length, 21 centimeters in width, and 13 centimeters in thickness. The inscription consists of sixty-two signs, and
a number of them seem to be repeated several times. The inscription
conforms to all standard criteria for a writing system: clear patterns of
sequencing, consistent reading order and distinct elements. It is without question a genuine writing system. Called "unprecedented" by

Brown University's Stephen D. Houston, one of the leading authorities on ancient writing systems, are signs that the stone has been repeatedly inscribed upon and then erased. Moreover, there are several paired signs that team archaeologists consider possibly the earliest indication of poetry in the New World (ScienceDaily 2006).

Houston elaborated: "It's a tantalizing discovery. I think it could be the beginning of a new era of focus on Olmec civilization. It's telling us that these records probably exist and that many remain to be found. If we can decode their content, these earliest voices of Mesoamerican civilization will speak to us today" (ScienceDaily 2006).

PREVIOUSLY UNKNOWN WRITTEN LANGUAGE DISCOVERED IN SCOTLAND

Recently a new written language was discovered—not buried in the deserts of the Middle East or the Indus Valley, but rather in the misty lands of Scotland. The language belongs to a race known as the Picts, an ancient pre-Christian Celtic people who lived in Scotland during the Iron Age, from 300 to 843 CE. The rocks on which the stylized engravings appear are called Pictish Stones. This language was originally thought to depict only symbols used to commemorate events and transfer other information, but after running the symbols through a system of computerized tests, a definite lingual pattern has been confirmed (Viegas 2010).

These data were compared with that of "numerous written languages, such as Egyptian hieroglyphs, Chinese texts and written Latin, Anglo-Saxon, Old Norse, Ancient Irish, Old Irish and Old Welsh. While the Pictish Stone engravings did not match any of these, they displayed characteristics of writing based on a spoken language" (Viegas 2010).

The Pictish Stone engravings are similar to Norse Rune Stones. It was first thought that they were linked to heraldry, yet it soon became apparent that these enigmatic symbols represent the long lost language of the Picts (Viegas 2010).

EVIDENCE OF A PREVIOUSLY UNKNOWN OLD EUROPEAN SCRIPT

A number of sacral plates were unearthed in Bulgaria. They were inscribed with an ancient form of Thracian writing not previously known to archaeologists. The script suggests that the Old European civilization that inhabited this region enjoyed a more advanced culture than its Western neighbors. It might even have been comparable to some of the civilizations of western and Central Asia. Old European civilization is believed to have comprised Greece, Bulgaria, Macedonia, Romania, eastern Hungary, Moldova, southern Ukraine, and locations in the former Yugoslavia. It opened the trade routes between those regions that lay more to the east and the European-dominated Mediterranean (Chouinard 2008, p. 10). Furthermore, archaeologists involved with the excavation believe that these examples of archaic script are the oldest in Europe and even antedate the Sumerian cuneiform and Egyptian hieroglyphs (Sophia Echo 2007).

This discovery, however, is not the first of its kind. Over the past century and a half there has been an explosion of new evidence hinting that Old European scripts are possibly the oldest writing ever invented. Archaeologist Zsofia Torma found a cache of uniquely engraved objects during an excavation in Transylvania in 1875. In 1908 inscribed objects were found in Vinca, a suburb of Belgrade (Serbia), and now that writing is recognized as just one aspect of what is now known as the Vinca culture. For more than a millennium such scripts spread throughout Old Europe. However, archaeologists still class these scripts as protowriting because they seem to convey direct ideas rather than retain any abstract or linguistic concepts (Winn 1981).

CHINA'S EARLIEST WRITING

Alternative archaeologists have now found a new rallying cry in the form of a discovery that could be as significant to global culture as the unearthing of the flood tablet of ancient Sumer. According to *China Daily* (2003), "Neolithic graves in central China may hide the world's earliest writing, if the 'signs' carved into 8,600-year-old tortoise shells can be deciphered by academics."

The artifacts were discovered at a site called Jiahu, in central China's Henan Province, which has been carbon dated to between 7000 and 5800 BCE. China's early writing consists of pictographic inscriptions known as jiaguwen. Researchers suggest that the pictographs on the tortoise shells predate the jiaguwen used in the Shang Dynasty, in existence from about the sixteenth century through the eleventh century BCE. If true, they would also antedate the writing in Mesopotamia by more than two thousand years. The researchers have met firm resistance from much of the archaeological community, which has labeled this seminal find as "nonsense" (China Daily 2003).

CONCLUSIONS

There is no doubt that identifying the first writing system is a pivotal goal in our search for the earliest civilization. This author subscribes neither to the theory that the cuneiform script of ancient Sumer is the first written language nor to the notion that the invention of writing was exclusive to the Old World. The next major discoveries will happen in the New World, and new finds suggesting an even greater antiquity for written language are looming on the horizon.

5

The Extraterrestrial Atlantis

There are those who believe that life here began out there, far across the universe, with tribes of humans who may have been the forefathers of the Egyptians, or the Toltecs, or the Mayans. Some believe that there may yet be brothers of man who even now fight to survive somewhere beyond the heavens.

BATTLESTAR GALACTICA,
OPENING NARRATION, 1978

In the orchards of the gods, he watches the canals . . .

ENUMA ELISH,
SUMER, 2500 BCE

In order to reach the Mountains of Mars, stand at the Foot of their awesome pyramids, and to reap the benefits of their energies, one must ascend the genetic ladder of one's forebears.

EDGAR RICE BURROUGHS,
THE CHESSMEN OF MARS, 1922

A SHARED HERITAGE

If there is one thing that the entire human race shares, it is a unique fascination with the universe and a distinct feeling that we are not alone. Since the earliest times, ancient writers have spoken of angels, demons, and gods who come down to Earth from the heavens, often to cause harm, at other times to instruct, nurture, and lead the human race into a new era of power and technological sophistication.

These ideas continue into the modern day, and some of today's most eminent scientists have faith that they are true. At the 1966 convention of the American Astronautical Society, Carl Sagan, the seer of modern science, stated, "Our tiny corner of the universe may have been visited thousands of times in the past few billions of years" (Steiger and Steiger 2003, 3:246). In 1966 Sagan coauthored a book with I. S. Shklovskii titled *Intelligent Life in the Universe*. In it he writes, "At least one of these visits occurred in historical times" (Shklovskii and Sagan 1966). This statement evidently planted the seeds of even bolder speculations on the part of UFO enthusiasts and independent researchers. The conclusion postulated by many Ufologists is that rather than evolving independently from more apelike ancestors, as the Darwinian theory states, we may have been seeded on this planet by an outside power, and not by the God of the Bible. The theory that eventually evolved is that ancient aliens caused a mutation among our hominid ancestors, leading to the intelligent and creative force of modern humanity.

Giorgio A. Tsoukalos, Erich von Däniken's business partner and associate in the United States, suggested a possible UFO connection to the Atlantis mystery. Tsoukalos believes that Atlantis was never a stationary landmass at all but rather a massive UFO or floating city. Rather than being destroyed, it launched itself back into space in a burst of fire, smoke, and ocean tidal currents. This corresponds directly to Plato's account. Tsoukalos supports his ideas by citing ancient legends that talk about floating cities that descended from the heavens, appearing suddenly and without warning. Then, just as quickly as they arrived, the mysterious floating cities returned to the lands beyond the stars, the home of the gods (Clotworthy 2011).

Carl Sagan was an exobiologist as well as an astronomer, and a visionary as well. He longed for a future age when people would put aside their endless warfare, dedicate themselves to the principles of science, and explore the universe for the benefit of all. Sagan believed that it was possible that a great galactic civilization could have visited Earth at one time in its prehistory. These visitations could have culminated in the establishment of bases within our own solar system, designed to spearhead future expeditions (Steiger and Steiger 2003, 3:246).

THE MARTIANS ARE COMING

In *Cosmos,* Carl Sagan poses an obvious but seldom-asked question.

Why Martians? Why so many speculations and ardent fantasies about Martians, rather than, say, Saturnians or Plutonians? Because Mars seems, at first glance, very Earthlike. It is the nearest planet whose surface we can see. There are polar ice caps, drifting white clouds, raging dust storms, seasonally changing patterns on its red surface, even a twenty-four-hour day. It is tempting to think of it as an inhabited world. Mars has become a kind of mythic arena onto which we have projected our earthly hopes and fears. (1980, p. 106)

Mars entered the public eye in the late 1800s when a wealthy Bostonian named Percival Lowell became convinced that life existed on Mars in the form of a wise and dying civilization, far more advanced than anything the people of Earth could imagine. Lowell was mesmerized by the reports by an Italian astronomer, Giovanni Schiaparelli, who wrote that he had observed canali, or channels, on the surface of Mars with his telescope. In Italian, *canali* means "channels," but to Percival Lowell the word signified *canals,* which was representative of intelligent design on the part of the Martians. The public became increasingly fascinated with anything the slightest bit Martian. Schiaparelli retired in 1892 because of failing eyesight, but Lowell vowed to continue his research (Sagan 1980, pp. 106–7).

In *Cosmos,* Carl Sagan wrote of Lowell's investigations.

[His] notebooks are full of what he thought he saw: bright and dark areas, a hint of polar cap, and canals, a planet festooned with canals. Lowell believed he was seeing a globe-girdling network of great irrigation ditches, carrying water from the melting polar caps to the thirsty inhabitants of the equatorial cities. He believed the planet to be inhabited by an older and wiser race, perhaps very different from us. He believed that Mars was, very closely, Earth-like. (1980, p. 108)

In 1898 H. G. Wells penned *The War of the Worlds,* an apocalyptic prophecy of a future Martian invasion. He opens with the chilling words:

No one would have believed in the last years of the nineteenth century that this world was being watched keenly and closely by intelligences greater than man's and yet as mortal as his own; that as men busied themselves about the various concerns, they were scrutinized and studied, perhaps almost as narrowly as a man with a microscope might scrutinize the transient creatures who swarm and multiply in a drop of water. With infinite complacency men went to and fro over this globe about their little affairs, serene in their assurance of their empire over matter. It is possible that the infusoria under the microscope do the same. No one gave a thought to the older worlds of space as sources of human danger, or thought of them only to dismiss the idea of life upon them as impossible or improbable. It is curious to recall some of the mental habits of those departed days.

At most, terrestrial men fancied there might be other men upon Mars, perhaps inferior to themselves and ready to welcome a missionary enterprise. Yet across the gulf of space, minds that are to our minds as ours are to those of the beasts that perish, intellects vast and cool and unsympathetic, regarded this Earth with envious eyes, and slowly and surely drew their plans against us. (pp. 1–2)

This fictionalized prediction of a Martian conquest was so frightening that on Halloween Eve, 1938, Orson Welles terrified American radio listeners with a fake news broadcast based on the novel. The program described an invading force from Mars with massive war machines equipped with death rays and poison gas. In the broadcast the announcer, before collapsing from a gas attack, claimed that the invaders were entering New York City and that poison gas had been released. This resulted in widespread panic and chaos in the streets.

These were uneasy times in American history: a depression gripped the country, and Hitler's forces were marching across Europe. Americans knew that war would soon come to them as well, and it terrified them. Many misunderstood the broadcast and thought that Nazi Germany was invading the United States.

Public interest in the fourth planet from the sun continued into the twentieth century. On December 4, 1957, Walt Disney aired "Mars and Beyond" as an episode of *Disneyland* (later called *Walt Disney's Wonderful World of Color*). It proposed a number of possible environments to be found on Mars. One suggestion was that human explorers to the Red Planet would find evidence of a highly advanced and now dead civilization, its remnants scattered across a bleak and devastated planet.

In the late 1980s, when I heard rumors of prehistoric ruins on the Martian surface, I jumped at the opportunity to investigate further. Graham Hancock clarified these interplanetary anomalies in his book *The Mars Mystery*. In a television interview in 2003, I was given the opportunity to speak with Mr. Hancock on the topic. He was a guest on my award-winning public access television show, *Archaeology TV*.

In his book Hancock says:

> Triangular and pyramid-like structures have been observed on the Martian surface. Located in the east central portions of the Elysium Quadrangle, these features are visible on the *Mariner* photographs, by frames MTVS 4205-3 DAS 07794853 and MTVS 4296-243 DAS 12985882. The structures cast triangular and polygonal shadows. Steep-sided volcanic cones and impact craters occur only a few kilometers away. The mean diameter of the triangular pyramidal structures at the base is approximately three kilometers and the mean diameter of the polygonal structures is approximately six kilometers. (1998)

In his book *Extraterrestrial Archaeology,* David Hatcher Childress writes:

> According to Australian science writer Brian Crowley, prior to 1976, the year of the *Viking* Mission, Dr. James J. Hurtak of the Academy of Future Science, California, published a series of articles highlighting NASA photographs from the previous *Mariner 9* expedition of 1971 that showed distinct pyramid-shaped "mountains" in the Elysium quadrangle region. . . . Hurtak even postulated that if there were pyramids on Mars, somewhere we may even find a Sphinx! (1999, p. 190)

Other Martian pyramids are located in an area of Mars known as Cydonia. It is here that some of the most bizarre and perplexing structures stand. They remain an enigma to this day. The pyramids of Cydonia were photographed by *Viking 1* during its first fly-by in 1976; they were elusive at first. Rather than jumping right out, they faded into the terrain of the Martian surface and initially appeared to be nothing but mountains, craters, and other natural formations. However, once the Viking team began to make a serious and critical examination of the site, the visual images they received were astounding. "Although the scale is grander," Hancock says, "it does look the way some archaeological sites on Earth might look if photographed from 1,000 miles up. The more you examine the frame, the more it becomes apparent that it really could be an ensemble of enormous ruined monuments on the surface of Mars" (1998).

THE FACE ON MARS

In addition to the ruins of pyramids and other structures, some investigators have remarked on the presence of an otherworldly "face" on the surface of the Red Planet. The "face" of Mars got its first major proponent in the person of Vincent DiPietro, an electrical engineer with more than fourteen years of experience in digital electronics and image processing.

In the motion picture *Mission to Mars* (2000), a great, obscured face is revealed to be a spaceship, built by the original race of Martians. This original race seeded Earth following a cataclysm that destroyed much of Mars, leaving it cold and barren. The story shows how humanity is the product of a four-billion-year-old program that has resurrected the Martian race in the image of humans.

Science-fiction movies aside, the most significant image to be taken by *Viking* is a gigantic Sphinx-like face that NASA dismisses as a trick of light and shadow. This distinctive Martian "Face," or "Sphinx" as it is called, is perhaps one of the most enigmatic structures ever found in the solar system. It is something that NASA has tried unsuccessfully to bury. Richard C. Hoagland strongly disagrees with NASA's assessment that it is the result of a play of light. "The second image, which had been acquired 35 Martian Days later than the first one and under different lighting conditions, made possible comparative views and detailed measurements of the Face" (Hoagland 1987, p. 133).

Hancock covers similar ground in his discussion of Martian archaeology. On the *Viking* photographs we find the distinctive headdress, or "helmet," as David Hatcher Childress calls it. The Sphinx of Mars has now been determined to be almost "1.6 miles in length from crown to chin, 1.2. miles wide, and just under 2,600 feet high" (Childress 1999, p. 189). More characteristics have been shown following further computer enhancement. This includes the presence of teeth and bilateral lines across the top of the headdress, making it quite similar to "the nemes headdress of ancient Egyptian pyramids" (p. 190).

Childress further writes:

Even more interesting to many researchers are the angular constructions about 7 miles (11 km) southwest of the Cydonia Face. This cluster of angled constructions of various sizes suggest pyramids, one of which appears to be under construction or partially destroyed. The Face of Cydonia and its attendant pyramids are not the only out-of-place objects scattered on the dusty plains of Mars. A *Mariner 9* picture features a strange series of cubical rectangular cells ranging from three to five miles in length and forming a pattern which has its closest comparison in early Inca mountain city remains found in northern Peru and Bolivia, as photographed from the sky. Geologists remain baffled by this unusual box-like patterning. (p. 192)

BEROSSUS'S MYTHOLOGY OF OANNES: A VISITOR FROM THE DEEP OR BEYOND THE STARS?

In addition to *The True History of Mankind over the Last 100,000 Years,* the Babylonian priest-historian Berossus also published another historical account, unnamed and also lost to history, which posits that before the advent of civilization the Mesopotamians were a crude and unruly mass of people, in constant turmoil with little technical sophistication and none of the elements necessary to create and maintain an advanced culture. According to him, the ancient Sumerians did not invent civilization independently but rather received instructions from a higher intelligence (Childress 1996, pp. 1–10).

Berossus writes that in the very remote past a half-human, half-fish entity known as Oannes surfaced from the waters of the Persian Gulf and gave the Mesopotamians the arts of civilization. Berossus claims that this strange aquatic being walked upon the Earth during the day and returned to the ocean each evening to regain his strength. During the day he educated the Sumerians in writing, philosophy, architecture, and science. He also taught them the basis of their laws and religion and imparted the knowledge of geometry.

The implications suggesting that Oannes was an extraterrestrial are not surprising. If one looks hard enough at the thousands of ancient folkloric and mythological accounts, from both advanced and primitive people all over the world, one may develop a firm belief that ancient humans were in intimate contact with a number of forces representing a higher intelligence.

ANCIENT ALIENS AND THE FIRST CIVILIZATION

In his 1968 book *Chariots of the Gods?* Erich von Däniken proclaimed with much gusto that "the past teemed with unknown gods who visited the primeval earth in manned spaceships" (1968). The mainstream scientific community reviled and ridiculed Däniken's assertions about ancient astronauts. Others, however, digested his ideas. They made *Chariots of the Gods?* one of the most successful bestsellers of all time, with a cult following second only to *Star Trek*.

Part of the ancient astronaut theory describes intercourse between the extraterrestrials and primitive humans, which produced a superior hybrid race. The proof of this outrageous claim, or at least the presence of the visitors themselves, can be found in the monuments, art, and artifacts of past civilizations. Primitive humans right out of the Stone Age, Däniken maintains, did not have the incredible innovation or the skill to build the statues of Easter Island or the pyramids of Egypt. His most compelling evidence is found in undeciphered art and symbolism depicting beings wearing what look like space helmets and scenes reminiscent of modern space travel.

In his book *The 12th Planet*, American author Zecharia Sitchin presents the idea that an intellectually superior race, otherworldly in origin, created Terrans some three hundred thousand years ago. Like Däniken, Sitchin proposes that the creation of modern humans was achieved by cross-breeding primitive humans with a superior race. After millennia, these progenitors of the human race returned. Sitchin calls them the Anunnaki, a name taken from Sumerian mythology (Sitchin 1976).

THE WANDERERS OF THE FOURTH WORLD: ALIENS OR ANCIENT GODS?

Author Philip Coppens called the Hopi "the most mysterious and mystical of all Native Americans" (2010). The Four Corners region of the American Southwest is home to a number of ancient Native American tribes. Included among them are the Navajo, Zuni, Pueblo, Hopi, and Apache, all of whom share some basic creation myths. The Hopi also describe a number of past cataclysms. At the beginning of a number of these cosmic events, the Hopi and other cultures claim to have received aid from a higher intelligence.

Hopi culture is replete with numerous legends describing times when the Earth was ravaged and became barren, and the people sought refuge at the center of the world. The Hopi accounts indicate that far back in prehistory a series of cometary or asteroidal impacts occurred, perhaps even aerial bombardment by an extraterrestrial armada of spacecraft. According to one legend the snake people then arrived, gathered together the ancestors of the Hopi, and took them deep underground into the safety of shelters, where they lived for countless generations until the falling stars fell no more. The Hopi also claim that at a different time they lived beneath the surface of the Earth with the ant people to escape an onslaught of fire and ice, very similar to some of the Norse legends from Iceland, Scandinavia, and Germany.

Hopi tradition calls this vast underground cavern where they were sequestered the Third World. According to all of these legends, when the fully evolved Hopi finally left this vast underworld behind and ventured to the surface, they passed through a crack in Earth's crust. They then emerged into our existence, which the Hopi creation stories call the Fourth World. Their arrival into the Fourth World occurred at a place known as Sipapu. This location is the site of a hot spring, which tops a six- to eight-meter-high salt dome near Desert View, not far from the Grand Canyon. Other tribes claim that Sipapu can be found at different locations (Coppens 2010).

But who were the "snake" and "ant" people? Did they represent an earlier form of life on Earth? Are they an unknown race of underground dwellers? Or are they representative of something else, perhaps otherworldly? Coppens points out that "for no obvious reason, the Hopi also deliberately flattened and broadened their skulls by binding the heads of babies against cradleboards. For some, this is suggestive evidence that they did as such to make their children resemble the people [or beings] who brought them their civilization: 'gods'" (Coppens 2010). This head shape is seen repeatedly in modern depictions of some extraterrestrials, such as the Grey aliens.

The Hopi accounts indicating that a series of cometary or asteroidal impacts occurred in the distant past correspond with some of the most recent theories presented by modern science. It is generally believed by most scientists that sixty-five million years ago, toward the end of the Cretaceous period, an object measuring ten kilometers in diameter impacted Earth (Gribbin and Gribbin 1996, p. 1). This resulted in a total disruption of the planetary environment. The object hurled so much debris and dust into the atmosphere that it blocked out the sun, and the planet descended into a global freeze similar to the projected effects of a nuclear winter (Sagan 1980, pp. 320–29).

According to authors John and Mary Gribbin in *Fire on Earth,* this "Mount Everest–sized asteroid traveled ten times faster than the fastest bullet, producing an impact so severe that the entire Earth shifted in its orbit by a few dozen meters and the length of the year changed by a few hundredths of a second" (1996, p. 1). This great cataclysm sixty-five million years ago, straight out of the Book of Revelation, pushed the dinosaurs and the majority of species living on Earth at the time into extinction. There may have been hope for the dinosaurs; some paleontologists theorize that some species of smaller dinosaurs evolved into modern birds, a hotly debated issue among today's paleontologists.

Another impact site, Tunguska in eastern Siberia, was probably caused by a comet impact in 1909. Native Siberians called the resulting fireball and mushroom cloud the breath of Agni the fire god. There have been many attempts to solve the riddle of that fateful morning more than a century ago. One of the most popular theories is that the impacting object was a downed UFO (Sagan 1980, pp. 73–76). Indeed, the popular History Channel series *UFO Hunters* made that suggestion in one of their recent episodes. Despite the plausibility of this argument, however, there is no evidence to support it. The object was most likely a fragment of a comet or a house-size asteroid that, although definitely extraterrestrial, bore no stamp of higher intelligence.

Much has changed in our scientific understanding of the world since Plato's time. We now are privy to knowledge about cataclysms millions of years in the past. Comet and asteroid impacts have, in recent years, captured the public's imagination with such blockbuster movies as *Deep Impact* and *Armageddon.* Between July 16 and July 22, 1994, Shoemaker-Levy 9, a titanic comet, split apart and collided with Jupiter, producing a scar more visible than the Great Red Spot (National Space Science Data Center 2005). All of Earth watched the event with amazement and foreboding. This was indeed a portentous event. Could it happen to this planet? Or has it already? Was this what caused other great civilizations to go extinct in the remote past? Did it cause the Great Flood, which is featured in the Bible, the *Epic of Gilgamesh,* and so many other cultural traditions? Are we next on the cosmic agenda?

CONCLUSIONS

The idea of ancient aliens being the driving force behind human evolution is unsettling, to say the least. It is far easier and more desirable to consider humankind to be heroic creators of our own destiny, struggling to survive, insignificant in contrast to the vastness of the universe, and slowly working our way up through the evolutionary process to become what we are now. How glorious it is to think of humans as the sole, absolute rulers of this planet, deriving the tools of success through our own brilliance and ambition.

But perhaps the story is bigger than that. Indeed, the presence of a humanlike face on the planet Mars can only make us pause and wonder if the story of humankind is far grander then we have ever imagined. In time, ancient alien contact may become a proven reality, signifying existence beyond our earthly domain and ushering in a new vision of an ever expanding, ever evolving human consciousness that is not exclusively confined to Earth but written in the stars.

6

Göbekli Tepe, Mt. Ararat, and the Mysterious Hittites

The great mystery is not that we should have been thrown down here at random between the profusion of matter and that of the stars; it is that from our very prison we should draw, from our own selves, images powerful enough to deny our nothingness.

ANDRÉ MALRAUX,
MAN'S FATE, 1933

Modern-day Turkey is the site of some of the oldest and most mind-boggling discoveries of ancient archaeology. Some of the most well-known sites include Mount Ararat (the possible location of Noah's Ark), as well as the underground cities of Cappadocia, first used by Christians to hide from the pagan authorities of Rome and then used by the pagans to escape the tyranny of institutionalized and enforced Christianity. In our voyage of discovery we must logically start at the very threshold of human history. We must travel back even further than the eight-thousand-year-old protocity of Çatal Hüyük in southern Turkey. It is necessary to visit the earliest known structures built by humankind.

GÖBEKLI TEPE

A recently discovered prehistoric temple is challenging the accepted paradigm of human civilization. Göbekli Tepe ("the hill of the naval" in Turkish) dates to around 12,000 to 10,000 BCE, or the time of the destruction of Atlantis. The site includes massive carved stones, including two T-shaped pillars. Surrounding these main megaliths, which tower some 5 meters high are a number of smaller stones facing inward. On the stones' broadsides are elaborately carved motifs of foxes, lions, scorpions, and vultures (Curry 2008).

The implications of this site are truly astounding. David Lewis-Williams, professor of archaeology at Witwatersrand University in Johannesburg, South Africa, says, "Göbekli Tepe is the most important archaeological site in the world" (Coppens 2009a). Many progressive archaeologists consider it to be the oldest built site ever found. People gathered together and worshipped there seven thousand years before the Great Pyramids were supposed to have been built. New Age author Philip Coppens further comments, "Five millennia separate us from the birth of ancient Egypt in ca. 3100 BCE. Add another five millennia and we are in 8100 BCE, coincidently the start of the Age of Cancer. Add another millennium and a half, and we have the date when Göbekli Tepe, in the highlands of Turkey near the Iraqi and Syrian borders, was constructed" (2009a).

Göbekli Tepe is even a few thousand years older than Stonehenge. Built by the ancient Britons, Stonehenge was completed several centuries before the Great Pyramid of Giza and was part of a series of constructions dating back as far as 6000 BCE. In comparison, Göbekli Tepe dates to the late Mesolithic to proto-Neolithic Age. According to mainstream archaeologists, this was an epoch before agriculture, the invention of pottery, the domestication of animals, and even the settlement of the first villages. Only the primeval Jomon of Japan displayed such sophistication.

Göbekli Tepe was the site of annual worship and sacrifices to the gods of the hunt and of nature. This temple's discovery is slowly changing the conventional view held on to for so many years by mainstream academics, that civilization began no earlier than 3500 BCE with the development of the ancient Sumerian culture. Scholars had always been skeptical of any claims to the contrary, even when such evidence was compelling. Now this attitude seems to be changing.

Ian Hodder, head of Stanford's archaeological program, voiced the following with pure shock: "Göbekli Tepe is unbelievably big and amazing, at a ridiculously early date . . . huge great stones and fantastic, highly refined art. . . . Many people think that it changes everything. . . . It overturns the whole apple cart. All our theories were wrong" (Collins 2010).

Andrew Curry, in a 2008 *Smithsonian* article, described the possible scene twelve thousand years ago: "Prehistoric people would have gazed upon herds of gazelle and other wild animals; gently flowing rivers, which attracted migrating geese and ducks; fruit and nut trees; and rippling fields of wild barley and wild wheat varieties such as emmer and einkorn." According to chief archaeologist Klaus Schmidt, "This area was like a paradise." In his view, it was human-kind's original sacred site, its first "cathedral on a hill" (Curry 2008).

Coppens mentions the discovery of "the biblical town of Jericho and its stone walls," which were dated to 8000 BCE. Like Göbekli Tepe, the discovery of Jericho pushed back the emergence of the first cities to a much earlier date. Jericho's discovery marked the first blow against the accepted world paradigm. It proved that the civilization of the Terran race, our human community, is far older than previously thought. This development was further solidified by the discovery of another Turkish ruin, Çatal Hüyük, in 1958 by British archaeologist James Mellaart.

THE MYSTERIOUS CAYONU

The lost city of Cayonu is located ninety-six kilometers from Göbekli Tepe and is just as mysterious. Cayonu is younger than Göbekli Tepe, dating to 7500 to 6600 BCE, roughly the time when the first earthen embankment at Stonehenge was created. Following the construction of Cayonu, Çatal Hüyük was built along similar lines but contained some innovations, making it (Çatal Hüyük) the ultimate evolution in that order of constructions.

When excavated, Cayonu was littered with human skulls and bone fragments. Experts discovered the residue of human blood on some of the skulls. Additional artifacts, such as obsidian blades and artwork with graphic depictions, suggest that the site may have been used for human sacrifice. These sites would not have been available for our study, if not for the builders of Göbekli Tepe; it was their daring and insight that developed the technology and economic system that made these structures possible.

The age of Göbekli Tepe is contemporaneous with the end of the last ice age—the era of Atlantis, Osiris, and the Rama Empire. What mainstream archaeologists have been saying about the human past for almost two centuries has at last been challenged by something more than mere speculation or conjecture. Ian Hodder was exactly right: "All our theories were wrong."

MOUNT ARARAT

Another location in Turkey that has inspired scores of adventurers and the Christian faithful to its enigmatic slopes is Mount Ararat. It is one of the highest mountains in Turkey, or the entire region for that matter, and lies near the headwaters of the Euphrates. The environment on these slopes is rugged, harsh, and unforgiving. There are barely "six to eight weeks of favorable weather," and the mountain itself is virtually impassible (Steiger and Steiger 2003, 2:217).

Ancient sources suggest that Mount Ararat is the resting place of Noah's Ark. Genesis 8:4 states, "And the ark rested in the seventh month, on the seventeenth day of the month, upon the mountains of Ar-a-rat." The ancestors of the Hebrews who would go on to write the Old Testament scriptures were familiar with these imposing peaks. Even Marco Polo, two thousand years ago, was told that the ark rested on the slopes of Ararat as he trudged on his way from his native Venice, Italy, to the mysteries of China and the Far East (Steiger and Steiger 2003, 2:217–18).

However, other locations have been put forth, even the mountains of Ethiopia. There are also claims, such as the one advocated by Childress, that there may be several arks, spread out not only on Mount Ararat but also across other mountaintops throughout the world, left over from the real flood that destroyed Graham Hancock's lost civilization (Steiger and Steiger 2003, 2:218).

But let us return to this mysterious peak. Just before the Russian Revolution of 1917, an Imperial Russian Air Force pilot was flying over Mount Ararat when he was stunned to discover what appeared to be Noah's Ark below! He immediately sent a communiqué to the Tsar in Saint Petersburg, and an expedition was immediately dispatched. The team took measurements, wood samples, and hundreds of photographs of the site. After the Bolsheviks seized power and discovered the stash of "religious poison," they immediately destroyed all evidence that had been collected in relation to the ark. There would be no biblical fantasies in the new atheistic Russia (Steiger and Steiger 2003, 2:218).

Another rumor that persists to this day is that in 1959, when the Turkish Air Force was undertaking a survey of the Ararat region, a Turkish army pilot and a liaison officer noticed an "enormous, rectangular barge on the southeast slope at about 12,000 feet altitude" (Steiger and Steiger 2003, 2:219). This continued to be considered authentic eyewitness testimony for decades, and even to this day among some researchers.

The quest for answers continues. In the 1980s James Irwin was the eighth human to walk on the moon and later dedicated his life to proving the credibility of the Book of Genesis. He renewed the quest for Noah's Ark and logged in many long days scouring the slopes of the great mountain, searching in vain. His will likely not be the final search for this lost relic, but before we contemplate future expeditions on Ararat's inhospitable slopes, we might first consider the true essence of the ark story.

Why has it been handed down through the millennia? Perhaps the remains of Noah's Ark do not actually exist in physical reality but is an intangible, metaphorical symbol representing an essential truth, as the late Joseph Campbell might say. Whatever can be gleaned in terms of physical evidence for the existence of the ark is not as compelling at its mythological evidence. The story tells us much about the hidden past of the human race and the idea that during a great cataclysm there were those with the fortitude to survive a probable demise.

THE MYSTERIOUS HITTITES

In the second millennium BCE a mysterious, unknown army ravaged the ancient Middle East. It attacked and sacked Babylon, waged war against mighty Egypt, and built an empire unmatched in its power, strength, and sophistication. Its glories rivaled that of Egypt itself, and it would go on to become the greatest empire of the Bronze Age, but as quickly as it appeared it vanished, leaving little trace of its existence.

Ancient historians and scribes record a time when the Near East was ruled by three great empires: Egypt, Assyria, and Babylon. But even by the nineteenth century evidence emerged to challenge this long held notion. Could there in fact be a fourth unknown empire previously lost to history, which had escaped the historical record? By the turn of the twentieth century many expert and archaeologists were busy trying to unlock the secrets of ancient mysteries and the myths and legends of the past. One culture in particular that was of extreme interest to archaeologists in their quest to discover the identity of this lost culture: the Hittites.

The English scholar Francis William Newman wrote that if the Hittites existed at all "no Hittite king could have compared to the King of Judah . . ." (1853, p. 179). This critical view was countered by renowned linguist Archibald Henry Sayce who made the suggestion that the lost Anatolion civilization "was worthy in comparison to the divided kingdom of Egypt" and was "infinitely more powerful than that of Judah" (1888, p. 123). Indeed, the Book of Genesis describes the mysterious Hittites trading cedar with the Israelites and giving them chariots and horses and becoming a trusted friend and ally of Abraham.

Tablets found at the Assyrian colony of Kultepe (ancient Karum Kanesh) containing records of trade between Assyrian merchants and a certain "land of Hatti" was the first real archaeological evidence to support the existence of the Hittite Empire. What was most tantalizing about these artifacts was that some of the names were neither Assyrian nor Hattic but rather Indo-European. This hinted at the possibility of an unknown Near Eastern empire of European rather than Semitic or Asiatic extraction (Ceram 1956, pp. 49–50).

In 1884 archaeologist William Wright discovered script on a monument at Bogazkoy in Turkey by a "People of Hattusas," which was found to match peculiar hieroglyphic inscriptions found at Aleppo and Hamath in northern Syria. The key to cracking the code of those ancient inscriptions came in 1887, when excavations at Tell Amarna in Egypt uncovered a diplomatic correspondence between Pharaoh Amenhotep III and his son Amenhotep IV, better known as the heretic pharaoh Akhenaton. Two of these letters were sent from the "Kingdom of Kheta" and contained Akkadian-style cuneiform featuring an unknown language. None of the examining archaeologists or linguists could decipher their meaning. Two references in Egyptian, however, linked the names "Kheta" and "Hatti," which prompted Archibald Sayce to identify the "kingdom of Kheta" as mentioned in Egyptian texts as the same as the mysterious Anatolion civilization and the biblical Hittites.

In 1906 the German archaeologist Hugo Winckler discovered a royal archive consisting of more than ten thousand tablets inscribed in cuneiform Akkadian and the same unknown language. They were the same as those found at Tell Amarna in Egypt and on the inscriptions on the monuments found in Turkey. This ancient language was eventually decoded by Czech linguist Derdich Hrozny. He announced this decipherment on November 24, 1915, during a lecture at the Near Eastern Society of Berlin.

In 1917 Hrozny published a book detailing his discovery. It was titled *The Language of the Hittites; Its Structure and Its Membership in the Indo-European Linguistic Family.* In his preface he states that it was his purpose to decipher "the mysterious language of the Hittites" to show that it is not Middle Eastern but rather an "Indo-European language." Of course, it is now open to speculation about where these people came from. Could it have been central Europe?

After a hundred years of intense study, the ancient tablets have come to life and revealed much about the history of this great, once lost but now found empire. They were named by the ancient historians as one of the great superpowers of their time, along with Babylonia, Assyria, and Egypt. Described as the Aryans of the Bible, they were clearly a totalitarian regime, with the kings ruling with absolute power and requiring absolute submission to the state. Their marriages, professions, work, religion, and family activities were all monitored and controlled. They also had a state-owned and operated economic system. This was similar to present-day Cuba or North Korea. All property was owned by the community, excluding private ownership.

Some proto-Hittites dwelled in east Anatolia at the time of the Assyrian trading colonies, or Karums, circa 2000 to 1700 BCE, but scholars disagree about the degree of their presence. For those who accept that the Anatolian tongues are a subfamily of Indo-European, they are viewed as part of the centum, or western branch, and not the eastern one, as with Iranian and Indic (or Aryan). The Neshites conquered the capital city of Hattusha at some point between 1750 and 1650 BCE, depending on which of several Mesopotamian chronologies is used. The importance of the latter was that the early Hittite king Mursili[s] I conquered Babylon, ending its first, or Amorite, dynasty. The date for the capture of Babylon, believed to be 1595 BCE, could be as late as 1506 BCE or as early as 1651 BCE (Caroli 2008, personal communication).

Mursili was either the second or third ruler of the first Hittite dynasty. He first took the name Hattusili I from the city of Hattusha. He might have been the son of a king named Labarnas, or the same person with a new name. Further back, two older kings named Anitta and Pitkana had captured Kanesh from the allies of the Assyrian merchants probably circa 1800 to 1750 BCE. Evidently they did use a name resembling Hittite (as previously mentioned, the Egyptians called them the "Kheta" and the later Greeks, "Khetioii"). Variants on the term likewise occur in the Bible, though referring to postimperial times in David's reign. Mursili overextended himself in taking Babylon and soon was forced to return north, where a rival assassinated him. The rival didn't last long, and the Hittites descended into civil war and weakness for more than a century (Caroli 2008, personal communication).

The Hurri Mitanni Empire grew, even ruling Assyria for almost a century. Egypt cast off the Asiatic Hyksos, or Aamu, and became a military power too. Another non-Indo-European and non-Semitic people called the Kassites came to dominate Babylonia. To the west the Minoans fell into decline, perhaps caused by Thera's great eruption (circa 1650–1525 BCE). The mainland Mycenaean Greeks came to replace them on the sea, possibly in competition with the Phoenicians and allied Cypriots. It appears that whatever Aegean goods reached the Levante did so through Cyprus. Egypt may have received a Mycenaean embassy during the reigns of Thutmosis III or his son, Amenhotep II, and appears to have sent one to the Aegean under Amenhotep III. Another might have gone to Egypt in the days of Akhenaton, but relations cooled by the time of Ramses II (Caroli 2008, personal communication).

In the days of Thutmosis IV the Mitanni had to ally with Egypt because Assyria had thrown off the yoke, and the Hittites were finally recovering their strength to the northwest. Amenhotep III wed two Mitanni princesses sent by two of their successive kings, but to no avail. When the Assyrians took their eastern territories the Mitanni were left with only a rump state as a buffer against the Hittites that survived maybe a hundred years. Egypt sent no help (Caroli 2008, personal communication).

Around the time of Akhenaton into the days of Tut and Aye, Suppiluliuma[s] I expanded the Hittite empire to its apogee, including territories once conquered by Thutmosis III. A mysterious epidemic seems to have started in Egypt perhaps as early as the old age of Amenhotep III, but definitely by the time of Akhenaton and Tut. Not long thereafter it spread into Asia. Meanwhile, an Egyptian queen, possibly Meritaton, daughter of Akhenaton and his wife or his successor Smenkhkare, sent a message to the Hittite king asking for one of his sons to rule beside her. She was being pressured to wed a courtier she viewed as a servant after her husband died. Often it is assumed that Ankhesenamon, Tut's widow and Meritaton's youngest sister, sent the letter. Despite being skeptical, Suppiluliumas agreed, sending his son Zananza, but the prince was murdered on the way to Egypt and war nearly resulted (Caroli 2008, personal communication).

Haremhab, the second successor after Tut, attacked Hittite territory but achieved little. Suppiluliumas died of the plague, as did his heir, Arnuwandas, within, at most, five years. Next came Mursilis II and Muwatalis, who again strengthened the empire. The latter gathered the largest recorded Bronze Age army (about thirty thousand to thirty-seven thousand men) to face Ramses II of Egypt, at Kadesh in Lebanon, in the young pharaoh's fifth year. The battle proved to be a draw, but both sides claimed victory at home. Still, it was the Hittites who kept their gains up to that point (Caroli 2008, personal communication).

While Muwatalis was away, northern tribes called the Kaska sacked Hattusas, though they did not occupy it. Muwatalis's son, Urhi Teshub, ascended the throne as Mursilis III. However, his reign was brief, and his uncle, Hattusilis III, usurped the throne. Urhi Teshub was allowed to live in exile but plotted a return to power. Eventually he fled to Egypt for asylum, briefly instigating strife between the two super factions again. In the twenty-first year of Ramses II, Urhi Teshub was sent home, and a treaty was signed between Egypt and Hatti. It lasted until the Hittite empire fell seventy to seventy-five years later. One of Hattusilis's daughters married Ramses II in his thirty-fourth year; Hattusilis and his queen visited them five years later (Caroli 2008, personal communication).

Not long after that Hattusilis died, and his son Tudhaliyas IV came to the throne. Hattusas was rebuilt under Hattusilis and Tudhaliyas. It was one of the greatest cities of the world, but it was not to last—the western provinces began to fall away before Hattusilis died. In the east the Assyrians were attacking—having conquered the Mitanni buffer state about the time of Kadesh. The mysterious "sea peoples" ravaged widely too, though Suppiluliumas II, the last Hittite emperor, defeated him in the only known Hittite sea battle. He regained the eastern copper mines from Assyria but also denuded the great port of Ugarit of its fleet, and it was destroyed like many other cities. A generation earlier famine stalked the empire, requiring Egyptian grain, sent by Merneptah, son of Ramses II, who was also forced to fend off the sea peoples and starving Lybian tribes.

Hattusas was savagely burned, though no trace of an enemy occupier has been found. The city never rose again. Suppiluliumas II disappeared from the record, and the Hittite Empire ceased to exist and was largely forgotten. Its language wasn't deciphered until 1900. The Hittites had an older pictorial script but in imperial times wrote in Mesopotamian cuneiform and used the East Semitic Akkadian tongue for commerce and diplomacy, as did contemporary Egyptians. Exactly what happened at the end may never be known. Egypt suffered more attacks, and numerous Levantine and Cypriot cities were destroyed. The Aegean civilization collapsed into a centuries-long dark age. Assyria and Babylon survived but later suffered their own shorter dark ages. Neighboring Elam, once a thriving civilization, disappeared from the record for 285 to 290 years. This slightly later wave of disaster circa 1110 to 1056 BCE saw the end of Egypt's New Kingdom as well and the final Aegean collapse (Caroli 2008, personal communication).

Still, city-states using the Luvian language survived or were rebuilt in southeast Anatolia and Syria, and these people called themselves Hittites. They endured until the expansion of the Neo-Assyrian Empire after the 880s BCE. The last of these city-states, Zinjirli, fell to Assyria in 707 BCE, less than a generation after the destruction of Israel.

CONCLUSIONS

In this chapter we have examined the ancient monuments of Göbekli Tepe and Çatal Hüyük and discovered the significance of their great antiquity. In addition we have reviewed the discovery of the ancient Hittite Empire, the decipherment of their Indo-European language, and the legacy of their brief yet bloody history. We have also seen firsthand what evidence exists for the physical existence of Noah's Ark.

We have also examined the Hittites, who have much to teach us about the fate of those who suppress human liberty and seek the path of conquest rather than global consolidation through peace and democracy. With these secrets now finally revealed we have been given the opportunity to understand some of the important cornerstones of world history, whether they be the reality of the Great Flood, the presence of ancient temples seven thousand to eight thousand years before the building of the great pyramids, or the existence of a warrior kingdom described in the Bible but nearly lost for three thousand years prior to being rediscovered by European archaeologists. This legacy is one of armies and war, temples and monuments, floods and conflagration, almost entirely lost to us but discovered again by human intelligence, the true candle in the dark.

7

Arktos

THE NORTHERN ATLANTIS

Buliwyf: 'Lo, there do I see my father. 'Lo, there do I see . . .

Herger the Joyous: My mother, and my sisters, and my brothers.

Buliwyf: 'Lo, there do I see . . .

Herger the Joyous: The line of my people . . .

Edgtho the Silent: Back to the beginning.

Weath the Musician: 'Lo, they do call to me.

Ahmed Ibn Fahdlan: They bid me take my place among them.

Buliwyf: In the halls of Valhalla . . .

Ahmed Ibn Fahdlan: Where the brave . . .

Herger the Joyous: May live . . .

Ahmed Ibn Fahdlan: . . . forever.

SACRED NORSE PRAYER,
THE 13TH WARRIOR, 1999 FILM

THE LOST CELTIC CIVILIZATION OF THE NORTH

Tens of thousands of years before recorded history there existed a Europe so utterly dark and ancient that humans have long since forgotten it. The glories and triumphs it enjoyed as well as its battles and long ages of peace have simply slipped from human memory and consciousness and exist now only in the form of mythology and folklore. In *The Chronicles of the Celts,* Peter Berresford Ellis said, "The mythology, legends and folklore of the Celtic peoples are among the oldest and most vibrant of Europe. The Celts were, in fact, the first European people north of the Alps to emerge into recorded history. They were delineated from their fellow Europeans by virtue of the languages which they spoke and which we now identify by the term 'Celtic'" (1999, p. 9).

The Celts who inhabited northwestern Europe at the time of Caesar and Vercingetorix took part in an oral tradition going back many thousands of years. This ancient record was Celtic Europe's link to an all but forgotten past. According to one series of narratives—the Irish Cycles—the Gaelic ancestors came to Europe from a great western continent, or large island, during a time of darkness and mysticism. In fact, Irish and Celtic wordsmiths told of a vanished kingdom very similar to Plato's Atlantis.

In his book *Lost Cities of Atlantis, Ancient Europe, and the Mediterranean,* David Hatcher Childress reports on a fascinating folktale relayed to him over a pint of stout in a pub in western Ireland. He told the man sitting next to him that he was on a quest to discover the roots of the Atlantis myth and that he had heard rumors that he could find it in Ireland. Tickled by this show of interest in Irish lore, the man guzzled his last drop of stout and told Childress the story of how Ireland was once an outpost for Tir na n'Og. The man concluded his story by saying, "On a misty day, when the light is just right, you can see the towers of Tir na n'Og beneath the sea from the southern cliffs of Inisheer" (1996, p. 450). This Irish Atlantis may in fact be connected to the old Greek idea of Hyperborea, or, as it was often called, Thule. It was considered one of the northernmost islands of the world beyond the land of the Celts and Germans (pp. 450–52).

This magical kingdom of "eternal youth" was located west of the Aran Islands in the middle of the North Atlantic (Childress 1996, 450). Tir na n'Og, like the mythical Atlantis, was said to have sunk into the sea thousands of years ago. Many of the various descriptions of this lost Celtic homeland resemble Plato's account.

One story about Tir na n'Og claims that centuries ago, when Ireland was still young and sparsely populated, two men, Fianna and Oissin, went out hunting in the wilderness. As they stalked their quarry they saw a beautiful blonde-haired girl riding a mighty white steed. Enchanted by this young beauty, the boys called out to her. She told them that her father was the king of Tir na n'Og and that her land, a land of eternal youth and untold splendor, existed across the sea. The girl fell in love with Oissin, so he agreed to go with her to her island.

They stayed there for centuries, happy and content, until one day Oissin longed for home. He missed the people he had left behind and wanted once again to see the Emerald Isle. So the young girl sent for her horse. She told him not to dismount the horse or touch Irish soil. He mounted the great steed and traveled back to his homeland, heeding her advice.

Upon his arrival he could see that things were vastly different. His loved ones were dead, and the land had changed forever. As he rode through the countryside he came upon two men working in a field. When he slowed down to speak with them, he fell off his horse. Upon touching the ground he immediately began to age and before long he was some three centuries old. There on the field he died, never to see the land of eternal youth again.

IRELAND'S MANY RACES:
ARE THEY SURVIVORS OF ATLANTIS?

Irish mythology is the most valuable resource in understanding the early prehistory of Ireland. *The Book of Invasions* is a long and detailed compendium of sagas that describes the rise and fall of Ireland's different races and how Irish civilization was born from a series of gory, blood-drenched battles and mortal catastrophes. Complete with vast lineages, intersecting plots, and archaic characters, these ancient chronicles parallel the works of J. R. R. Tolkien, known for the mythical proto-European world called Middle Earth. Indeed, ancient Europe was once called *Mittel-erthen.*

Tolkien received much inspiration from *The Book of Invasions* and liberally borrowed from these stories throughout his major works. It's not well known that, along with creating epic fantasies, he was trying to reconstruct what lay behind the myths he loved. For years, he and one of his sons both had a recurring nightmare that featured a tsunami. For Tolkein senior the nightmare only abated when he began to write about Numenore, his version of Atlantis, in the late 1930s. Although he was a devout Catholic, Tolkien believed the tsunami dream could be explained as either a "racial memory" or as an event from a past life, and indeed he used the concept of reincarnation for his elves.

The Book of Invasions serves as an expanded explanation of the four cycles, which are the chief epics of Irish literature. It describes how waves of warring factions took control of the country and how each one added to the ethnic and racial composition of their island. Most of these early tribes were members of a master, godlike race that was said to have created Ireland from the foam of the sea and whose roots probably could be traced back to the European mainland (Childress 1996, pp. 423–25).

The invasion of the Milesians and their conquest of the people of Danu are the central stories of Irish culture even now, even after centuries of Catholicism. *The Book of Invasions* begins with the aftermath of a great flood. A tribe known as the Partholon traveled from the west across the Atlantic to escape the deluge and found refuge on Erin. The Ireland that they found was not the one we would recognize today. Childress describes the early Irish nation: "There were just nine rivers, three lakes and one plain, called the Old Plain. Partholon and his people cleared away some of the forests and fought against a people called the Fomorians. Partholon and his group were eventually wiped out by a terrible plague and Ireland is deserted for 30 years" (1996, p. 424).

Thomas Rolleston, an expert in Celtic myth, described the Fomorians as follows:

> Huge, misshapen, violent and cruel people, representing, we may believe, the powers of evil. One of these was surnamed Cenchos, which means The Footless, and thus appears to be related to Vitra, the God of Evil in Vedantic mythology, who had neither feet nor hands. With a host of these demons, Partholon fought for the lordship of Ireland, and drove them out to the northern seas, whence they occasionally harried the country under its later rulers. (1911, p. 97)

The second wave of invasions came when the Nemedians, led by Nemed, traveled from the Greek homeland. Amber was widely traded throughout Europe. The Nemedians exchanged amber, which they acquired in Denmark, Germany, and Scandinavia, in the bustling port cities of the Mediterranean. The Invasion Cycle tells us that the Nemedians had thirty-four ships that traveled the open sea in search of new lands. They eventually caught a vision of a great golden spire reaching high above the horizon. They sought it out, hoping to steal its treasures, but before they could find it, gigantic waves converged upon them, drowning most of the Nemedians in the deep, cold waters of the North Atlantic. Despite this setback some of them survived. The remaining Nemedians then wandered the ocean for more than a year, looking for a place to settle. Finally, along the misty horizon, the Emerald Isle appeared. The Nemedians beached their vessels, settled throughout Ireland, and declared it their own. However, their new-found hopes were soon beset by catastrophe (MacManus 1944, pp. 19–22).

The Nemedians faced more than just the troubles of a new colony trying to establish a home. The mountain lakes burst and flooded huge tracts of fertile land. According to Childress, the Nemedians then faced another problem: the Fomorians returned to Ireland in their second major invasion of it. On the order of their chieftain, Conan, the Fomorians constructed an inner tower on Troy Island, off the northwest coast of Donegal, where Conan assumed absolute power over Ireland (1996, p. 452).

This new ruler was far from benevolent. He was a powerful tyrant who demanded an annual tribute of two-thirds of the wheat, milk, and children. The Nemedians requested a three-year grace period from the harsh taxes levied on their people, while at the same time they sent a messenger to Greece, their original homeland. The Greek king, who was related to Nemed through a royal marriage, summoned forth a vast army of druids and druidesses, as well as an invasion force of vicious animals and diabolical creatures, including scorpions and snakes. The animals and druids breached the tower and put to death many of those inside, including Conan (Rolleston 1911, p. 105).

However, the Fomorians escaped and then returned with a great fleet, threatening to attack and eliminate the enclave of Nemedians. Nemed prepared to wipe the Fomorian race off the face of the Earth, but as his troops entered the port, a titanic tidal wave thousands of meters high crashed upon the harbor and destroyed almost everyone. Thirty Nemedians and one ship of Fomorians survived. The single group of Nemedian survivors then ventured forth and divided into three camps. The first consisted of those who went back to Greece. The second remained in Ireland under the jurisdiction of the Fomorian clans, and the third, under their leader Briton Mael, traveled to Scotland.

The Nemedians would not remain in exile for long. Waves of returning Nemedians from Greece, stronger than ever before, reconquered much of Ireland. Their triumph was short-lived, however. A race of Celtic god-men named the Tuatha Dé Danann came to Ireland, known as Eire, with blood axes and magical swords. They also brought other items, both mystical and powerful in nature, such as the Stone of Destiny and the enchanted cauldron of Dahgda, which might be the forerunner of the Holy Grail of Christian tradition.

The name Tuatha Dé Danann means, literally, "the folk of the god whose mother is Dana" (Rolleston 1911, pp. 103–4). Dana also sometimes bears another name, that of Brigit, a goddess held in high regard by pagan Ireland and whose attributes are in a great measure transferred in legend to the Christian Saint Brigit of the sixth century. Her name is also found in Gaulish inscriptions as "Brigindo" and occurs in several British inscriptions as "Brigantia" (Caroli 2011, personal communication).

Eire, then, may be said to be the god whose mother was Dana, and the race to whom she gave her name are the dearest representatives we have in Irish myths of the powers of Light and Knowledge. Yet they do not appear as gods in the Irish legends that have been passed down to us. Christian influences reduced them to the rank of fairies or identified them with the fallen angels. They were conquered by the Milesians, who are conceived as an entirely human race and who had all sorts of relations of love and war with them until quite recent times. Yet even in the later legends a certain splendor and exaltation appears to invest the people of Dana, recalling the high estate from which they had been dethroned (Rolleston 1911, p. 106).

THE LOST GERMANIC CIVILIZATION OF THE NORTH

In 600 BCE the Greek lyric poet Alcaeus wrote a series of narratives describing a vast northern kingdom located far beyond the lands of the Germani and Keltoi. Others suggest that a race of humans evolved separately in the Arctic. If true, this would defy everything we have been taught about human evolution. Traditional sources dating as far back as the first millennium BCE describe a civilization that once existed there, when the Arctic region was suitable for human habitation (Godwin 1993, p. 14).

More recently, author Robert Scrutton has presented his own collections of speculative texts, *The Other Atlantis* and *Secrets of Lost Atland,* to support his theory of a "proto-Viking Atlantis located in the North Sea" (Childress 1996). In *Secrets of Lost Atland* he describes the wisdom of the ancients with enormous attention to detail, explaining that the main thrust of the prehistoric technological civilization was a "coordinated system" of "psycho-electric science or cosmology" that was employed on a global scale. Scrutton further maintains that prevailing evidence for such a system is in the "stone circles, artificial hills, sacred sites, meditation chambers and altars. All of these were connected by ley lines and underground streams that formed an energy network that surrounded the globe" (1978).

John Michell, a genius in the science of alternative studies, supports Scrutton's views. Michell's work could well be considered an epilogue to this thoroughly researched topic. In 1998 near the great stone circle of Avebury, in England, Michell made the following comments in an interview with Douglas Kenyon, which was part of an Atlantis Rising video presentation called *English Sacred Sites: The Atlantis Connection.* The time period he was discussing was the late Neolithic Age, which was the time period of Old European civilization. In Britain this was dominated by the Beaker Folk and later the Wessex culture. "[Avebury] was the great center; the land was very sacred. It was farmed only for the high priests and those who came to the festivals. There were tribes or nations who were actually responsible for it, they held the games and protected the rites of the sanctuary. If you look at this land it is all ritualized, it's full of monuments" (Kenyon and Michell, 1999).

Hence it was Michell's viewpoint that Avebury, Stonehenge, and the other megalithic sites of southeastern England were in fact vast ceremonial centers for the practice of religious and spiritual activity. Researcher, aviator, and photographer Busty Taylor also appeared on the video, and he has made it his life's work to document and find connections between the ley lines and the modern phenomenon of crop circles. Taylor and Kenyon believe that many of the stone circles now scattered across the English countryside were, in fact, built on and around ancient crop circles. According to Kenyon, many of the churches now seen in the region were actually built on sites "revered" by the ancient populace, and this in itself hints that a far older order of civilization once dominated Europe.

THE *OERA LINDA BOOK*

Scrutton's primary source in bolstering his argument of a proto-Viking Atlantis in the North Sea is a Dutch manuscript, the *Oera Linda Book*. It has been acclaimed as "the oldest book in the world and a number of authors believe that this ancient book holds a key to the Atlantis riddle" (Childress 1996). Although the book is controversial and some believe it to be a fairly recent work of fiction, others hold that it is an incredibly valuable text from the mists of history.

One story tells us that in February 1871, the year Germany was unified for the very first time, a Frisian antiquarian located the *Oera Linda Book*. It had been in the possession of his family "for generations" and had been "handed down from father to son as a holy obligation" (Childress 1996). Scholars were struck by the fact that it appeared to have been written in an unknown language. This mystery was soon solved, however, when it became clear that the script was an ancient form of Frisian. Scrutton describes northern Atlantis, drawing on the *Oera Linda Book*.

A large, semi-circular land-mass, a sort of silhouette halo around the north and east of the British Isles, was contemporary with the conjectured Atlantis. It survived the traditional Atlantis, however, by many thousands of years. Its name was Atland, and there may be reason to suppose that Atland was the archetype of the Hyperborean tradition.

Although situated between what are now the storm-stricken Hebrides and the Greenland permafrost, Atland was no impoverished continent. On the contrary, its climate was subtropical, yielding abundance of everything for full and happy human existence. . . . In the year 2193 BCE, some cosmic calamity struck Earth; perhaps some imbalance proposed by Immanuel Velikovsky . . . perhaps an asteroid collided with the Earth. At any rate, from descriptions in the *Oera Linda Book,* something consistent with the tilting of the Earth's axis took place and within about three days, climatic change of overwhelming severity took place. Atland was submerged and her history lost . . . or nearly so. (1978, pp. 1–4)

According to the *Oera Linda Book,* the Atlanders were a maritime people who charted the seas of the world, including the Mediterranean. They established colonies in Scandinavia, northern and southern Europe, Africa, and Greece (Childress 1996).

Unlike Hancock, who places the great flood between 13,000 and 10,000 BCE, Robert Scrutton bases his chronology on the *Oera Linda Book* and sets it at 2193 BCE. At this time the Atlantic tidal waves enveloped the continent of Atland and smashed into the Mediterranean. This formed the basis of what Scrutton calls the "myth" of Noah's Ark at Mount Ararat (Childress 1996).

THE HYPERBOREAN TRADITION

Although Scrutton, as noted earlier, speculated that Atland may have been the archetype of the Hyperborean tradition, it was the Eastern idea of racial purification that laid the foundations of the modern Hyperborean myths. While biblical tradition states that all humankind descended from Adam and Eve in the Garden of Eden, and later from Noah and his sons, Eastern philosophy is replete with references to the root races and the independent evolution of all living beings. It was this Eastern mystique that enabled "Western imagination to entertain so different a view of human origins," namely the Hyperborean, Lemurian, Atlantean, and the ideas of Ignatius Donnelly, Helena Patrovna Blavatsky, Edgar Cayce, and others. This transfusion of Eastern ideals came first from Jesuit missionaries like Pere Amiot.

The myths of Hyperborea and the northern Atlantis of the Celts, Germans, Norse, Slavs, Balts, and Finns share common elements and could well be linked. In the nineteenth century this northern kingdom became associated with a distinctive "Germanic Atlantis," from whose shores great maritime fleets departed for trade, conquest, and settlement. Some believe that the major migrations of early civilization began there. Contrary to popular portrayals of the ancient Germans as wild barbarians, some propose that they maintained a vast and sophisticated Nordic culture, but then Christian Romans purposely destroyed that society, erasing all memory of its existence. The seers of those forgotten times depicted the saga of Germanic history on the grandest scale imaginable, visions of a dark, spiritual world illuminated from above by three suns and inhabited by giants, gods, and monsters (Goodrick-Clarke 1992, pp. 1–21).

This society, born of Teutonic pagan tribalism and governed by sacred kingship, survived until the end of what I call the fourth Cataclysmic age (roughly based on the terminology of Howard), around 11,000 BCE. The remnants of that civilization scattered across

Europe and Asia. Their knowledge was preserved in the oral traditions of the people they conquered or their descendants in the lands they colonized. Europe and India were the richest centers of Aryan culture that survived the Cataclysmic age.

The Aryan culture was comprised of the tall, blond, and fair-skinned ancestors of today's northwestern population, and also the partial ancestors of much of modern Europe and Asia. Contrary to the beliefs of the twentieth-century National Socialist movement, the Aryans were a very real, very ancient people with a rich archaeological and mythological heritage. This race descended from the Hyperborean culture and initially escaped the highlands and mountains of Tibet; afterward they migrated back to Central Europe. Among the Hindus—the descendants of the great Aryan invasion—the Rig Veda and Upanishads remain vestiges of that race. These texts, written by members of this elite warrior society, document the purest strain of the Aryan race that had conquered much of India and whose culture was preserved through the rigid caste system.

THULE AND THE ANCIENT ARYANS

When Hitler drafted a counterclockwise swastika as his emblem, he proclaimed that it represented how the glorious Nordic sun looked to the ancient Aryans in their northern continent of Thule as it spiraled across the sky. As mentioned earlier, Thule is another name for the northern Atlantis, also known as Hyperborea, Arktos, and the Celtic Tir na n'Og. Thule is the ancestral homeland of the lost Aryan race. One of the proponents of a northern home for the so-called Aryan race was the Nazi philosopher Alfred Rosenberg. He was a Baltic national who escaped the scourge of the Bolshevik Revolution of 1917 by immigrating to Germany (Shirer 2008, p. 262).

The idea of Thule struck a chord with many Europeans, especially the Germans and English who spent much of their existence asserting their supposed racial superiority and engaging in violent colonial endeavors. Rosenberg wrote extensively about a northern Atlantis and offers the following thoughts concerning the lost continent of Thule.

Today, historical visions can see deeper into the past than was imaginable at an earlier time. The monuments of all peoples now lie spread out before us, excavations of the very oldest examples of pictorial art allow a comparison of the driving forces of cultures, the myths from Iceland to Polynesia have been collected, the treasures of the Mayans in great part unearthed. In addition, modern geology enables us to draw maps as things were tens of thousands of years ago. Underwater exploration has raised solid masses of lava from great depths of the Atlantic Ocean, the summits of suddenly submerged mountains in whose valleys cultures had once arisen before one—or many—frightful catastrophes destroyed them. Geographers depict for us continental masses between North America and Europe whose fragments we see in Iceland and Greenland. On Novaya Zemyla, in one area of the far north, old water lines are revealed more than 100 meters above the present ones. These suggest that the North Pole has shifted and that a much milder climate once prevailed in the Arctic. All in all, the old legends of Atlantis may appear in a new light.

It seems far from impossible that in areas over which the Atlantic waves roll and giant icebergs float, a flourishing continent once rose above the waters, and upon it a creative race produced a far-reaching culture and sent its children out into the world as seafarers and warriors. Even if this Atlantis hypothesis should prove untenable, a prehistoric Nordic cultural center must still be assumed. We have long since been forced to abandon the theory of an identical origin of myths, art and religious forms among people.

On the contrary, the strongly substantiated proof of the frequent traveling of Sagas from people to people, and their taking root among many different groups, shows the majority of basic myths have a fixed point of radiation—their place of creation. Thus, in their outward form, they are only comprehensible on the basis of a completely distinct point of origin, and the migrations of races also become a certainty in the most prehistoric times.

The solar myth, with all of its ramifications, did not arise spontaneously as a stage of general development, but was born where the appearance of the sun must have been a cosmic event of profoundest significance, that is, in the far north. Only there would the year be sharply divided into two halves, and only there would the sun represent a certainty in man's innermost being of the life renewing, primal creative substance of the world. And so today the lone derived hypothesis becomes a probability, namely that from a northern center of creation which, without postulating an actual submerged Atlantic continent, we may call Thule, swarms of warriors once fanned out in obedience to the ever renewed and inaccurate Nordic longing for distance to conquer and space to shape. It may still be uncertain where the original home of the Nordic race lies . . . many details are still doubtful . . . but whatever may be the result of further investigations one great fact cannot be challenged: the fact that the race which provides the "meaning of world history" is found to originate in the North and has spread from the North over the whole Earth; that it was a blue-eyed, fair-haired race which in several great waves formed the spiritual features of the world—even where the race itself was bound to perish.

These migration periods we call: the march of the Atlantic people—round the ancient traditions sprang up—through North Africa; the migration of the Aryans to Persia and India; followed by Dorics, Macedonians, Latins; the migration of the Germanic peoples; the colonisation of the world by the West under dominant Germanic influence. (1982, p. 20)

Beowulf, the *Nibelungenlied,* Irish and Norse sagas, Arthurian romances, and many other examples of ancient and medieval literature stand as lasting remnants of those forgotten times. The *Kalevala,* a Finnish epic, is perhaps one of the most extensive sacred texts that far north, and the Eddas retell what is left of the glorious Teutonic gods and mystery cults of the first Germans.

THE PIONEERING WORK OF JEAN-SYLVAIN BAILLY

During the eighteenth century Jean-Sylvain Bailly (1736–1793), a French astronomer and orator who was key figure in the early French Revolution, fused the collective knowledge of classical antiquity and the Bible with the newly discovered treasure trove of mystical knowledge that was gained from India and other Eastern cultures. Uniting them with modern astronomical science further strengthened the basic points of these cosmologies.

Bailly thought that Egyptian, Chaldean, and Indian scientific and philosophical knowledge were in many ways superior to those of other nations and cultures. This admiration was tempered, however, by the racist assertion that this was merely "the half-remembered residue of a far-superior culture: the antediluvian North" (Godwin 1993, p. 24).

Godwin quoted Baily as saying, "It is a very remarkable thing that enlightenment appears to have come from the North, against the common prejudice that the earth was enlightened, as it was populated, from South to North. The Scythians are one of the most ancient nations; the Chinese descend from them. The Atlanteans themselves, more ancient than the Egyptians descend from them" (1993, pp. 27–29).

Bailly firmly believed that during the Taurean Age, a distant astrological age some ten thousand years ago, the titans, gods, goddesses, and heroes of classical Greece and other parts of the world were, in fact, sages to the historical Noah. He also asserts that Hercules was originally an Eastern figure, perhaps Chinese, whose fame and relationship with the great northern race spread like wildfire, so much so that he was eventually renamed in the Hellenic world. Hercules was linked to the great northern race by the fact that some of the most ancient branches of the Hellenic race came not from the Aegean but migrated from the impenetrable Norse, thus making both the Greek gods and the demigods such as Hercules extensions of existing Germanic deities and heroes. Indeed, there are many similarities between Norse and Greek gods and heroes.

According to Bailly, as humanity began to rebuild after the deluge, the purest stream of civilization descended from northern Asia into India, a region that to this day carries evidence of having the most ancient astronomical system on Earth. Thus, Bailly introduces the idea of a northern homeland for humanity, or at least for what he considered the most important branch of it. One of his favorite arguments for this is that the fable of the phoenix is found both in Egypt, as reported by Herodotus (484–425 BCE), and in the Eddas, the epic poetry of the north.

Bailly prefers the Nordic version: "[The Phoenix's] head and breast are the color of fire; its tail and wings sky blue. It lives for 300 days, after which, followed by all the birds of passage, it flies off to Ethiopia and nests there; it burns itself together with its egg, from which ashes there emerges a red worm, which, after having recovered its wings and the form of a bird, takes flight again with the same birds to the north" (Godwin 1993, p. 22). The imaginative Bailly used the migrations of the Nordic phoenix as a spiritual representation of the flight of Nordic humans from the far north southward to the rest of the world.

Comte de Buffon, one of the first natural scientists prior to Charles Darwin, reported on Bailly's findings.

Bailly found records of subsequent stages of the great racial migration in the mythology of Egypt and Syria, where the dying and resurrected gods, Osiris and Adonis, were mourned for 40 days: this would correspond to the sun's annual absence at 68° latitude, he says . . . but surely not quite accurately, since that is practically on the Arctic Circle. Again, in the Zend-Avesta, the sacred book of the Persians that had recently (1771) been translated by Anquetil Duperron, Bailly read that the longest day of the year is twice as long as the shortest. This is the case at 49°, by no means an Arctic latitude, but still far to the north of Persia. (Godwin 1993, p. 42)

The natural conclusion was that these various legends preserved the racial memory of an origin in the far north and a gradual migration to the south. This worldview, or "Weltanschauung," thrilled Comte de Buffon because he had posited the age of the Earth at seventy-five thousand years; according to Buffon, the North Pole was the first to cool following Earth's separation from the sun. This happened some thirty-five thousand years ago. This, of course, is not a correct time frame but was an essential step toward developing a modern geologic and evolutionary timescale. Working from legends and scientific data, Buffon "placed the first civilizations in northern and central Asia; east of the Caspian Sea" (Childress 1996, p. 327).

OTHER PROPONENTS OF
A LOST NORTHERN CIVILIZATION

Another scholar with an interest in these matters was William F. Warren, the first president of Boston University and author of such books as *The True Key of Ancient Cosmology* (1882) and *Paradise Found—The Cradle of the Human Race at the North Pole* (1885). He was trained in esoteric studies and later joined the Mystical Seven, which was a secret society embracing ancient symbology and the occult. Suprisingly enough, he was a staunch Creationist who stood against the Evolutionist leanings of his colleagues. As an anti-Darwinist he rejected the standard idea that humans evolved from less-developed primates, as well as the notion that all life evolves from simpler forms to more advanced stages. He firmly believed that the Garden of Eden was not to be found in the Near East, but in the Arctic, where the antediluvian race of humans built their splendid cities and were all but annihilated by the onslaught of the great deluge.

Concerning the paradise of the far north, Warren makes an eloquent statement: "Whoever seeks a probable location for Paradise the heavenliest spot on Earth with respect to light and darkness, and with respect to celestial scenery, must be content to seek it at the Arctic Pole. Here is the true city of the sun. Here is the one and only spot on Earth respecting which it would seem as if the creator has said, as of his own heavenly residence, 'There shall be no night there'" (Godwin 1993, p. 21).

In 1954 Jurgen Spanuth, a German scientist and minister, came to the conclusion that a lost civilization, a now submerged island that existed in the North Sea many thousands of years ago, was the basis of the Atlantean myth. However distorted by Plato's account, it came from the Nordic and other European races, as well as the cultural influence that spawned global civilization. In his book *Atlantis of the North,* he claimed that he had "explored a sunken, walled city fifty feet below the shallow North Sea waters" (Spanuth 1980, p. 22). He identified this wall with the wall described in Plato's account that surrounded the temple and citadel.

COSMIC ICE THEORY

The cosmic ice theory, also known as the world ice theory, or Welteislehre, was presented to the skeptical, pre-Nazi intelligentsia of Europe in a book called *Glazial-Kosmogonie,* written by Erich von Däniken's mentor, Hans Hoerbiger, and a schoolteacher named Philip

Fauth. Hoerbiger's cosmic ice theory states that world history—indeed the entire existence of the Earth itself—includes a legacy of cataclysmic events initiated by the interaction of ice and other natural elements (Gnostic Liberation Front 2003).

The Hoerbigerians accepted the theory of Thule and used it to explain and support their world ice theory. The solar system began, in Hoerbiger's view, with the collision of two stellar objects, a supergiant star and a smaller body, perhaps a dead sun or a gigantic comet, that were soaking wet to the core with water. When the smaller star or comet crashed into the supergiant, the heat of the latter vaporized the water and other elements as huge chunks of the star spewed into space. These chunks eventually formed a system of rings that became the Milky Way. Out of this ring system our solar system, one of many, was born (Gnostic Liberation Front 2003).

The solar system, during its primeval stage, had many more planets than there are today, and the gas giants and their planet-size moons existed in different locations. It is plausible that many of the worlds in the solar system, now barren and lifeless, once were home not only to life but civilizations as well. It is even likely that at one time there were multiple suns within the solar system (Gnostic Liberation Front 2003).

The evolutionary history of the solar system is long and complex. For countless eons the orbits of the outer planets have been in decay, and one by one they plummet toward the inner solar system, including the Earth. This is due to a significant amount of hydrogen between the planetary orbits. From beyond the orbit of Neptune, huge interplanetary icebergs are in a trajectory toward Earth, and they have caused many of Earth's natural disasters that are spoken of in legend. They are also the basis for many of the flood myths and end-times legends so prevalent in the Hindu, Teutonic, Christian, and pre-Columbian American traditions. The raining of hailstorms and sunspots signifies their arrival. As they smash into the sun they produce a blanket of vapor and thin ice that covers the inner planets (Gnostic Liberation Front 2003).

The Earth has had many natural satellites since its formation eighteen billion years ago. These moons were once planets but were captured by the Earth's gravity. These world-lets eventually spiraled in until they disintegrated and were swallowed up by the Earth, becoming part of the planet's geography. This is evidenced in the geologic record. The rock strata, when examined, show the full history of this cosmic evolutionary process.

The most recent episode of moon-Earth collision occurred when the Cenozoic moon fell from the sky, and the present moon, Luna, took its place. This event resides in the collective racial memory of the human species and manifests in the great myths and legends related to mass destruction, galactic battles, and the end of the world, most notably in Ragnarok and the Book of Revelation (Chouinard 2008, p. 450).

Hans Schindler Bellamy, a loyal follower of Hoerbiger and a British citizen during the mid-twentieth century worked out many ideas in detail and created the basis of pre-Lunar culture, a term comparable to "antediluvian" or "pre-flood" culture currently used by Christian creationists. During the age of the fall of the Cenozoic moon, the moon pulled the oceans into a "girdle tide" as it fell into the Earth's surface. This, according to Bellamy and Hoerbiger, forced many advanced civilizations to seek refuge in mountaintops and highlands such as Tibet and the Andes (Gnostic Liberation Front 2003).

Meanwhile, much of the Earth was forced into an ice age. The moon now loomed close in the sky, and its rapid revolutions around the Earth, nearly six times a day, resulted in eclipses of the sun. Bellamy believes that this is where so many of our Norse and Christian legends about the end of the world come from, and why the idea of demons and powers of mass destruction permeate so much of humanity's cultural lore.

As the old moon disintegrated, Luna finally entered orbit around Earth. Then there was a long period of tranquillity and virtual paradise, followed by more horrendous events that may have led to the destruction of Atlantis (Gnostic Liberation Front 2003).

CONCLUSIONS

The descriptions of primeval Thule and Hyperborea are a sobering view of the Atlantis myth. They depict an Atlantis based not on the quality of culture and sophistication, but rather aggression, fear and blood, fire and battle. It is a staging ground for the ancient Teutonic gods and, as we have seen, even the ancient Celtic tribes who shared a common Nordic heritage with the ancient Germanic peoples.

It is clear that the true picture may never become fully visible, that the truth about the Nordic Atlantis may never be totally known. But through the wild speculation of ingenious men and women, we are coming ever closer to that ultimate understanding. Let it be known that the fundamental consequence of investigating the truths about the northern Atlantis can only result in a better understanding of ourselves as a species—now and forever.

8

The Lost Germanic Civilization

[Conan's father is speaking] Fire and wind come from the sky, from the gods of the sky. But Crom is your god. Crom, and he lives in the Earth. Once giants ruled the Earth, Conan. And in the darkness of chaos they fooled Crom and took from him the enigma of steel. Crom was angered, and fire shot down from the sky and destroyed the giants. But in their rage, the gods forgot the enigma of steel and left it on the battlefield. And we who found it were just men. Not gods, not giants, just men. Steel has always carried with it a mystery, and it's up to you to learn its riddle, Conan. For no one—no one in this world can you trust. Not men, not women, not beasts. This you can trust! [Conan's father points to the sword]

CONAN'S FATHER,
CONAN THE BARBARIAN, FILM, 1982

GERMANIC VISIONS OF ATLANTIS

Unlike their Greek and Roman brothers to the south, the Teutons developed myths concerning the end of the world, or "end times," an idea that is also very pronounced in the Christian tradition. The early Germans thus shared this intimate connection with their Christian converters. According to ancient Germanic myths as relayed by Christian monks who took down these pagan stories, a final, great battle will come to pass between the forces of good and evil, wherein the gods who dwell in Asgard (the countryside surrounding Valhalla, the resting place of the slain) will fall to their death, and the world will be consumed by a maelstrom of steel and fire. That sinister hour will be presaged by many terrifying omens. First, a bitter cold will descend upon the Earth, followed by a devastating winter that will last three arduous years. The union of nations will be shattered, the bonds of kinship will be demolished, and global warfare will break out as humankind commits insufferable acts of murder, rape, incest, and betrayal.

A giant wolf called Fenris, son of Loki (the Nordic god of evil, strife, and discord), will arrest the sun, causing it to grow dim and pale, and then he will swallow it whole. As he advances he will gluttonize the moon and cause the stars to fall from the sky and crash to the Earth. Finally, with his jaws agape, he will fill the gap between the firmament and the atmosphere. The mountains will collapse into fragments as the entire planet quakes and shudders in an immense bedlam of molten lava.

The Serpent of the World will soar from the sea, excreting poison upon the land, while Loki, bound and gagged for centuries, breaks loose from his strangling chains and destroys everything, liberating hideous monsters from their shackles and commanding them to pillage the thwarted world. Nagflar, a boat made from the fingernails of the dead and navigated by Loki himself, will sail the oceans of the world, delivering wicked giants to distant regions and summoning the primordial waters to rise and flood the land (Davidson 1990, p. 26).

Surt, the fire giant, and his many adherents will rise from Muspelheim (a fiery realm between the Earth and sky that helped create the world) with blood axes and magical swords, pursuing their ultimate goal of attacking and killing the gods and goddesses of Asgard and Valhalla. Surt's forces will eventually join the frost giants as they storm the Bifrost (the rainbow bridge connecting Earth with the home of the gods) and trample it beneath the hooves of their preternatural steeds. Then, as the giants storm the gates and the Twilight of the Gods looms imminent, the supernatural armies will meet on the great plain known as Vigrid, and there, as in the Christian Armageddon, the final battle between good and evil will transpire, and the gods will fall to their knees in a blaze of enormous intensity (Davidson 1990, p. 68).

Thor will battle the Midgard Serpent, his eternal opponent and succeed at last in slaying the brutal beast. But not before the serpent penetrates Thor's body with its venom, a final mortal wound from which Thor will ultimately perish. At that moment the nine worlds and all the gods and goddesses will be consumed in a maelstrom of steel and fire. Only Surt will remain to burn the heavens and Earth to ashes, and then he too will perish as the thrashing waters envelop the entire universe. Yet, beyond this traumatic catastrophe is a glimmer of hope: the sons of the old gods shall remain alive, and Balder, the Germanic god of purity and justice, will be reincarnated and create a new race of divinities to rule a newly purified and rejuvenated universe (Davidson 1990, p. 70).

Earth will rise from the ashes new, fresh, and fertile, more beautiful and more enduring than ever before. A man and a woman, Lif and Lifthraser, will take shelter from the holocaust in Yggdrasil, the World Tree: "Neither the sea nor Surt's fire had harmed them, and they dwell on the plains of Ida, where Asgaard was before" (Joseph 2004, p. 127). There they will repopulate the new world. A new sun, outshining its predecessor in radiance and beauty, will travel across the azure sky, and the heavens at night will be illuminated by a brilliance unlike any that humankind has ever known. The new universe, purged of treachery and corruption, will endure for all eternity (Davidson 1990, pp. 78–80).

The Christian monks who recounted these stories were attempting to set a precedent for the spread of Christianity to the north. The stories were compiled nearly three centuries after the Norse conversion. It was implied that the two survivors, Lif and Lifthraser, represented the purely Nordic Adam and Eve. Their arrival marked the beginning of God's world and the end of the old one with its many deities.

FRANK JOSEPH AND THE ASGARD OF THE CANARY ISLANDS

Author and scholar Frank Joseph put his own spin on things in his first book, *The Destruction of Atlantis*. He writes that the sagas specifically indicate in several locations that Asgard was not a mighty fortress in the sky, as commonly believed, but rather an island in the Atlantic Ocean. This is further emphasized when, in the sagas, Asgard is depicted as actually sinking into the depths of the sea at Ragnarok. Joseph identifies the location of the mythical plains of Ida at Tenerife in the Canary Islands, which lie off the northwest coast of Africa.

During the preconquest period the indigenous peoples of Asgard were the native Guanches who were of European ethnicity. They called their sacred volcanic mountain "Aide." This indigenous name is strikingly similar to the name "Ida" from the Norse sagas, the mythical plains on which Asgard once stood. So similar are these two names, in fact, that it speaks to us of some form of common identity. The Guanches told their own story of Atlantis, a mythological tradition now forever lost due to the Spaniards' brutal campaign of extermination against the natives that drove them into extinction.

GUIDO VON LIST AND THE LAST REMNANTS OF WOTANISM

Guido von List was an early-twentieth-century political and racial thinker, philosopher, and theorist who developed a new model of human history called Ariosophy. This was based primarily on an

Aryanization of Madame Blavatsky's teaching, depicting the Aryan, or fifth root race, as being uniquely Germanic in heritage and appearance. List believed that Germany, before Roman colonization, was the center of a great Ario-Germanic civilization of untold glory and importance. He firmly denied that the Germans displaced the Celts and believed that Charlemagne was not the first to establish a civilized German presence in the region. He identified Charlemagne as the "slaughterer of the Saxons," and considered Charlemagne's conversion of the northern Germans and his forced consolidation of Christian power to be a historical crime (Goodrick-Clarke 1992, p. 95).

List claimed that the ancient Teutons practiced a primordial gnostic religion that dominated prehistoric Germany and served as a medium between humankind's modern existence and an ultimate initiation into the nature mysteries of old. He dubbed this pagan faith Wotanism. The name was derived from the chief god of the Germanic pantheon, Wotan, King of the Gods and Master of War. For List, this religion revealed itself in the Eddas—ancient sets of verses, sagas, and hymns that vividly recall the Old Norse religion and culture—and the runes, which were the magical script of the Germanic tribes and the Vikings.

According to List the inhabitants of Iceland are refugees from the persecution of paganism in northern Germany following the defeat of Widukind, the most famous of pagan German martyrs. Widukind was a heroic figure, as significant to German history as King Arthur is to the British, with one exception: Widukind's existence has been verified. He stands alongside such figures as Hermann and Barbarossa as a shining example of German nobility.

List claimed that his knowledge of prehistoric Germany came to him during strolls on the Hermannskogel, a hill that lies just north of Vienna, and through a dream he had while spending the night in an old hill fort in Geiselberg in western Germany. These ancient sites, according to List, were centers for the Armanenschaft, an elite branch of German priests who carried with them the eternal knowledge of Wotan and the Aryan race. Additional sites in the German holy land include Vienna, the earthen burial mounds at Gross Mugl and Deutsch-Altenburg, and the hill forts of Gotschenberg, Leisserberg, and Oberganserndorf. These were some of List's first inductees into a long list of holy Teutonic cities and sacred Armanenschaft sites. In addition, the town of Ybbs, Austria, List claimed, was erected upon a shrine to the Teutonic goddess Isa. While these locales were thought to be associated with good spirits, the cryptlike ruins of Aggstein, Austria, were linked with the evil spirit Agir (Goodrick-Clarke 1992, p. 97).

List saw remnants of the once universal Wotanist faith wherever he went. Situated in the region of the southern Danube, near the modern-day Austrian city of Melk, a vast Armanist temple stretched over many square kilometers. The towns of Osterburg and Burg Hohenegg, along with "the woodland church," a small stavelike church such as those of medieval Scandinavia, which once stood in Osterburg, were in his view remnants of the great complex of religious strongholds. He interpreted place-names and surnames as uniquely Teutonic and directly related to a Germanic god. Among the Wotan-inspired designations were Wutterwald, Wulzendorft, Wultendorf, and Wilfersdorf. The names dedicated to Frigga, Wotan's wife (also known as Freya and Holla), were remembered in such titles as Hollenburg, Hallabrunn, Hollarn, Frauendorf, and Frauenburg (Goodrick-Clarke 1992, p. 98).

KARL MARIA WILIGUT AND THE IRMINIST LEGACY

Karl Maria Wiligut, an early-twentieth-century German occultist and one of the most bizarre and psychotic of the lesser Nazis, believed that he was the last descendant of the Asa-Uana-Sippe, a long line of Ario-Germanic sages whose origins can be traced back to the dimmest chapters of antiquity. He claimed to possess the esoteric knowledge of a once glorious Germanic past. Through his visions, he was able to observe the movement and evolution of the ancient Germans over thousands of years. His noble sword, which his ancient clan carried into battle, is still rumored to be located at a stone grave in Steinamanger, and his crown in the imperial palace of Goslar (Goodrick-Clarke 1992, pp. 69–92).

Wiligut was a proponent of Irminism, a religious faith that traces the Germanic tribes to 228,000 BCE, at a time when the world had three suns as well as giants, dragons, dwarves, and other fantastic creatures. Irminists have a savior called Krist, a figure who they believe was co-opted by the Christians, and they claim that the Bible was originally written in Germany. Irminists have long been enemies of the Wotanist religion (Goodrick-Clarke 1992, pp. 91–93).

Wiligut believed his family history began with the coming of the Alder-Wiligoten, who ended a devastating world war, ushered in the "second Boso culture," and established the world capital Arual-Joruvallas, or Goslar, in 78,000 BCE. Great migrations and conflicts ensued, as continent after continent was subjugated and ruled by the ancient Aryans. In 12,500 BCE the Germans universally accepted Krist and his Irminist faith as the only religion of the Teutonic race, but this ended when challenged by the Wotanists several hundred years later. In 9600 BCE the Wotanists crucified the holy Irminist prophet Baldur-Chrestos. After this, he disappeared from the ancient runic texts, but rumors held that he broke loose and vanished into the Asian steppes, while the carnage and bloodshed of the great holy war continued for centuries. The advancing Wotanists eventually obliterated the Irminist center in Goslar, but a new temple was built near Detmold. The Wotanists also demolished this in 460 CE (Goodrick-Clarke 1992, pp. 91–93).

The aristocrats of the antediluvian world, known as the Wiligoten, received their potent powers from the Asen and the Wanen, the gods of air and water. Following the fall of Irminism and Wotanism, this powerful clan assumed supreme authority in the Burgenland, and one of the more highly populated regions of primordial Germany. This region is comparable to southern France today. Wiligut associated many of Germany and Europe's twentieth-century locations with the great cities of Goslar and Steinamanger—metropolises that exist in ruins underneath Vienna (Goodrick-Clarke 1992, p. 95).

THE NORDIC PANTHEON

According to ancient Nordic cosmology, the world of the gods consists of two houses of deities, the Aesir and Vanir. The Aesir were the aristocratic, warlike divinities—the largest and most dominating house of the Nordic pantheon. Among them were Odin, Thor, Balder, Tyr, Bragi, Hodr, Heimdall, Vithar, Vali, Ullr, Ve, and Forseti. The Vanir, on the other hand, were agricultural deities, led by Njord, Freyr, and Freyja. Loki was the Norse trickster deity, not a being of pure evil like the Christian Satan, but definitely a being up to no good, much in the same way the original snake figure in the garden of Eden was content with redressing the balance set forth by God.

Loki also features prominently in dealings with the god Thor in that he was a mediator between Thor and the mountain giants when their leader, Thrym, stole Thor's hammer and promised only to return it if he was given Frejya's hand in marriage. Loki dressed Thor as a woman and manipulated events so that Thor decimated the giants and seized back his mighty hammer.

The Vanirs' endless blood feud with the Aesir, on the other hand, has often been likened to a historical conflict between different religious beliefs: the native agriculturalists (for some, the Megalithenvolker) and their conquerors (the Streitaxtvolker)—the Aryan invaders of Germany, Scandinavia, Eastern Europe, and other western lands (Eliade and Trask 1984, p. 39). As Mircea Eliade and Willard R. Trask explain in *From Gautama Buddha to the Triumph of Christianity*:

To be sure, the invasions of the territories inhabited by the Neolithic agricultural populations, the conquest of the autochthonous by militarily superior invaders, followed by a symbiosis between two different types of societies, or even two different ethnic groups, are facts documented by archaeology. Indeed, they constitute a characteristic phenomenon of European proto-history, continued in certain regions, down to the Middle Ages. But, the mythological theme of the war between the Aesir and the Vanir precedes the process of Germanization, for it is an integral part of the Indo-European tradition. (1984, p. 42)

The Aesir and the Vanir were involved in skirmishes for millennia. After the conflict ended the groups became close comrades. Three gods in particular assumed the position of the Norse trinity: Odin, Thor, and Freyr (Guerber 1895, p. 8).

Odin

The chief deity, Odin, was considered to be the very embodiment of Norse culture. Because of Christian influences he is often considered the supreme all-father progenitor of all the living gods, but clearly that was not his original role. As the undisputed master of battle and victory, kings, heroes, and Viking warriors prayed to him before entering combat. In the *Heimskringla,* written in about 1230, Snorri Sturluson wrote an in-depth description of Odin

> Odin could make his enemies in battle blind, or deaf, or terror-struck, and their weapons so blunt that they could no more than cut a willow wand; on the other hand, his men rushed forward without armor, were as mad as dogs or wolves, . . . and were strong as bears or wild bulls, and killed people at a blow, but neither fire nor iron told upon themselves. (Sturluson and Hollander 1964, p. 13)

It was said that while a Viking longboat moved through the mist, and the water seemed to vanish beneath them, they shot flaming arrows into the fog, screaming the words, "Odin! Odin!" They cried as each arrow pierced the vapor, as if to rouse him from Asgard to point the way to land. Odin's primary palace was Glads-heim, and he had another in the mystical grove of Glasir. Before Odin's throne in the main chamber were twelve majestic thrones of smaller size, each made from the finest of materials, for the gods to sit in council. Each had a footstool of solid gold, the basic metal besides silver from which their abode and all their fantastic artifacts were made (Davidson 1993, p. 109).

Odin sacrificed his eye to the giant Mimir's sacred pool to obtain secret knowledge. In this he is reminiscent of the Greek god Prometheus, who also sacrificed part of himself for the dignity and worth of human concerns and society. Odin realized that his new-found knowledge of the future could aid in his battle against the giants, thus helping to protect the men and women of Midgard. To obtain the knowledge of runes, Odin hung for nine days and nights on the World Tree, Yggdrasil, peering into the eternal wintry abyss of Nifelhiem, one of the primordial realms—an image reminiscent of Christ on the cross. After his ordeal, Odin arose with runes chiseled on his spear and on the teeth of Sleipner, his magical eight-legged horse. He granted the knowledge of runes to humankind (Grimm 1882, p. 355).

From his glorious throne, Hildskialf, Odin ruled over the Earth with solemn reflection. While resting one massive hand on Gungnir—his giant, magical spear—he peered below with his one remaining eye and saw the elves, dwarves, and giants scurry about in filth, treachery, and deceit, while the Germanic heroes fought gallantly to show their worthiness for Valhalla, the resting place of the slain. Some of his wives were said to sit upon the throne, looking downward on the northern nations, yet Odin was a jealous god, and he seldom allowed his wives the pleasure of peering from his sacred vantage point. Upon his precious ring, Draupnir, loyal followers swore the oath of allegiance, and fruitfulness and glory came to all those who had the courage to do this (Davidson 1993, p. 109).

When he marched with his warriors into battle, Odin wore a splendid eagle helmet. Yet he often wandered the domain of Midgard disguised in a long, gray robe and a huge, broad-brimmed hat that cast a shadow over his eyeless socket to keep his identity unknown. He shouldered two ravens, Hugin (thought) and Munin (memory), and at his feet were his pet wolves, Geri and Freki, snarling, snapping, and foaming at the mouth but loyal to their master to the very end (Davidson 1993, p. 109).

In battle Odin galloped astride Sleipner, screaming the immortal battle cry, "Odin has you all!" Blood always followed, turning the ground crimson with the saturated flesh of corpses (p. 111).

Valhalla was Odin's sacred abode of the dead, the holiest of mead halls. He traveled there to revel and rally the departed spirits in great orgies of food, drink, and sex from the prettiest of maidens. It was said to have 540 doors, large enough for the passage of almost one thousand warriors. Its walls were made from millions of brightly shining spears that reflected off one another, producing an eerie light, and the roof was constructed from thousands of golden shields that shot a shimmering ray into the sky above, high into the outreaches of nine worlds. A gargantuan eagle perched atop the structure, its eerie glance piercing the world below, noticing everything that moved in every region of the Earth (Grimm 1882, p. 360).

A quasi-historical Odin correlates with many of the myths about the Nordic deity. He was the chieftain of a great race of warriors in Asia Minor called the Aesir. They supposedly left their homeland around 70 BCE to escape Roman aggression. H. A. Guerber explains the mortal Odin's legacy as follows: "According to other very ancient poems, Odin's sons, Weldegg, Beldegg, Sigi, Skiold, Saeming and Yngvi, became Kings of East Saxony, West Saxony, Franconia, Denmark, Norway, and Sweden and from them descended the Saxons, Hengist and Horsa, and the royal families of the northern lands" (1895, p. 10).

The new faith that followed became quickly confused and confounded with the personage of the wise ruler, and an almost entirely different religion came into being, one based on his deeds and those of his followers. In Uppsala, the temple of the Teutonic race, great sacrifices and rituals were performed. Nordic art flourished for thousands of years, yet most of the objects were made from wood and were burned to ashes by Christian aggression. So the images of Odin—the focal point of the glorious days of feasting and rejoicing—were gone forever. Yet Odin lives on, and someday he will rule again (Rydberg 2007, p. 22).

In the myths of the British Isles, King Uther Pendragon, father of the legendary monarch King Arthur, thrust the sword of power, Excalibur, into a large stone, declaring that only the most noble man (Arthur) could withdraw it from its rocky embrace. A similar story is told of Odin and his sword, one that had been forged by dwarves, whose sole purpose was to vanquish a clan of red dragons that once terrorized Asgard (Guerber 1895, p. 150). As mentioned previously, Odin frequently disguised himself as a one-eyed wanderer to walk among people to observe and listen. One day he thrust his sword into a tree, declaring that only the greatest warrior could withdraw it and that the man who could achieve this feat would have the right to possess the shining blade. Sigmund, a noble warrior, was the only man able to yank it free. He then used it to set right crimes committed against him and his family (p. 148).

Before Sigmund passed away he gave the sword to his son, Sigurd. Sigurd used it to slay the fierce dragon Fafnir, then drank its blood to commune with the mystical power of nature and the cosmos. He subsequently rescued a Valkyrie known as Brynhild and made passionate love to her, living the rest of his life for her.

Thor

Throughout the dark ages—a time when paganism was annihilated by the followers of Christ—Saint Boniface was a key figure. In the eighth century this dedicated zealot came upon a horrifying scene while wandering through the forests of northern Germany. A group of heathen worshippers were congregated around an oak, symbol of the Teutonic god Thor. They were preparing to sacrifice the son of their king, little Prince Asulf, hoping to ensure the well-being and continuation of their race. With one thundering blow of his bare fist, Boniface knocked down the tree. In its place grew a tiny evergreen, which, according to legend, became the first tannenbaum. This was the beginning of the end for Thor and his many adherents (Andrews 1974, pp. 7–8).

Thor was Odin's favorite son and heir, and perhaps second only to his father in the hearts of the people. When medieval historian Adam of Bremen visited the temple of Uppsala, he saw that Thor, along with Odin and Freyr, was situated in the center and appeared to hold the most venerated position. Indeed, in many German minds he remained the quintessential embodiment of the common man, as opposed to the haughty Odin who seemed too distant for many Germans to relate to (Davidson 2007, p. 24).

Thor was a fighting man, down in the trenches, battling for the fatherland and its people. The ancient Nordic people knew this; therefore, they proclaimed him the mightiest of all. Thor was also the lord of thunder and rain. He was bound by a solemn oath to protect mortals from the filth and treachery of giants. Using his will he manipulates every aspect of the weather, making him a favorite of sailors and merchants. With his mighty arm he casts magic and throws lightning. He was married to the giantess Larnsaza, and from the fertile union two sons were born: Magni and Modi. His second wife, Sif, bore him a son named Loride and a daughter named Thrud (Grimm 1882, p. 398).

Thor's giant hammer was known as Mjollnir and, like the Arthurian Excalibur, it was capable of penetrating any armor or shattering any sword. It also returned to its master whenever and wherever thrown, with magical swiftness. Thor's power belt increased his strength, and his iron gauntlets allowed him to wield his mighty hammer. Blazing across the grayish cloudscapes of the North Sea, he followed the retreat-ing sun, known as Sol, on a chariot driven by two mountain goats named Tanngrisner and Tanngjost.

On one occasion, Thor challenged Hrungnif of the giants to engage in single combat in order to settle long-held disputes. This was a com-mon occurrence, even in the mortal world, where Viking kings would settle their grievances by dueling instead of committing their sons to die in battle. Hrungnir and Thor met for battle where the land of the Aesir and the giants met. Fearful of Thor's growing strength and indomitable spirit, the giants built a cyclopean clay warrior called Mokkurkalfi and gave him a mare's heart to animate him. Thjalfi, Thor's devoted ser-vant, decided to stage a ruse. He said that he wished to betray Thor and told the giants that Thor's attack would come from beneath. Thus, they braced for the attack by standing on their shields, but, of course, Thor plowed over them from above. He hurled his hammer, which split Hrungnir's skull. Bits of shattered bone showered over Thor, with sharp pieces becoming lodged in his own skull. The witch Groa then removed them (Grimm 1882, p. 429).

There were many different stories regarding Thor and the giants, and they differed essentially from the tales of the Greeks in that unlike the Greek deities the Germanic gods could easily be killed and were far more mortal than their Hellenic counterparts. But essentially, there are no other myths on the planet filled with more somber realism and grotesque imagery than those of the ancient Germans.

Freyr

Freyr is perhaps one of the most pretentious of the Germanic gods. He is the supreme god of fertility and holds a position of prestige in the great Norse trinity. His outward appearance is that of a handsome young man, with a square jaw, blond hair, blue eyes, and a strong, ath-letic build. However, he is also thousands of years old, as are all the gods who dwell in the sacred places of divinities and half-gods. He provides humans with sunshine, rain, peace, joy, and happiness. He symbolizes and protects the union of marriage, and ensures conjugal bliss. He is also the master of horses, controlling horses on Midgard and protecting their honor in battle (Grimm 1882, p. 460).

Freyr commands a ship called *Skidbladnir,* the product of skillful dwarven craftsmanship, which can be folded up and placed in a pouch. At its maximum size, it supports all the gods of Asgard and can instantaneously transport them anyplace in the nine worlds, enveloped in a cloudlike aura. This is part of an ancient tradition, going back to Bronze Age Scandinavia and even the ancient Celts (Rydberg 2007, p. 45).

Freyr was also said to have impregnated mortal women. The peasantry regarded these children as a good omen for a plentiful harvest and as a sign of beneficial relations with the gods. Freyr remains to the end a true Nordic hero (Grimm 1882, p. 460).

THE NORDIC NARRATIVES

The ancient Germans and the Norse and Celtic brethren were gifted in storytelling. When the tales were finally written down centuries later, there was a rich oral tradition to draw from. One of these tales was told by an individual called the Voluspa. The Voluspa was a seer who, like many clairvoyants in Germanic society, committed her prophecies to a narrative. These narratives were usually carried on by oral tradition, but some eventually appeared on rune stones and in the sagas of latter-day Iceland.

A popular poem was "The Thrymskvida," which was first copied down in the early fourteenth century by historians living in Iceland. Today one can find it in many collections and public domain anthologies from the Internet to one's local library. This was a very original comedy, in which the giant Thyrm abducts the goddess Frejya only to be confronted by Thor in the guise of a young bride—a bride who devours an ox, seven salmon, and two vessels of mead, belches a repugnant scent, and farts a smelly gust of air at the dinner table.

In yet another story, Sigi, Odin's son, murdered another man's slave girl and was cast out, left to wander through the world, unable to love, unwilling to hate. Odin took pity on his son and directed him to Hutland, where he seized the mortal throne. There he married and produced a son named Rerir. When Rerir was away on a brief excursion, Sigi's brothers-in-law slaughtered Sigi and declared the right to ascend the throne. Rerir returned and killed them, decapitated their bodies, and threw their guts into the air for the vultures to feed upon.

THE NORSE AND ALGONQUIN CREATION MYTHS: A COMPARISON

The creation myths of the Norse, originally from Scandinavia in northwestern Europe, and the Algonquin of northeastern North America share much in common. The Norse were great warriors, traders, and explorers, and from 800 to 1000 CE they erupted on to the world stage in what became known as the Viking Age. These pagan seafarers became the scourge of Christendom and Western Europe. They invaded and settled parts of France, Great Britain, Ireland, the Baltic, Russia, and Asia Minor and peacefully explored and established settlements as far west as Iceland, Greenland, and America.

Leif Erikson, the son of Eric the Red, founder of the Greenland colony, made his way at least as far west as Newfoundland, but probably farther, five centuries before Columbus. Evidence suggests that during one expedition Leif and his crew made contact with the ancestors of the Algonquin, intermarried, and thus seeded Native American culture, mythology, and their gene pool with elements from the Nordic race.

The Norse creation myth is told in the medieval Icelandic saga known as the Elder Eddas. According to this pagan Teutonic myth, in the before-time there were no heavens, no Earth, no cool waves, nor soft breezed. All that existed was a dark, bottomless abyss called Ginngungagap. However, there remained at this early stage in cosmic evolution two distinct worlds. The first was known as Nifelheim, a land of eternal ice, cold, and darkness. Twelve sacred rivers, known as the Elvigar, flowed from a fountain welling up in the center of Nifelheim. These rivers then froze as their ancient course flowed beyond the sanctuary of Nifelheim. The result was the formation of huge glaciers and mountains of ice.

South of the realm of ice and mist was a land of eternal fire and heat, known as Muspelheim, the second world. A warm current of air burst forth from this fiery realm and began to melt the ice. The warm air and ice created clouds of hot steam, which condensed to form the frost giant Ymir, whose name means "seething clay."

Ymir arose out of his cradle of hoarfrost and rime and looked over the primordial universe. He took a step forward and sent forth a tremendous thud that reverberated throughout the cosmos. Licking her way out of the ice was another creature, the giant cow Audhumbla. Ymir knelt beside her and drank from her teats, and then the milk coursed through his body, increasing his reproductive powers. From under his armpits a new race of giants was born.

From the union of Bor, the first manlike creature, and Bestla, a female giant, three gods were born: Odin, Vili, and Ve. These three gods then murdered the frost giant Ymir, decapitated him, and used his salty blood to create the oceans, lakes, rivers, and streams; his bones became the mountains, and his flesh the Earth. His brainpan became heaven, from his brains all dark skies were created, and the maggots from his stomach became the dwarves. From his hair the gods formed any number of trees and plants. Among these first trees was Aske, the ash tree, and Embla, the elm. Odin made the first man from the ash and the first woman from the elm. The similarities between Aske and Adam and Embla and Eve are obvious and might be attributed to the thirteenth-century Christian writers who recorded these pagan myths almost three centuries after Iceland's conquest by Christianity.

Lewis Spence (1874–1955), a poet, occult writer, and compiler of Scottish folklore, marked some similarities between the idea of the Norse gods creating human beings from trees and an Algonquin Indian legend that attributes the birth of humans to "tree creation" rather than "animal transformation." Spence writes the following:

> But although Malsum [in the Algonquin myth] was slain he subsequently appears in Algonquin myth as Lox, or Loki, the chief of the wolves, a mischievous and restless spirit. In his account of the Algonquin mythology Charles Godfrey Leland appears to think that the entire [North American] system has been sophisticated by Norse mythology filtering through the Eskimo. Although the probabilities are against such a theory, there are many points in common between the two systems as we shall see later, and among them few more striking that the fact that the Scandinavian and Algonquin evil influences possess one and the same name [Loki]. When Glooskap had completed the world he made man and formed the smaller human beings, such as fairies and dwarfs. He formed man from the trunk of an ash-tree, and the elves from its bark. Like Odin, he trained two birds to bring to him the news of the world. . . ." (Bierlein 1994, p. 45)

The apparent similarities between Norse and Algonquin and other Native American myths are striking. Perhaps, they are due to interbreeding and diffusion. There is much evidence to support the theory that the Vikings explored and settled the North American continent centuries before the arrival of Columbus. Indeed, a Viking settlement in Newfoundland has been confirmed that dates to 1000 CE, nearly five centuries before Columbus made his epic voyage. There is also the possibility that both the Algonquin and the Norse had similar supernatural experiences, and that they both had encountered a more advanced race that both myths were based on. Regardless, these parallels provide for ample discussion and debate and will continue to do so for many years to come.

CONCLUSIONS

The Germanic world is a bizarre and chilling one. The world from which the ancient Norse emerged was one dominated by a deep primordial darkness, both in terms of lack of sunlight and in terms of a brooding and depressed view of the world. The Vikings faced life and death daily, their life was a constant struggle and contrasted between total darkness and an ever-present midnight sun.

Ice dominated their existence, and as in Iceland fire was also second company. Through this constant shifting from light and show, fire and ice, there grew pessimism and the indomitable spirit of the warrior, which knew only loyalty and honor, strength and power. It is easy to say that the kinfolk of the northern European community, the Celts, Slavs, and Germans, and their latter-day brethren the Norse Vikings believed that strength was a virtue, indifference to pain and weakness a virtue, and that the sick and defenseless did not deserve salvation. As horrible as this worldview seems to us today, this was their essential law of life. It creeps into every aspect of their mythology and culture, and rightfully so. Let it never be forgotten the sacrifices these ancient people made so that strength and human ingenuity could in the end prevail.

9

The Earliest Europeans
FATHERS OF ATLANTIS

A fire-mist and a planet,
A crystal and a cell,
A jellyfish and a saurian,
And caves where the cave-men dwell;
Then a sense of law and beauty
and a face turned from the clod,
Some call it Evolution,
And others call it God

WILLIAM HERBERT CARRUTH,
"EACH IN HIS OWN TONGUE," 1902

THE EARLIEST SETTLEMENT
IN NORTHERN EUROPE

Recent excavations at Happisburgh, England, near the southeastern city of Norwich, reveal that ancient Europeans settled there at least eight hundred thousand years ago. This is a far earlier date for the habitation of northern Europe than previously believed, according to archaeologist Simon Parfitt of the University College of London. At a number of sites excavated from 2005 to 2008 anthropologists unearthed more than seventy-eight palm-size stones in several sediment layers. These stones displayed intentionally sharpened edges, indicative of early human tool-making (Bower 2010; ScienceDaily 2010a).

Chris Stringer of the Natural History Museum in London says, "We suspect these tools were made by the last dregs of a larger hominid population that had come when the area was warmer but hung on and survived under challenging conditions as the climate cooled" (Bower 2010a).

A zone of thick forests covered much of northwestern Europe 800,000 years ago. At the time there was a land bridge connecting the British Isles with continental Europe, and rather than being a coastal community subsisting on the waters of the North Sea, the Happisburgh community thrived on an ancient course of the River Thames. The Thames then connected with the Rhine as a single river. According to archaeologist John Gowlett, "Analysis of clasts found in gravels show that material from northwestern Wales, more than 150 km beyond the current catchment of the Thames, was transported into southeastern England by an ancestral river" (2006). The inhabitants of these regions no doubt utilized the river system as a travel route.

The early residents of Happisburgh took advantage of freshwater pools by the river that provided mollusks and barnacles for sustenance. Along the marshy floodplain of the ancient Thames thundered mammoths, rhinos, horses, and red deer. Predators included hyenas and the saber-toothed cat. Experts narrow the timing of human occupation to relatively warm periods either around 840,000 or 950,000 years ago (Bower 2010; ScienceDaily 2010a).

Perhaps the forested landscape of ancient Britain provided the inspiration for human belief in nature spirits and powerful deities. The forests always represented the unknown, the unfathomable, and the eternal. These early settlers had to learn to live within the ancient woods because they had no strong axes or other technology to chop down trees and clear the land for settlements.

Another site, Beeches Pit, contains evidence of early fire use. This Middle Pleistocene archaeological site in East Anglia is approximately four hundred thousand years old. Several hearths were found preserved here; some were separated by two stratigraphic levels denoting a pond or some other body of water. In addition to the fire pits, there is extensive stratigraphic evidence of various microfauna as well as mollusks. According to Gowlett, "The site represents a place, or a set of localities, where early humans occupied the north bank of a pond, probably attracted by those features which so commonly recur in the record: freshwater springs, protection on one side by a body of water, access to flint raw material, and perhaps to other resources" (2006, p. 302).

The oldest examples of protohuman fossil remains found in Western Europe were found in a cave in Atapuerca, Spain, and are believed to be those of *Homo antecessor.* At that site a jawbone and a tooth from the same individual were also found. These are the oldest examples of protohuman fossil remains discovered in Western Europe. Although some scientists believe that these remains are examples of *Homo antecessor,* not all of them do. Some maintain that these early fossils are just an adapted form of a well-known hominid discovered more than a century ago—*Homo heidelbergensis*—dating to approximately 600,000 years old, not the 800,000 to 1.2-million-year-old specimen that antecessor-theorists vehemently maintain.

Stringer hopes to find the remains of *Homo antecessor* at the Beeches Pit site in England—to his mind they are the most likely candidate. He maintains that the *Homo antecessor* was the precursor to European Neanderthals and even modern humans. He also posits that both *Homo erectus* and *Homo floresiensis,* the famed real-life hobbit of Flores Island, Indonesia, existed around that time but that they were entirely in Asia and Indonesia, far too distant to be our mysterious toolmakers (Bower 2010; ScienceDaily 2010a).

DMANISI AND SIBERIA:
THE FORGOTTEN CRADLES OF MAN

A new discovery in the former Soviet Republic of Georgia now links a major phase in human evolution to Europe, not Africa. This discovery is a portion of a skull that exhibits features similar to a *Homo habilis*. What perplexed those who found the skull was the fact that a very primitive hominid species, which was 3.7 million years old, had been found in Europe at a time prior to the supposed colonization of the Old World by *Homo erectus*. According to mainstream science, 3.7 million years ago was the time of Lucy, a more primitive hominid called *Australopithecus;* more advanced hominid species were not in Europe at that time (Gore 2002).

This find in Georgia suggests that Europe played a pivotal role in the evolution of the human species and that many of us share a direct lineage *from* Europe. The Dmanisi fossils have not been conclusively identified, but they may be an earlier form of *Homo erectus,* or possibly a new species, *Homo georgicus*. It now seems possible that the first of our species to become a habitual upright walker did so in Eurasia, in a region whose climate at the time, 3.7 million years ago, was similar to that of modern-day Europe (Gore 2002).

The accepted paradigm of human evolution, maintained for half a century, says that fully evolved specimens of *Homo erectus* left Africa more than a million years ago to establish themselves throughout Europe and Asia. But the Dmanisi finds change all of that. Now it seems that more primitive forms of hominids made it as far as Europe and the Caucasus, and once there they continued to evolve into more modern forms.

It would have seemed preposterous just a few short years ago to even suggest that Europe, not Africa, could play such a decisive role in human evolution or that the birthplace of the proto-Indo-Europeans could also be the nursery of our human ancestors.

THE "X-WOMAN": FORGOTTEN ANCESTOR OR EVOLUTIONARY ANOMALY?

Yet another hominid species, nicknamed "X-Woman," was discovered in Siberia in early 2010. This possible ancestor was identified using samples of DNA, the very first time DNA has been used to identify a species that lived alongside modern humans and Neanderthals thirty thousand to fifty thousand years ago. The tissue used for the procedure was taken from a single finger bone, the only remaining part of her skeleton. The nature of the find did not fully crystallize until the final DNA results were in.

The DNA report indicates that X-Woman's ancestors left Africa five hundred thousand years ago and settled in Siberia, before the ancestors of the Neanderthals left Africa. Modern humans made the arduous trek much later, approximately fifty thousand years ago.

THE NEANDERTHALS AND THE MYTHICAL ATLANTIS

An excavation by Ralph Solecki and his team from Columbia University from 1957 to 1961 yielded the first adult Neanderthal skeletons in northern Iraq, dating to approximately 80,000 BCE to 60,000 BCE. Located in the Zagros Mountains near Kurdistan, these burials contained what appeared to be carefully laid-out human remains and grave goods, including bear skulls, which launched speculation about possible Neanderthal bear cults. In *Santa Claus, Last of the Wild Men*, Phyllis Siefker says, "Some of these bear skulls had little stones arranged around them; others were set on slabs; one very carefully placed, had the long bones of a cave bear (no doubt its own) placed beneath its snout; another had the long bones pushed through the orbits of its eyes" (1997, p. 193). In *The Masks of God: Primitive Mythology*, Joseph Campbell makes mention of bear-worship in Europe dating from about 75,000 BCE among late Neanderthal populations, to 30,000 BCE with the Cro-Magnons (1959, p. 123).

Religious artifacts produced by the Neanderthal's successors, the Cro-Magnon, including their beautiful cave paintings, displayed mixed human and animal imagery and symbolism that reflected the concept of a god or goddess. This in itself allows for speculation and wonder. Even though the hard evidence has yet to be revealed, these finds indicate that some sort of religious activity took place among these prehistoric people. If this is so, it is not hard to imagine a primitive human community seeking shelter from the cold.

During the Mesolithic period, 11,000 to 10,000 BCE, a number of advances were made, including the growth of populations and the dispersal of archaic peoples to even more remote regions of the world. This age ended with the proto-Neolithic period, in which a limited agricultural technology prevailed. This was a pivotal moment in the evolution of the human race.

The Mesolithic period brought new innovation and an increasingly sedentary lifestyle for many peoples in India, the Near East, and Europe. China, Japan, Korea, and Southeast Asia experienced similar evolutionary adaptations. Some of the protomegalithic monuments found in Britain, Ireland, Scandinavia, and France date to this transitional period, though they were not as fully developed as those of the Neolithic period. Two such examples include Stonehenge (England, circa 8000 BCE) and Carrowmore (Ireland, circa 5400 BCE). Around 9000 BCE the short-lived Mesolithic cultures of Europe were supplanted by the proto-Neolithic cultures; they began in the Near East and spread throughout the West.

In the 1950s Lithuanian American archaeologist Marija Gimbutas first presented her Kurgan theory of the origins of the Indo-Europeans: that a matriarchal, Neolithic civilization of pre-Aryans lived in Europe before the invasion of Indo-European tribes in the third millennium BCE. She describes this race in her book *Goddesses and Gods of Old Europe*. The lost civilization of pre-Aryans covered the lands of what are now Poland, Ukraine, Slovakia, the Balkans, and northern Greece.

These people established the first cities in Europe and made advances in primitive tribal law, but most important, they laid the foundations for a permanent religion (1982, p. 1).

Gimbutas was drawn to the idea of her own native region of Lithuania as a possible northern frontier of the Old European civilization. In examining the archaeology of the area, she found evidence of a matriarchy, complete with a bird goddess and a bear goddess. She believed that feminine cults and goddess worshippers dominated all of Neolithic Europe. In this author's opinion these artifacts are remnants of a vanished Europe that we have long since forgotten. (These ideas have found a following among certain groups of feminists as well as the feminine faction of the Wicca faith, a form of reconstructed paganism, or neopaganism.)

In Old Europe proper—in the Balkans, Adriatic, and Aegean, as well as nearby Eastern Europe—an upsurge in creativity and imagination led to more complex deities. The Neanderthals, after they evolved, ruled Europe for more than two hundred thousand years. They truly were the first Europeans, and they were uniquely adapted to its cold climate, especially the frigid centuries of the European ice ages. A November 30, 2007, article in *Science* details variations in skin color, eye color, and hair type among the main classic Neanderthal populations, indicating they were as diverse in physical characteristics as modern humans. The article's abstract explains:

The melanocortin 1 receptor (MC1R) regulates pigmentation in humans and other vertebrates. Variants of MC1R with reduced function are associated with pale skin color and red hair in humans of primarily European origin. We amplified and sequenced a fragment of the MC1r gene (mc1r) from two Neanderthal remains. Function analyses show that this variant reduces MC1R activity to a level that alters hair and/or skin pigmentation in humans. The impaired activity of this variant suggests that Neanderthals varied in pigmentation levels, potentially on the scale observed in modern humans. Our data suggest that inactive MC1R variants evolved independently in both modern humans and Neanderthals. (Lalueza-Fox et al. 2007)

British anthropologist Chris Stringer was one of the first to champion the "Out of Africa" theory. Both Stringer and his theory were mentioned previously: that modern peoples originated in Africa and then displaced all other peoples of the world. Stringer, in an interview with NOVA, explained, "If we look at the fossil record, Africa is the place that has the oldest modern humans, and so Africa, I think, is our original homeland. Within the last 100,000 years, from that homeland, our ancestors dispersed across the world. They replaced archaic peoples, and gave rise to the people we find everywhere today" (NOVA 1997).

Australian anthropologist Alan Thorne strongly disagrees. He believes that isolated populations of *Homo erectus* evolved locally into what we now consider *Homo sapiens*. Thorne says, "I think we all agree that there's an Out of Africa, but I feel strongly that Out of Africa has to be at least a million years ago. So, you know, since that time, over the last million years, with people in Africa and Asia, Europe and Southeast Asia, various populations are making their own adaptations to different environments and landscapes, but all are the same evolving and expanding species" (NOVA 1997).

Thorne envisions human evolution on a grand scale: *Homo erectus* spreading and evolving into the modern races of today in Europe, Asia, and most certainly Africa. Between three hundred thousand and thirty thousand years ago, the Neanderthals ruled as absolute masters of their domain. Scientists are now becoming aware of the unique role Neanderthals played in modern human evolution. The Neanderthal genome has been mapped, and it seems that about 4 percent of our DNA comes from Neanderthals. Many of the features of these early people hint at a common heritage. But more than a decade ago, such revelations were yet to come. Chris Stringer voiced the typical views of the day.

> The Neanderthals had a long and successful evolutionary history. They evolved and survived in Europe over a period of at least 200,000 years. But in that time, they also developed their own special features, and these occur through the skeleton, but in particular, they are concentrated in the face. The face is dominated by the nose, a very large and projecting nose, and the whole middle of the face is poured forward, taking with it the teeth, as well. And for me, this, in particular, marks them off as something different, probably a different species from us. And this is difficult to grasp, in a sense, because we're saying they were human beings; there's no doubt about that. And yet, they were different kinds of human beings, different from us, not part of our lineage, not our ancestors. (NOVA 1997)

Alan Thorne countered in a PBS interview.

> When we look at the bones of the Neanderthals and other peoples, it's easy to see the differences. But as living people with flesh on those bones, those differences would have been much less significant or noticeable. I mean, today, there are people of extraordinarily different physical characteristics: different skin colors, different face and eye shape, different hair forms that meet, marry and have children. When I look at Europeans, I see the evidence of that mixed Neanderthal parentage. So, Neanderthals must be a part of our species. They must be a part of us [Europeans]. (NOVA 1997)

A HYBRID DISCOVERED

Amid all of this debate, something quite unexpected happened in the study of these first Europeans. On Tuesday, April 21, 1999, BBC News reported, "A hybrid skeleton showing features of both Neanderthal and early modern humans has been discovered, challenging the theory that our ancestors drove Neanderthals to extinction." The skeleton was of a young boy and it was found in Portugal. Erik Trinkaus of Washington University further stated, "This skeleton, which has some characteristics of Neanderthals, and that of early modern humans, demonstrates that early modern humans and Neanderthals are not all that different. They intermixed, interbred and produced offspring" (BBC News 1999).

In early 2010, DNA testing at the Max Planck Institute of Evolutionary Anthropology in Leipzig, Germany, was undertaken in an effort to settle the Neanderthal/modern human hybrid theory. It was based on the collection of material found in Croatia during the 1980s. According to Gina Gomez, reporting for the *Thaindian News,* "A sample, the size of a small pill, was dug out from the center of an almost 38,000 year old bone. This sample was then ground and the powder was mixed with chemicals to release the DNA of the bone fragments. Small fragments of the DNA samples had to be multiplied a million times, only then could the scientists in Leipzig arrive at the conclusion" (2010). Subsequent to this initial attempt to determine ancestry, the Neanderthal genome was successfully mapped and compared to modern humans. It now seems definite that Neanderthals and members of our own species mixed and produced offspring, and many Europeans, even peoples from other populations entirely, can now trace their ancestry to this group of hybrids.

Neanderthals are often depicted in modern art as having dark, matted hair, swarthy skin, and dark eyes. Genetic testing now indicates that Neanderthals were in fact fair-skinned and freckled and had ginger or even blond hair. Their eye color was predominately green or grayish blue.

In February 2010 a team of Polish scientists announced that they unearthed what they believed to be three Neanderthal teeth from Stajna Cave on the north side of the Carpathian Mountains. The teeth are similar to those of modern humans, indicating how close both species are to one another. Hammers made out of deer antlers were also discovered, and scattered around the area were the bones of woolly rhinoceros and woolly mammoths. Flint tools were also found throughout the site. From these discoveries scientists can glean much about the eating habits, environment, and technology of these ancient peoples (Science News 2010). Even if the Neanderthals of one hundred thousand years ago were nothing more than primitive hunters, with only a slight inclination toward creativity, innovation, and independent thought, it still seems appropriate to think of them as something else, something more *like* us.

In *Atlantis and the Kingdom of the Neanderthals,* Colin Wilson reports on an excavation in 1989 conducted by a group of Israeli archaeologists led by Professor Naama Goren-Inbar. They discovered a priceless relic from the age of the Neanderthals.

It was a part of a planned and polished wooden plank, ten inches long and half as wide. It had obviously been ripped out of a larger plank, and the digger had cracked it across the middle. On its lower side, the plank was slightly convex and had obviously not been planed or polished. What was odd about the find? Only that the layer from which it came was half a million years old, the time Peking Man, who belonged to a species of early man—the first "true man"—called *homo erectus*. Presumably their brain was about half the size of modern man's. Yet they had made this polished plank, which Professor Goren-Inbar confessed that she was unable to explain. (2006, p. 270)

Wilson cites a number of examples in which brave scholarly individuals suggested that there was something more to the Neanderthals' culture than previously thought. Stan Gooch, for instance, proposed that Neanderthals were the first "stargazers." This idea was presented in Gooch's book *Cities of Dreams: The Rich Legacy of Neanderthal Man Which Shaped Our Civilization*. According to Wilson, "This book challenges the orthodox view that nothing worth the name of civilization existed prior to the last Ice Age and the subsequent emergence of modern man some 30,000 years ago" (2006. p. 272). Wilson also mentions that Gooch inferred that the religion of the Neanderthals included a moon worship cult of immense sophistication. Finally, "*Homo sapiens*, he said, were not an evolutionary leap" beyond Cro-Magnon man, but only a gentle step from Neanderthal" (p. 275).

CONCLUSIONS

The story of the first Europeans is the story of our Western origins. It was the nations of Europe that went on to subdue and civilize the entire world. Without the evolutionary edge the earliest Europeans initially had, the history and fate of the world would have been quite different. By examining who the Neanderthals were, and what ultimately happened to them, provides guidance for us as a species. It prepares us for the task ahead, which is to survive and evolve into the splendid greatness that awaits us. The study of other races within the confines of Europe shows us that we are merely a link in a chain that goes back 800,000 years—and we are only now beginning to fully understand the significance of that heritage, a legacy as inexplicable as the evolutionary process itself.

10

The Caucasian Mummies
of China

Eons ago when your ancestors were defending their caves
against the tiger and the mammoth, with crude spears of
flint, the gold spires of my people split the stars! They are
gone and forgotten, and the world is a waste of barbarians,
white and black. Let me, too, pass as a dream that is
forgotten in the mists of the ages . . .

ROBERT E. HOWARD,
THE MOON OF SKULLS, 1930

THE ANOMALOUS PEOPLES OF ASIA

In the late 1980s Chinese archaeologists unearthed hundreds of
Caucasian mummies along the western frontier of China. Other
ancient corpses, located in Mongolia, Siberia, and Central Asia, were
also discovered. These prehistoric Chinese remains were unknown to
much of the outside world until a security breach led to their announce-
ment in 1994. The mummies date back to at least 3500 BCE, while still
others have been determined to be far more ancient, dating to around
5000–4000 BCE. The odd thing is that, although they dated back to

Chinese prehistory, they showed no evidence of Asian ethnicity. They wore Western-style clothing and closely resembled Europeans. It is most likely that they are related to an Indo-European-speaking group of Caucasians known as the Tocharians (Baumer 2000, p. 28).

While the discovery of Caucasian mummies in China was a surprise to many, for many long-term researchers, the findings were not new. Groups of yellow-bearded peoples from the steppes had been reviewed and discussed by many ancient scholars, and they were even mentioned in Roman sources. Pliny the Elder (circa 23–79 CE) reports on a curious description of the Seres (in the territories of northwestern China) made by an embassy from Ceylone to Emperor Claudius—these people "exceeded the ordinary human height, had flaxen hair and blue eyes, and made an uncouth sort of noise by way of talking"—a possible reference to the ancient Caucasian populations of the Tarim Basin (Coppens 2009a).

Since the turn of the twentieth century, many European explorers reported finding numerous ancient mummies with distinct Caucasian features dotting the Tarim Basin on the western frontiers of China. Among these stalwart explorers was Sven Hedin, a Swede whose brash and relentless drive and wanderlust resembled the expeditionary leaders of his Norse forebears. Some of the notable historical figures who honored him include Theodore Roosevelt, Paul von Hindenburg, and even Adolf Hitler. Other noteworthy explorers who blazed the trail of discovery include German archaeologist and ethnologist Albert von Le Coq and British archaeologist Sir Aurel Stein, whose investigations produced one of the first known photographs of a Tarim mummy in 1910. Neither Hedin nor Stein fully understood the historical and evolutionary significance of their discoveries.

Another famed explorer of the early twentieth century was Sven Hedin's Swedish countryman Folke Bergman, who added much to our early knowledge of the Tarim Basin. He provided one of the very first descriptions of the Lop Nor Desert and the many graves he visited. He remains a significant figure in the quest to further understand the significance of the Tarim Basin within the larger story of the human race. In his journal he writes:

> As one approaches the hill, the top of it seems to be covered by a whole forest of upright Toghrak trunks but standing too close together to be dead trees. They were presently found to be erect posts with the tops splintered by the strong winds. On the surface of the hill, particularly on the slopes, there were a lot of strange, curved, heavy planks, and everywhere one stumbled across withered human bones, scattered skeletons, remains of dismembered mummies and rags of thick woven materials. Some of the mummies had long, dark hair and incredibly well preserved faces, even an almost fair complexion. From others a ghastly-looking skull grinned out of a partly preserved blackened skin. I shall never forget the sublime expression on the face of the mummy! On the dark, flowing hair, parted in the middle she wore a yellow-pointed felt cap with red cords; her brow was high and noble, her eyes slightly closed, as if she were on the point of falling asleep; she had a fine aquiline nose and thin lips, slightly parted, and showing a glimpse of the teeth in a quiet timeless smile. (1935)

Several other Late Bronze Age burials are scattered in and around the Tarim Basin region. These include the gravesites at Bozdong, Aqsu-Konashadar County, near the northwest edge of the Tarim Basin, which were first unearthed in 1985, under much secrecy. Shui Tao from Nanjing University, explains:

> One of the tombs, M41, is an oval-shaped grave with a mound of stone on the ground above it. In the grave, about twenty skeletons consisting of 8 males, 11 females, and 1 child were placed in confused positions. Grave goods include pottery, bronze, iron, bone,

stone, and golden wares. The pottery includes bowls with round bottoms, cups with handles, and teapots with handles and spouts. All of the pottery is shaped by hand and has no decorations on the surface. Bronze objects are mainly ornaments, consisting of buttons, bells, and pendants. Iron objects are small tools and weapons. They include knives, arrowheads, nails, and band hooks. Bronze objects are mostly pendants, as well as ornaments and the like. (1998, pp. 162–63)

Based on the descriptions of mummies and reports of long-lost populations of Caucasian nomads, Frenchman Ferdinand Grenard in 1893 concluded that the original inhabitants of the Tarim Basin were Caucasian (Baumer 2000, p. 21). According to conventional wisdom, Indo-Europeans migrated into the Tarim Basin, Mongolia, and west China in two main waves. The first is the aforementioned Tocharian wave, which was divided into two groups: Tocharian A and Tocharian B. The first entrance into Central Asia was supposed to have occurred between 3500 and 2000 BCE.

The second wave of immigration took place around 1150 BCE and lasted for several centuries, concluding in 900 BCE at the beginning of the Central Asian Iron Age. These later immigrants were identified as a northern Persian group known as the Saka. Near the Qäwrighul cemetery and close to the Lop-Nor Desert at a place called the Ordeck necropolis, numerous Saka or Indo-Iranian tombs were found. Evidence in these tombs, including grave offerings and human remains mixed with animal remains, indicate that the inhabitants practiced both agriculture and pastoralism and lived sometime between 1200 and 700 BCE.

Ancient Chinese texts identified a group of people known as the Wusun and also as the Yuezhi. Much has been documented about their dealings throughout the Tarim Basin, Outer Mongolia, and in the Central Asian state of Bactria. They were depicted as treacherous yellow-haired barbarians with a propensity for destruction. In his monumental and controversial work *The Passing of the Great Race,* first published in 1916, Madison Grant said the following with regard to this people.

> These tall, blue eyed, Aryan-speaking Sacae were the most easterly members of the Nordic race of whom we have record. The Chinese knew well these "green eyed devils," whom they called by their Tatar name, the "Wu-suns," the tall ones, and with whom they came into contact in about 200 BCE in what is now Chinese Turkestan. The Zendic form of the Iranian group of Aryan languages continued to be spoken by these Sacae who remained in old Bactria, and from it is derived a whole group of closely related dialects still spoken in the Pamirs, of which Ghalcha is the best known. (1936, p. 115)

These early reports precipitated future revelations made by scholars and explorers alike. Some of the later discoveries were made by such stalwart individuals as Russian explorer Pytor Kuzmich Koslov (1863–1936). He explored western China in an effort to enter the sacred Tibetan city of Lhasa and meet the Dalai Lama, a goal he achieved. This success eventually led to additional excavations that Koslov organized. Among the noteworthy sites was Khara Khoto, highlighted by the unearthing of a tomb fifteen meters beneath the ruins in which the body of a mummified queen was discovered, "accompanied by various scepters, wrought in gold, and other metals" (Coppens 2009b). Koslov was permitted to take a considerable number of photographs that were later published in *American Weekly,* but he was not allowed to further disturb the site or remove any of its contents, specifically the body. He continued onward with a series of significant expeditions from 1923 to 1926, culminating in the discovery of Xiongnu royal burials at Noin-Ula (Coppens 2009b).

For more than seven decades, virtually unknown to the West, numerous mummies and desiccated corpses with Caucasian ethnic traits have been unearthed at key locations throughout the region. They were removed from their tombs, analyzed, and displayed at various Xinjiang museums, including the one at Urumchi. Han Chinese scholars suppressed the knowledge of their existence to the outside world, much to the chagrin of international academia. Many of these distinctly anomalous "Western" bodies, however, are now available for study by archaeologists, even non-Chinese scholars, which is only a recent development.

According to Christopher Thornton and Theodore Schurr in their article, "Genes, Language and Culture: An Example from the Tarim Basin":

> The mummies share many typical Caucasoid body features (elongated bodies, angular faces, recessed eyes), and many of them have their hair physically intact, ranging in color from blond to red to deep brown, and generally long, curly and braided. It is not known whether their hair has been bleached by internment in salt. Their costumes, and especially textiles, may indicate a common origin with Indo-European neolithic clothing techniques or a common low-level textile technology. (2004)

THE AMERICANS WEIGH IN

Also seeking answers to this ancient riddle was an American team led by Dr. Victor Mair, professor of Chinese literature at the University of Pennsylvania, and a group of his colleagues, including Jeannine Davis-Kimball, executive director at the Center for the Study of Eurasian nomads. The aim of the team's exploration of the Xinjiang region was to fully investigate previously excavated and studied remains that the Red Chinese had, until that point, kept from Western scholars. These finds were housed in a number of museums all around the region. Each museum was another piece to the puzzle. The remains contained in them varied in form from being decomposed, almost entirely skeletal, to immaculately preserved (Mallory and Mair 2000, pp. 24–26).

In the Korla Museum the investigating team found a twenty-year-old maiden lying half-covered in a thin, orange-brown dress drenched in blood. Her face was distorted with agony, and she had bitten her tongue. Her eyes were gouged out, her limbs had been ripped out and placed directly under her pelvis, and her arms above her elbows were gone. She appeared to have been sacrificed.

When the team arrived at their next destination, the Urumchi Museum, they were waved into a large chamber filled with rows of mummies, some looking as if they had died within the past forty-eight hours, others seriously deformed or in a state of advanced decomposition. Many appeared to be Mongolian, perhaps the ancestors of Genghis Khan, but others, as shocking as it might seem, were clearly Western, dating as far back as 2000 BCE (Barber 1999, p. 44).

These were not the only archaeological gems found at the Urumchi archaeological museum. There was the red-haired Chärchän Man, dubbed "Ur-David," who bore the indelible stamp of the West, both in terms of ethnicity and his beautifully colored pants and clothing, the earliest examples of such clothes in known history. His cause of death remains inconclusive. Wisps of blond Nordic hair could be seen peeking from beneath the rim of a red and blue felt cap, and, echoing ancient Greek tradition (see Homer), blue stones had replaced the eyes, likely part of a death ritual in preparation to meet the gods in paradise.

Their clothing seemed reminiscent of those worn by the Celtic tribes of Ireland, Britain, and Gaul for among the styles were unmistakable plaid tunics. Textile expert Dr. Elizabeth Wayland Barber notes that although it was once thought that the Scots adopted plaid twill fabric relatively recently, it is now clear that the Celts and the Western European Grooved Ware culture before them had been using this stylized fabric for thousands of years. The fact that the people of the Tarim

Basin possessed this fabric as well speaks of a European, even proto-Celtic origin for them. One might speculate that this was a story of a reverse migration and that the Celts can trace their ancestry to Central Asia instead of Central Europe. According to Barber, "The dominant weave [of the Urumchi people] proved to be the normal diagonal twill and the chief decoration was plaid, as in the woolen twill material of the Scottish kilt" (1999, p. 23).

Knight and Lomas end their speculation by writing, "These European settlers used a woven-wool textile technology, and Barber comments that woolly sheep with a coat suitable for making woolen yarn did not appear in Europe until 4000 BCE (Knight and Lomas 2001, p. 307).

Another mummy was found with clear Caucasian traits—a forty-year-old brown-haired woman. The team leader of the original Chinese expedition that found her, Mu Shun Ying, was impressed by her immaculate state. She called her the "Loulan Beauty," because her appearance seemed beautiful even in death. In fact, many of the mummies of the Tarim Basin exhibited an equal prettiness. Radiocarbon dating set this mummy at around 3,800 years old. Found in close proximity to the "beauty" in the same wooden tomb was another mummy. Radiocarbon dating on the materials used to construct the tomb placed its origins as early as 4000 BCE (Barber 1999, p. 132).

Removed from the same tomb as the two others were the remains of a third individual, clearly of Indo-European origin. She was tall, long-nosed, and had a narrow visage and blond hair. "She must have been a real beauty when she was alive," said Wang Binghua, one of the archaeologists who initially worked on her. Her long blond hair, almost perfectly preserved, caressed her narrow shoulders and ran downward toward the middle of her chest. She had been removed from an ancient burial site in 1978 by Chinese archaeologist Wang Binghua at Qizilchoqa, east of Urumqi, which is the capital city of Xinjiang-Uyghur Autonomous Region (Barber 1999, p. 93). As with the other mummies consigned to the dusty reaches of the Xinjiang museum at Urumchi, the anomalous nature of the once-glorious blond woman led this discovery to be intentionally buried by the Communist regime for almost twenty years (NOVA 1998).

Also presented to the team was a far later relic, known as the "Hami Mummy," dating to around 1400 to 800 BCE, with a distinctive head of red hair. Still another group, known as the Witches of Subeshi, managed to turn a number of heads. Dr. Barber commented in amazement about the bone-chilling scene of discovery—and its apparent mythological implications.

> Yet another female—her skeleton found beside the remains of a man—still wore a terrifically tall, conical hat, just like those we depict on witches riding broomsticks at Halloween or on medieval wizards intent on their magical spells. And that resemblance, strange to say, may be no accident. Our witches and wizards got their tall, pointy hats from just where we also got the words magician and magic, namely, Persia. The Persians or Iranian word Magus (cognate with the English might, mighty) denoted a priest or sage, of the Zoroastrian religion in particular. Most distinguished themselves with high hats; they also possessed knowledge of astronomy, astrology, and medicine, of how to control winds and the weather by potent magic and how to contact the spirit world. (Knight and Lomas 2001, pp. 304–5)

One collection of mummies, found at the settlement of Qäwrighul that dated to 1800 BCE, were of Caucasoid physical type whose closest affiliation is to the Bronze Age populations of Kazakhstan and the Lower Volga (Mallory and Mair 2000, p. 237). The cemetery at Yanbulaq contained twenty-nine mummies dating from 1100 to 500 BCE, twenty-one of which are Mongoloid—the earliest Mongoloid mummies found in the Tarim Basin—and eight of which are of the same Caucasoid physical type found at Qäwrighul (Wikipedia, "Tarim Mummies"). This is where the oldest remains have been found thus far.

In March 2010 the archaeological community was stunned by the discovery of yet another Caucasian skeleton, this time in Mongolia. DNA extracted from this individual's bones confirms a direct genetic link with the West. In essence, these remains were clearly European, if not Western Eurasian. This time, however, the ancient corpse was a much younger find. It dated to around the first century CE, about two thousand years ago. This corresponds roughly to the time of Christ (Bower 2010).

The date of Western arrival or habitation of China and East Asia is continually being pushed backward in time to an ever earlier date. The origin of some Caucasian mummies can be traced back to 4000 BCE, and some are even older. But this most recent unique specimen is no less significant in our quest to understand the truth surrounding the Lost Caucasian Civilization. This individual was apparently a major player in Mongolia's Xiongnu Empire, an ancient state that is now believed to have been a multiethnic melting pot of former Eurasian nomads. This ancient conglomeration of foreign tongues and non-Mongoloid races no doubt consisted of a large number of Indo-European-speaking peoples (Bower 2010).

THE THEORY OF MARIJA GIMBUTAS

By and large, the discoveries of the Caucasian mummies of China and similar finds have fueled more speculation concerning Lithuanian American archaeologist Marija Gimbutas's Kurgan theory. She identifies the origin of the Indo-European tribes with the culture that constructed the earthen burial mounds known as Kurgans, in the Pontic Steppe region of southwestern Russia nearly 6,400 years ago. This group later left their ancestral homeland and invaded Old Europe, replacing their matriarchal and megalithic way of life with a male-centered, sky-god cult (Gimbutas 1982).

The argument for the Kurgan hypothesis is the discovery of large wheels found among the hundreds of blond mummies that were spread from the Pontic Steppe to the Western frontiers of China and then onward to the Gobi Desert and the plains of Mongolia (Gimbutas 1982).

Authors Christopher Knight and Robert Lomas suggest that the people of the Tarim Basin were associated with the Grooved Ware culture of Western and Central Europe. Knight and Lomas made the mistake of linking the Grooved Ware people with those described in the Book of Enoch and the Old Testament as giants. According to Knight and Lomas, they migrated to Central Asia in search of "high ground" to escape the Great Cataclysm foretold to them: "All the mysteries had not yet been revealed to you. . . . You have no peace. . . . Behold, destruction is coming, a great flood, and it will destroy all." This is a purely mythological explanation; it is not to be interpreted as science (2001, pp. 202–3). Furthermore, this link between the offspring of the Watchers and archaeologically verifiable European culture is less than convincing. The idea that the Tarim mummies were related to the Grooved Ware culture, however, is scientifically viable.

It is clear from both the historical and archaeological record that Asia was once home to a lost tribe—an indigenous and racially dominant Caucasian population. East Asian ethnicity, as it is known today, is relatively recent. There is even stronger evidence suggesting that the native Caucasoid peoples intermarried with the later Mongoloid cultures advancing from Siberia. Yet evidence for this only emerges in the physical and genetic record around 900 BCE, the dawning of the Central Asian Iron Age.

A. C. Haddon, in his classic work, *The Wanderings of Peoples,* affirms that ancient China was directly influenced by an Indo-European presence during the Neolithic and Bronze Ages. Colin Renfrew, one of the preeminent Indo-Europeanists, suggests that, linguistically, the inhabitants of the Tarim Basin developed from an early group of pre-proto-Indo-Europeans that emerged from Anatolia in 7000 BCE.

Some share the opinion that it was the European races, rather than the Asiatic ones, that led to the establishment of early Chinese civilization. It is evident that there was an ethnic migration of Tocharians from Central Europe, possibly from the lower Danubian basin, through Caucasia, Russia, and the Pontic Steppe, reaching the borders of China in 800 BCE. In 1951 German archaeologist Robert Heine-Geldern showed similarities of metallurgy in Europe and China around 800 BCE (Deavin 1997). With regard to this, Heine-Geldern makes the following comments.

> The early swords of China (9th and 8th centuries BCE), several daggers of the Dongson culture of northeastern Indo-China, as well as various Far Eastern designs correspond closely to those of the fifth period of the Bronze Age of Northern Europe. This can only be due to the participation in the eastward migration of a group of those Scandinavians who, as Tallgren (1911:169–183; 1937:30–41) has shown, settled on the Volga around 800 BCE. The very conspicuous elements of the Hallstatt culture in the Far East would seem to correspond to the relation between the Tokhari languages which Sapir thought to have existed.

Socketed battle axes and spearheads used in abundance in early China were compared to those of Hallstatt and the Indo-European homeland, and results indicated they were brought to China by nomadic Indo-Europeans some three thousand years prior. Although it might be considered an erroneous concept—the product of an overactive imagination—Heine-Geldern also claims that the first Chinese Empire, ruled by Ch'in Shih Huang Ti beginning in 221 BCE, was created by Indo-European invaders (Deavin 1997).

Now many scholars' once disputed theories are being exonerated. David W. Anthony, an anthropologist at Hartwick College in New York, linked the awesome migration patterns of the Indo-European race to the invention of wheeled wagons. They were used to great effect by Steppe cultures such as the Andronovo and Afanasievo. The latter,

Anthony believes, provides a direct link to the Tocharians of the Tarim Basin (Deavin 1997).

In his book *The Horse, the Wheel and Language,* Anthony writes:

> Mallory and Mair have argued at book length that the Afanasievo migration detached the Tocharian branch from Proto-Indo-European. A material bridge between the Afanasievo culture and the Tarim Basin Tocharians could be represented by the long-known but recently famous Late Bronze Age Europoid "mummies" that are found throughout "the northern Taklamakan Desert, the oldest of which are dated 1800–1200 BCE." If Mallory and Mair were right, as seems likely, late Afanasievo pastoralists were among the first to take their herds from the Altai southward into the Tien Shan; and after 2000 BCE their descendants crossed the Tien Shan into the northern oases of the Tarim Basin. (2007)

Paramount in this evolutionary migration is the utilization and mastery of first the horse, then the wagon, and finally, the chariot.

Like their Tocharian predecessors, later Eurasian nomads such as the Alans, Huns, and Tartars of the Golden Horde and the Mongols also perfected the use of the horse as an innovation of culture and warfare. According to Otto J, Maenchen-Helfen in his book *The World of the Huns,* "Horses played a prominent role in the economy of the Huns. Although our authorities do not mention that the Huns ate horse meat—perhaps because this went without saying—they certainly did, like the Scythians, Sarmatians, and other steppe people" (Maenchen-Helfen 1973, p. 220). Records also say that the "Huns, too, drank the blood of their horses" (Maenchen-Helfen 1973, p. 220).

The Roman writer Ammianus commented that while undergoing negotiations with the Romans, the leaders of the Huns remained mounted on their horses (Maenchen-Helfen 1973, p. 203). Maenchen-Helfen continues:

On their migration to the Don and from the Don to the Danube, the Huns probably transported their old people, women, and children in wagons. Toy wagons found in Kerch show what the wagons of the later Sarmatians looked like. Some have pyramidal towers, doubtless movable tents, others are heavy four-wheeled vehicles. The wagons of the Huns must have been similar to the toy wagons from Panticapaeum. (1973, pp. 219–20)

Extensive excavations in southern Russia and Kazakhstan have revealed five-thousand-year-old burial mounds containing traces of numerous wagon wheels. Not only were such artifacts found in Eastern Europe but also in the Gobi Desert, which lies on the northeastern border of the Tarim Basin (Deavin 1997). It is now accepted by almost all twenty-first-century archaeologists that the birthplace of mounted culture was Ukraine, contrary to earlier assertions that horse riding and the chariot originated in China or the Middle East. These mummies of the Huns are a link not only to the human past but also to the evolution of Chinese and Eastern culture, just as much as Western culture. It is not the story of one culture overtaking the next, but rather an East-West synthesis.

In addition to the Huns distinctive European appearance, DNA testing of their mummies proved they were of Caucasian origin. As many more corpses became unearthed, it became evident that the original inhabitants of the region, far from being Mongoloid, were actually Caucasian. A number of later samplings indicated that not only do these bodies have a direct genetic link to Western Europe, and even the Pontic Steppe around the Black Sea, they also show traces of inbreeding with other tribes ranging from Mesopotamia, the eastern Mediterranean, and India. Indeed, the Tarim Basin could be considered a major thoroughfare for many of Eurasia's Caucasoid peoples.

CONCLUSIONS

The findings articulated in this chapter lay down the foundation of another argument this author wishes to make in future chapters. They indicate a genetic population far older than even the Mesopotamian or Bactrian cultures, and far older than the European or Indian cultures. Indeed they are a possible link to a once dominant Caucasian population that, at one time, inhabited much of the Earth. If this is true, the history of East Asia and the world would have to be rewritten. The noted German anthropologist Max Muller stated one hundred years ago that the "first Caucasians were a small company from the mountains of Central Asia" (Coppens 2009b). It is clear that something unusual is linked to these ancient peoples, as there is widespread evidence of anomalous Caucasian-like peoples appearing in remote corners of the world—regions thought to be untouched by European and Western influence.

11
The Lost Caucasians of Ancient America

By Crom, I do not like this place, where dead men rise,
and sleeping men vanish into the bellies of shadows!

ROBERT E. HOWARD,
XUTHAL OF DUSK, 1933

All the glory of the godhead had the prophet Quetzalcoatl
All the honor of the people sanctified his name and holy;
And their prayers they offered to him in the days of ancient
Tula

SAHAGUN,
FLORENTINE CODEX

THE NORTH ATLANTIC CRESCENT

A group archaeologists and paleoecologists formed the North Atlantic Biocultural Organization some twenty years ago to explore the available wealth of data pertaining to both human habitation in the region as well as specific fauna indigenous to it. This organization has undertaken the daunting task of studying the striking similarities between the paleo-population in Europe and North America.

The question of where the first Americans came from is being answered, in part, by a new theory, which illustrates how North America developed and how the dispersal of peoples across the North Atlantic could have formed a circumpolar Mesolithic culture. This Mesolithic culture was responsible not only for mass migration between the two major continents but also the interbreeding and establishment of hybrid cultures (Chouinard 2008, p. 156).

A great migration of ancient sea peoples in the North Atlantic dates to the final glacial epoch of the ice age (ten thousand to fifteen thousand years ago) during Mesolithic times, or the Middle Stone Age. The aforementioned concept, known as the "North Atlantic Crescent," is now gaining traction. Scientists studying the dispersal of archaic clans across the great northern ocean are prophets of a new planetary gospel, teaching not the dead theory of Clovis Man, but the idea that the northern Atlantic, including the circumpolar environment, was the decisive factor in molding both Old and New World cultures (Chouinard 2008, pp. 155, 159).

The Center for the Study of the First Americans at Oregon State University recently began genetic testing of human remains found both along the East Coast of North America and in Western Europe. Further examination of the human mitochondrian cells may prove a Caucasoid link to the first Americans dating as far back as 28,000 BCE. Known as the "power packs" of DNA, these cells helped scientists form four categories of ancestral groups, or lineages, which are viewed as the founding genetic material on which Native Americans are based. Congruent with existing dogma, and fueling the argument in favor of Asiatic origins for the New World population, they could be traced back to Siberia and northeast Asia, specifically the Baikal and Altai-Sayan regions. However, a fifth lineage is also credited as one of the founding genetic strains of present-day Native Americans. Known as "haplogroup X," this genetic signature is the vestige of either a later population found in Europe and the Middle East or possibly a primeval population of Caucasoid ethnic groups that inhabited Asia and was also part of the tribes that followed the coastline on small boats to a point where they could disembark and settle (Chouinard 2008, p. 160).

KENNEWICK MAN

On July 28, 1996, two young men, William Thomas and David Deacy, were wading in the Columbia River near Kennewick, Washington, while attending a hydroplane exhibition. They were about to stumble upon the greatest and most controversial find in North American history. The Kennewick Man would have far-reaching implications not only for science but also for European American identity.

What the two men found appeared to be a human skull, perhaps ten to twenty years old, by their reckoning. Shocked by this discovery, they made their way to the park rangers. After a brief examination, the skull was considered to be a relatively recent deposit. As the immediate area was searched, more and more remains were found. Jim Chatters, a forensic scientist called to the scene, explains: "Most of the large bones were visible. The big parts of the pelvis were there, there were parts of both thigh bones, pieces of both arms just lying there on the mud" (NOVA 2000).

Impressions of the teeth were made. The considerable wear on the enamel pointed to a male somewhere in his late forties. When the skull was examined, it showed Caucasian characteristics. If it was a European American, "then I'm thinking it was a fairly recent person," Chatters recalls. The man stood approximately 2 meters tall, considerably taller and leaner than the Amerindian races. The back of his skull was not flattened, a trait shared by many Native American skulls. His visage was slender, narrow, and resembled those of the Cro-Magnon of prehistoric France. Everything about this man pointed to European rather than Mongoloid origins, the latter being the supposed ancestors of present-day Native Americans who, according to conventional wisdom, crossed the land bridge, Beringia, connecting Siberia and Alaska near the end of the last ice age (NOVA 2000).

Nothing seemed out of place about this discovery until a small gray projectile was found embedded in the man's hip. This sparked the supposition that he may have been a white settler who met an untimely demise at the hands of a hostile Indian tribe. After numerous tests, however, including a CAT scan, the projectile was found to be a prehistoric spear point. After a series of additional tests aimed at estimating its age, the scientists dropped a bombshell. It turned out that this being was no recent homicide victim or even a nineteenth-century white settler, but a Native American of possible European descent who lived and died near the Columbia River some nine thousand years ago! His traits were typical of Caucasians of Europe, the Middle East, and India (NOVA 2000).

Jim Chatters further explains his view of the find.

This fellow told more of a story than most people I've ever dealt with. I mean, he not only had the spear point stuck in him—and it was healed there, he'd had it for quite a long time—but he had a whole series of other injuries too. If you sort of start from his youth, he broke his left elbow and appears to have gotten an infection or some serious bone damage. He had his chest crushed with a massive blunt blow, breaking the ribs off either side and leaving them separate. That's an often fatal wound. It healed. He has a little skull fracture on the front left side, the kind that's consistent with that of a right-handed person wielding a club, and that had healed. In a few words, the man had a perilous existence. (NOVA 2000)

When Jim Chatters wrote up his report about Kennewick Man, he used the phrase "Caucasian characteristics." The press politicized his comments, and headlines around the world posited that Kennewick Man was white. (Indeed, the re-creation of Kennewick Man's face resembled the actor Patrick Stewart in his role as Captain Jean-Luc Picard of *Star Trek: The Next Generation*.) As a result, Jim Chatters was wrongfully accused of inciting a racist rampage. But perhaps feelings both for and against the idea of Kennewick Man being a European were overblown (NOVA 2000).

The actual testing of Kennewick Man's DNA links him to the Ainu of Japan. Only one hundred Ainu remain alive in their racially pure form, but they inhabited all of Japan before immigrants from Korea made their way there two thousand years ago. Labeled the "Caucasians of Asia," the Ainu strongly resemble Caucasians in facial features as well as eye and hair color. They also have distinctly non-European characteristics. It is possible that during prehistoric times there was a previously unrecorded population of which both the Ainu and Kennewick Man were a part (NOVA 2000). In addition to Kennewick Man, another fair-skinned ancient American, Spirit Cave Man, was found, this time in Nevada. Anthropologists have conservatively identified these rare specimens as the Ainu of Japan. Other discoveries contradict this notion (NOVA 2000).

Kennewick Man and Spirit Cave Man are two of the most compelling pieces of evidence supporting the idea that Europeans settled and lived in North America thousands of years before the first Viking expeditions. New evidence also hints that this mass migration during the Stone Age some nineteen thousand years ago—the Solutrean epoch—was one of the main movements of early peoples into the Americas, thus discounting the archaeological model that maintains that the land bridge from Asia was the only artery into the New World (NOVA 2004).

The reality is that America could have been a crossroads of human exploration and settlement. Indeed, there are many more examples of people who shouldn't be in pre-Columbian America but seem to creep from the undergrowth to stun the world. However, belief in the conventional theory as to how the Americas were populated—by Asian migration across the Bering Strait—has almost reached biblical proportions. It is a story that most archaeologists are raised to believe and trained to try to prove beyond a shadow of a doubt.

But why?

People have always gone forth in boats to explore, trade, and find new places to live. It is fundamental to human nature. Indeed, in the past it was relatively easy for human beings to get from one place to another. That is why it is highly probable that America was frequently visited and inhabited by peoples not related to the Paleo-Indians. If the Vikings found America five hundred years before Columbus, then what about all the other rumored sightings of another land beyond the Old World?

DISCOVERIES IN SOUTH AMERICA

In 1996, the year that Kennewick Man was found, another indication of outlanders in America was uncovered in a place called Monte Verde in southern Chile: evidence of human habitation dating back approximately 12,500 years, predating any human sites yet found in North America. Then in Brazil a discovery as significant as Kennewick Man in the Northern Hemisphere was made in the Southern Hemisphere: the eleven-thousand-year-old skeleton of a being now known as Luzia, in reference to Lucy, one of the earliest known hominids, or ancestors of the human race.

Luzia's physical characteristics were not consistent with those of Paleo-Indians; indeed, she seemed to be descended from a whole other group of Asians altogether. Her features were very similar to those of Australian Aborigines (NOVA 2000). According to Joseph Powell, who worked on the site:

The date of 11,000 makes her potentially the oldest skeleton in the New World, and the fact that Luzia looks so very different may imply that she was part of a different population. The question of how she got there is another one altogether because her early age, combined with data from Monte Verde which is at least 12,000 to 13,000 years old, certainly means that people must have been migrating into South America much earlier than we previously thought. (NOVA 2000)

David Meltzer, also involved in the project, told NOVA:

That's a complicated issue because what it means is that they must have come in long before this ice-free corridor opened. And that raises lots of questions about the route that they took, how early they got here, what population or populations we're talking about here, whether there were single or multiple migrations. (NOVA 2000)

They may not have come from Australia. Perhaps they were derived from a common group of ancestral races living in Asia who then split apart—one going to South America and the other to Australia. Change is an inevitable characteristic of all living things. Our own species, with its many races and populations, has changed many times over. From a population of dark-skinned humans in Africa, all the other races emerged—from European white to the yellowish-skinned Mongolians. It is possible that these races, found in North and South America, represent an earlier stage in American evolution.

THE MUMMY PEOPLE OF THE ALEUTIAN ISLANDS

The northern circumpolar region is now yielding new discoveries. Traditional models of the Far North are dying fast as new theories emerge about how migrations occurred from one continent to the other. With the demise of the Cold War, anthropologists from the United States and the Russian Federation have gathered their talents together in an attempt to prove that intercontinental wanderings were the norm and not the exception. Although Russia has, in recent years, been somewhat suspicious of American intentions with regard to their internal affairs, researchers from both countries have been able to combine their data concerning the history of the circumpolar world (NOVA 2000).

Seven thousand years ago Alaska's Aleutian Islands were inhabited by an ancient Caucasian-like race that maintained its role as the dominant race on the island until historic times. The long-headed "Mummy People" are still a mystery. It is uncertain where they originated. Only a very few archaeologists have studied their physical remains. Some connections have been drawn between the Mummy People and the Ainu of Japan. Both the Mummy People and the Ainu had long skulls; wore wooden armor and helmets; both wielded broad swords and pikes. The Mummy People hunted the surrounding waters for food and material such as ivory and bone for tools, weapons, and religious artifacts. They also practiced mummification, which is typically indicative of higher civilizations, but nonetheless practiced by more primitive people such as the Chinchorro of northern Chile and southern Peru (Pettyjohn 2001).

The Mummy People developed an advanced technology based on the natural resources surrounding them and their own creativity. In his article titled "The Caucasian Mummy People of Alaska," F. S. Pettyjohn writes:

The Aleuts used a decimal system that could tabulate up to 100,000 and used a 12-month calendar. They manufactured white parchment that had endured through the ages. They made fishing nets, harpoon lines, and bidarka ropes from the core of seaweed, and wove baskets and sleeping mats from the roots of tall grass. Geese were domesticated by catching them during the molting season and then clipping their wings, thus, a yearly supply was assured. They had a working knowledge of astronomy and anatomy: human and animal, setting simple fractures and performing some operations, one in particular being the removal of eye abscesses. (2001)

FLORIDA'S EIGHT-THOUSAND-YEAR-OLD CAUCASIAN CEMETERY

Even with such finds as Kennewick Man and Spirit Cave Man, the true physical nature of those who preceded us in the Western Hemisphere remains clouded in mystery. But the enigmatic veil parted somewhat in 1983 when a local development company discovered an ancient burial site at a bog called Windover Pond at Cape Canaveral, Florida. It was dated to the Early Archaic Period, some eight thousand years ago. It was the cemetery of a prehistoric community that once inhabited northeastern Florida. Did they possess what could be defined as "civilization"? The answer seems to be a resounding yes—this was a civilized society (*Archaeology TV* 2003).

According to experts, although they were hunter-gatherers they had remarkable artistic gifts and practical knowledge. The burial site contained ninety-one skeletons in all, and these remains are linked genetically to other sites all across the United States. The largest concentration of remains with similar DNA is in the Los Angeles area. More than fifty human remains at a single location, at such an excellent level of preservation, all in the same burial or cemetery site, is an extremely rare occurrence. In other words, something unique happened in prehistoric Florida. Buried amid the peat, their skulls still contained preserved specimens of brain tissue—90 percent complete in some cases. Genetic tests link these people to western Europe (*Archaeology TV* 2003).

The sheer number of skeletal material and their excellent condition created intense interaction in the scientific community, and word finally spread to Dr. Glen Doran, now of Florida State University. Ever since 1982 he has worked extensively at Windover Pond and has become the leading expert on its archaeological history and the idea of proto-Caucasoids in Florida and other parts of North America. He recently appeared on *Archaeology TV*, a local Florida television series produced and hosted by this author. Dr. Doran stated that the Windover Pond area was continually occupied from 8000 BCE to roughly 4000 BCE. This would place it in the Early to Middle Archaic Period. The types of races we are familiar with today and the various geographical distinctions associated with race did not exist or, at least, were quite different (*Archaeology TV* 2003).

Dr. Doran cited the emergence of typical Mongoloid racial traits that do not seem to really become noticeable until around 4000 BCE. The people who inhabited North and South America may have been from Asia, but they also could have simply been a different type of human being who left no known descendants (*Archaeology TV* 2003).

For example, the Ainu of Japan represent a proto-Caucasoid race that must have inhabited much of East Asia at one time. The racial makeup of the New World during the Early and Late Archaic periods may have appeared quite different with many ethnic groups migrating to and fro throughout the country, but it does not exclude the possibility that they were, in fact, related to northwestern Europeans, perhaps the Paleolithic culture known as the Solutrean. Such a condition is highly probable and is what I believe to be true.

In any case, Windover Pond has demonstrated some fairly convincing evidence that prehistoric North America was home to more peoples than the Mongoloid immigrants from Asia. The continent could have been the crossroads of civilization itself. The site will no doubt continue to spark debate and intense investigation for many years to come.

LOST CAUCASIAN KINGDOMS
OF ANCIENT AMERICA

During the 1940s and 1950s, a significant archaeological stash was discovered that further legitimizes the search for the lost Caucasian kingdoms of ancient America. Not far from Clarksville, Virginia, by the Roanoke River near Jeffries, a farmer named James V. Howe found a treasure trove of ancient ironworkings. According to David Childress in his seminal work, *Lost Cities of North and Central America,* additional sites were also uncovered. They revealed a considerable number of artifacts that were found in Brunswick County, some eighty kilometers to the east. Included in the discovery were swords and other forms of iron weapons, chisels, nails, and even threaded nuts (1992, p. 434).

In addition to these artifacts, Howe uncovered a broken bronze cup, a bronze spindle whorl, and two other bronze fragments. He believed that the Bronze Age artifacts must have been brought from another site, because no evidence existed of copper or tin deposits anywhere near the location of the find. Moreover, Native Americans did not possess knowledge of such advanced forms of metallurgy or anything that could produce artifacts that were identical to those found in Europe.

The mystery only intensified in 1950 when Roman inscriptions were found on rocks located a mile apart just outside the village of Dolphin, nearly eighty kilometers away. Mainstream archaeologists refused to subject them to radiocarbon dating, and many of the artifacts are now lost. The Smithsonian took some of the artifacts, but their current location remains unknown. This is just one more royal example of how the establishment continues to suppress theories and discoveries that challenge accepted scientific wisdom. But isn't challenging accepted dogma the very embodiment of scientific inquiry? As discussed in previous chapters, the knowledge filter remains a clear and present danger to science.

In his book Childress also tells us that

> another "Roman" artifact was brought up from the ground while men were boring a water well opposite Elizabeth, Virginia, in September of 1833. It was a coin, brought up from a depth of 30 feet, about the size of an English shilling of the period. It was oval in shape, and unlike anything ever seen there before by even the oldest inhabitant. According to historian W. S. Forrest, the figures on the coin were distinct, representing a warrior or hunting and other characters apparently of Roman origin. (1992, p. 434)

Today, hard evidence suggests that the Celts visited the New World prior to the arrival of Columbus, and they may have colonized and intermingled with existing North American populations. Investigators have found Ogam inscriptions all over North America. Ogam is the ancient Celtic script that many believe was transplanted to the Americas during a forgotten epoch of European civilization. Throughout the Americas there are also many examples of cairnlike structures that are reminiscent of European or Irish forms. For some, it is clear that the Celts left their signature all across the East Coast of North America, but others remain skeptical. But if the Celts indeed visited or settled in North America, did they come straight from Europe or did they make their way through an indirect route, perhaps at a much earlier date than currently thought?

Barry Fell, a maverick in the field of ancient European and American cultures and their interrelationships, was the first to recognize the presence of the Celts. He articulated this in his groundbreaking book, *America BC*. If Atlantis existed, and it was in fact Tir na n'Og, then the Celts could have moved across all three continents, North America, Atlantis, and Europe, with relative ease. Fell and others would eventually go on to find Keltic and Iberian inscriptions etched into the surface of rocks and what are possibly their monuments all across North America.

A site that may be Celtic in origin is found in New Hampshire. Dubbed "America's Stonehenge," it is a possible Bronze Age Celtic settlement. Its owner, Dennis Stone, has spent much time compiling evidence to support this assertion. This evidence includes what appears to be an Ogam inscription found in one of the underground chambers on his property.

These finds generated enormous interest in this particular field of amateur archaeology, and soon everyone was appearing out of the woodwork with some type of ancient script that they hoped Fell, in his supposed divine wisdom, could decipher, which would then gain them entry into the history books. Unfortunately, many of these finds turned out to be quite recent, such as eroded grave markers and half-finished works of a relatively recent age. But some proved to be perplexing, and thus caught Fell's critical eye. Needless to say, Fell's theories did not fit well with conventional archaeologists.

The Mississippi Valley is home to yet another series of finds. Evidence suggests large-scale Celtic expeditions to the region. Among the physical evidence are Ogam inscriptions in Arkansas along the Cimarron River, and many more in Kentucky. The first date for such an expedition is roughly one thousand years ago. It is clear that if these were pre-Christian Celts, then the date must be much earlier.

A small, flat-topped island known as Manana, situated off the coast of Maine near Monhegan Island, was the location of yet another discovery. Remnants of Goidelic Celtic script (unfortunately no longer extant) were found there, which seem to argue for the island's inclusion as a stopping point for the many voyages that took place to the New World during the European Bronze Age. These inscriptions made reference to Roman and Carthaginian rulers.

Hanno was a historical figure, a Phoenician seafarer who is remembered for his exploration and colonization of the African coast five centuries before Christ. Inscriptions from the Temple of Baal in Carthage, which were copied to manuscript from approximately 1000 CE, tell of his exploits. These records indicate that Hanno circumnavigated the northern Atlantic around 480 BCE. His feat of exploring the coast of Africa and making his way to India indicates his superior abilities, as this kind of a trip is twice as long as an Atlantic crossing.

Evidence suggesting global navigation at such an early point in the evolution of human civilization gives credence to the idea that such voyages were possible and did in fact occur. We are already certain of the voyages led by Norse explorer and navigator Leif Erikson. But there is growing evidence that many more Europeans ventured west in the centuries and millennia that preceded him. Contrary to popular belief, ancient people were very knowledgeable about the sea and were inordinately skilled in navigation and shipbuilding techniques. An abundance of evidence suggests that ancient peoples such as the Chinese, Middle Easterners, and Europeans did in fact visit the New World in the centuries before Columbus. The evidence remains inconclusive as to whether any of these European powers established true Caucasian kingdoms in North America, but the evidence is steadily mounting.

ATLANTIS AND THE GREAT WHITE GOD

In 1773 a Spanish friar named Ramon de Ordonez left the town of Ciudad Real in Chiapas, southern Mexico, and entered the dense Mesoamerican rain forest. He then wandered through the jungle for some 113 kilometers until he finally paused to rest. As he looked around he beheld the most magnificent sight he had ever seen. His gaze fell upon elaborate ruins, nearly consumed by the thick tropical vegetation. Through the climbing vines and thick underbrush there stood a wonder beyond description: a variety of fallen structures, including a pyramid. Carvings of serpents, perched on the side of the stone edifices, stared ominously back at him. Ordonez called this place the City of the Serpents. This site would later be known as Palenque (Wilson 2006, p. 108).

The founder of the city was a godlike individual named Votan, a being that Ignatius Donnelly associated with the Germanic god Wotan. Votan was a tall, fair-skinned, bearded individual. Legend has it that he appeared in the New World from the Near East. His homeland was called Valum Chivim. While journeying in his homeland, Votan encountered a people who were building a temple in a city, with a tower high enough to reach heaven. The date was 2500 BCE and without question presents more than an obvious connection to the Tower of Babel. It is therefore possible that the city was linked with ancient Babylon.

Votan became revered as a god and was known as the Great White God as well as by other names: Kukulkan, Quetzalcoatl, Kon-Tiki, and Viracocha. According to author Colin Wilson, "In the 'sunken temple,' in front of the Kalasasiya in Tiahuanaco, is a statue of a tall, bearded European who is assumed to be the great teacher, Viracocha. He must have been European, since native Indians cannot grow beards" (2006, p. 108).

In *Lost Cities of North and Central America,* David Hatcher Childress explains that the story of Quetzalcoatl, the Great White God, is on an equal standing to those of any other major religion, whether of today or ancient times. When compared with Buddha, Confucius, Lao Tzu, Zoroaster, or Jesus of Nazareth, the Great White God has the same religious and cultural significance for the peoples of ancient America and the Pacific as any of these figures.

All three main civilizations, Olmec, Maya, and Aztec, had a profoundly rich heritage of oral tradition related to Atlantis. In Mexico the lost continent is referred to as Aztland. This particular homeland is indelibly linked to the Great White God Quetzalcoatl. Depicted as a feathered serpent, he has a human avatar that is tall and white-skinned, again with a full, long beard and even, some say, light-colored eyes. He is considered one of the most prominent, if not the paramount, deity in Mesoamerican tradition. Scholars consider him a combination of fact and myth (Rosenberg 1994, p. 492).

Like the Romano-British hero King Arthur, Quetzalcoatl may have been based on a real person, or he could be the culmination of a number of earlier events or legends that developed into a composite character. Some cultural anthropologists suggest that Quetzalcoatl was either partly or almost wholly based on Topiltzin (Our Prince), the great leader of the tenth-century race known as the Toltecs, which were ancestral to the Aztec Empire and contemporaneous with the classic Mayan civilization. But many would argue against such a suggestion, especially because Topiltzin did not share the same Caucasian facial features and other attributes that the Great White God was noted to have.

In addition to being known as Quetzalcoatl to the Toltecs and then to the Aztecs, he was known as Kukulkan among the Yucatec Maya and Gukumatz Tohil among the K'iche' Maya. These deities are part of a hemispheric tradition. The Inca god Viracocha was proclaimed to be the founder of their race and culture, and unlike the Inca themselves, he had distinct Indo-European features. He also promised one day to return and raise the Inca to the pinnacle of their spirituality. This would ensure that they alone would become the dominant race.

When Quetzalcoatl first created the world, he created a race of giants whom he gave acorns for nourishment. It was this race of giants that ultimately would build the largest structure of the ancient world: the great Mesoamerican pyramid of Cholula that three successive civilizations—the Toltec, Maya and Aztec—labored over centuries to construct. According to myth, however, the giants built it to reach the heavens. Sixty-four meters high, it covers eighteen hectares.

The pre-Conquest Mexican legend about Cholulu is very similar to the biblical account of the Tower of Babel. According to the legend, after the deluge that destroyed the primeval world, seven giants survived, one of whom built the great pyramid of Cholula to reach heaven, but the gods destroyed the pyramid with fire and confounded the languages of the builders (Childress 1992, p. 230). Childress also mentioned that according to *Facts and Artifacts of Ancient Middle America,*

Cholula was the "seat of the Olmeca-Xicalanca who was finally driven out by Toltec-Chichimecs in 1292 CE; that the pyramid of the Cholula is dedicated to the 'white god' Quetzalcoatl" (1992, p. 231).

The symbolism surrounding the Great White God is far from simple. He shifts from being a human but paradoxically European avatar who is tall, with a gray or blond beard, white skin, and light-colored eyes, to the almost repulsive likeness of a crested rattlesnake with feathers. It seems in most circumstances both visions are accepted simultaneously and without question.·

As Harold T. Wilkins describes in his now famous *Secret Cities of Old South America* with regard to the ancient Mayan civilization of Belize, "A remarkable Atlantis figure [was] found bearing a great mass of stone and earth on his shoulders in the Mayan temple of warriors at Chichen-Itza of the Classic Maya period. Almost side by side with it is that superb profile of a fair, white, handsome Atlantean supporting a massive stone table-like altar in the sanctuary of the same temple" (1998, p. 94).

Temples like the ones of Chichen Itza were built all across Mesoamerica in the name of Quetzalcoatl. From the Pacific to the Atlantic his name reigned supreme. No other god was more important. He remains one of the most perplexing of the Mesoamerican deities. He stands alone, due to the simple fact that in addition to his manifestation as a feathered serpent, his avatar was a fair-skinned, blond-bearded, and blue-eyed warrior. Such a vision would be impossible for an ancient race who had never looked upon a northern European; one who didn't know there was indeed a land to the east.

Prior to the final cataclysm that ravaged and then sank the continent of Atlantis, the Great White God Quetzalcoatl and his followers traveled as far north as what is now British Columbia. On Native American totem poles in British Columbia are engraved figures wearing costumes very similar to the type that the Atlantean peoples of Brazil used to wear at the festivals of Viracocha. Inhabitants of British Columbia claim to have been visited by Qoagalal, a variation on the name of Quetzalcoatl

(Wilkins 1998, p. 95). His preeminence throughout North America is now known, from the Adena and Hopewell to the Mississippians and the Anasazi. Even Florida Indians often spoke of an ancient white master.

The Great White God was perhaps western Europe's first encounter with legends of out-of-place Caucasians. The vision of him being master of a lesser race was very inviting and comforting to Europe's colonial and racist leanings. But they were missing the point. This issue goes beyond a few hard-line Europeans twisting the truth in their favor. There is hard evidence not only in oral and written traditions but also from the artifacts themselves depicting a Great White God. There had to at least have been some Caucasian presence at some time. Remains such as Kennewick Man and Spirit Cave Man are a testament to this, and there is no doubt to *their* authenticity. The Great White God lived, and the questions surrounding the forgotten Caucasians of ancient America have yet to be answered.

CONCLUSIONS

Through the efforts of a select group of mainstream archaeologists, geneticitsts, and scholars, we are nearing a final solution to the problem of New World population and the rise of its earliest civilizations. We are learning, in the case of the North Atlantic Crescent, that the transference of humans and their technology from northern Europe to North America was a very real possibility and most likely happened in actual fact. We are also learning through newly discovered anomalies such as Kennewick Man, Lutzia, and Spirit Cave Man, as well as the findings at Windover Pond, that the racial composition of North and South America has been one of infinite change and fluidity.

We are learning that the Americas was a land of lost and ancient kingdoms, as well as forgotten Caucasian civilizations that are only now being explored. It will be up to the explorers and investigators of the future to come to some final conclusions regarding any or all questions that these explorations pose.

12

Atlantis, Mesoamerica, and the Five Suns

Heaven is founded,
Earth is founded,
Who now shall be alive, oh gods?

THE AZTEC CHRONICLE,
THE HISTORY OF THE KINGDOMS, 1522

There is an Aztec prophecy foretelling a future time when Earth will "become tired" and the "seed of Earth" will be ended. The Aztecs believed that when that day of darkness and death arrives, the sun, moon, and stars would fall from the heavens and crash to the Earth. This is a fitting end of the world scenario for a group so synchronized with the cosmos, astronomy, and the passage of time (Sagan 1980, pp. 231–32).

According to the Aztec religious cosmology, there have been four creations, or "suns," each ending in a great cataclysm, after which there is a rebirth, and society begins anew. In Aztec tradition the termination of each epoch, or sun, is achieved by one of the four main elements—water, earth, fire, and water—including one destruction by flood, another by a conflagration, another by an earthquake, and still another by a violent windstorm (Campbell 1949, p. 224). Each of these cycles, which we will discuss further, is associated with a deity.

As with the Mayan prophecy, the Aztecs hold that we are presently living in the fifth creation, or fifth sun. The reassuring aspect of this worldview is that there will be another world after us, another chance for life, and the inhabitants of Earth will able to build back their power and momentum.

In 1790 a four-meter-wide disc, the Aztec calendar stone, was found near the former site of the Aztec Temple in Mexico City. This disc is one of the most beautifully impressive and unique religious creations that the human race has ever produced. Positioned in the center of the stone is an image of the sun god Tonatiuh. Two giant claws and four boxed figures symbolizing the four previous suns surround the image of this god. These suns, or cosmic realities, are dedicated to the jaguar, wind, fire, and water, which are the sacred forces that control and determine all things in nature. There are also images representing day signs belonging to the sacred calendar.

According to Frank Joseph, author of *Atlantis and 2012,* the Mayan and Aztec calendars appear to describe "a worldwide memory of global cataclysms so traumatic they became defining moments in ancient man's prehistory and his reckoning of time. They appear in the squares clustering around the hub of the Stone, beginning particularly with the most recent catastrophe, the great deluge, a clear reference to the destruction of Atlantis in every respect" (2010).

Joseph also mentions Mayan cosmology: "The Maya legend of the Four Suns recounted how death came to their overseas' ancestors from out of the sky: 'It rained fire upon them. They were swallowed up by the waters.' This was the Unuycit, when an ancestral homeland, Patulan-Pa-Civan, perished with all but a handful of survivors, who sailed to the shores of the Yucatan during the remote past. Mentioned in the Dresden Codex, the Haiyococab was the Water over the earth, from which the Earth-upholding gods fled when the world was destroyed by the Deluge" (Joseph 2010, p. 49).

The origins of the Aztec and other Mesoamerican calendars are seen in the earliest evidence of Olmec culture. As Eliade and Adams pointed out, their calendrical system is based on the "indication that the political and social order not only was closely linked to the universe, but also conceived in measurements of time, all of whose moments are bearers of destiny" (Eliade and Adams 1987, 9:393). In an ancient proto-calendar known as the Stelae of the Dancers at Monte Alban I (epoch I) in Oaxaca the human figures are described by Eliade and Adams "as an expression of political and ritual power" and are accompanied by hieroglyphs. These ancient inscriptions apparently denote the names of individuals and places of divine origin. Most likely they describe an early pantheon of gods and their dwelling places (Eliade and Adams 1987, 9:393).

The Aztec calendar no doubt evolved along with the development of the earliest astronomic observations. Its early presence throughout Mesoamerica suggests a very ancient and common origin. It eventually came to determine all divine and human activities. Images of humans are depicted in many Olmec monuments, such as those at Basalt Altar 4 in La Venta, which emerges from a chasm or out of the dark mouth of a dragonlike god, thus symbolizing the womb and the birth of humanity (Eliade and Adams 1987, 9:393).

As Joseph Campbell points out, the Aztec, Mayan, and other mythologies of Middle America adopted a worldview shared by the Greek philosopher Heraclitus, who wrote, "We must know that War is common to all, and Strife is Justice, and that all things come into being from Strife. This world, the same for all, was not made by any god or man, but was always, and, is and shall be an ever living Fire, with measures of its kindling and measures of it being extinguished" (Campbell and Abadie 1974, p. 166).

The symbol for the sun in Aztec myth was the eagle. This was linked directly to ancient sacrifices, as the eagle is kept in flight by clutching two human hearts, which is seen in the central image of the Aztec calendar, its two earlike projections tipped with eagle claws, grasping human hearts (Campbell and Abadie 1974, p. 151).

Aztec and indeed much of Mesoamerican mythology centers on an eternal struggle between light and darkness, but this might not necessarily denote a battle between good and evil, as in European and Near Eastern religions. For the Aztec in particular, the sun, and indeed all heavenly bodies, were sacred, and there was an ongoing fight against the darkness, to keep the lights of the sky and of the heavens burning. This ideal is embodied in the Aztec creations, or "suns."

In the beginning there were only the male and female lords of duality: Ometeotl and Omecihuatl. Out of their cosmic union the four Tezcatlipoca were conceived and born. These new gods consisted of Xipe-Totec, symbolizing the east; Huitzilopochtli, the south; Quetzalcoatl, the eternal west; and Black Tezcatlipoca, the north (Cotterell and Storm 2004, p. 285).

Eventually there was a whole community of divinities, including Tlolac the rain god and his companion the water goddess, named Chalchiuhtlicue. It is not clear where all of these gods came from in the line of creation, but this is not uncommon among ancient myths (such as those of Norse cosmology). A series of primordial wars between these ancient and bloody deities eventually led to the formation and destruction of the first four worlds, a cycle of blood, death, and honor that dwarfs anything conceived in the Mayan codexes.

During the first sun giants walked the Earth. An epoch dominated by the jaguar, it lasted for almost seven centuries. Finally, the Great White God Quetzalcoatl banished the presiding deity, Tezcatlipoca, into the eternal waters, after which the jaguars rose and destroyed the Earth (Cotterell and Storm 2004, pp. 283–85).

The second sun saw the world ruled by Quetzalcoatl. This world was noble and just, but it was quickly destroyed when Tezcatlipoca returned, pushed the White God from his throne, and obliterated all life with an immense hurricane. The third sun was dominated by fire and was ruled by Tlaloc, the rain god. A rain of fire obliterated this world. The fourth sun, which immediately precedes our own, was ruled by Chalchiuhtlicue, the goddess of water. This world was destroyed not by fire or an act of the gods, but by a Great Flood that destroyed the advanced civilization that was under her rule (Cotterell and Storm 2004, p. 285).

After all of these imperfect worlds met their final destruction, a fifth sun, known as the fourth movement, was born. Quetzalcoatl became ruler of the underworld and promised to return someday and lead his people to true freedom. Mixing the bones of those who perished in the great deluge and the blood of the gods created a new race of humans. To provide light and warmth for the new race, the gods gathered at what is now the ruins of Teotihuacán and summoned the god Nanahuatzin to throw himself on the cosmic fires. He ignited and became the sun. He is fed through blood and blood alone. Without it he dies, and so does the fifth sun, at which point darkness, chaos, and eventual destruction will roar forth upon the Earth (Cotterell and Storm 2004, pp. 285–87).

THE POPOL VUH

In *Voyages of the Pyramid Builders,* Boston University geologist Robert M. Schoch noted that the K'iche' Maya believe that their distant ancestors came "from the other side of the sea, where the sun rises" (2004, p. 103). The belief in some primordial migration from a mysterious unknown land, often associated by some scholars with the idea of Atlantis, is a recurring theme in many cultures. The Popol Vuh is the sacred religious texts of ethnic Mayans in Central America, which was preserved in oral tradition after the Spanish Conquest of 1521 and written down several decades later by Roman Catholic monks. It is the sacred scriptures of the K'iche' Maya, and it further explains that the people dwelt in darkness in the east and journeyed west in ships in search of the eternal sun. After reaching the Promised Land they disembarked on the shore and made their way to the highlands of Central America. As with the Hebrew scriptures, the Popol Vuh mentions that as the Mayan tribes made their way to the New World, they "crossed the sea, the waters having parted when they passed," an occurrence with undeniable links to the Old Testament and the depiction in Exodus of the parting of the Red Sea (p. 104).

The Popol Vuh describes the Mayan creation myth, which was transcribed directly from Mayan scripture after the Spanish conquest. In the beginning the twin gods of creation, Gugumatz and Hurakan, divided the mountains from the water and the Earth from the firmament. Then they went forth and created all the vegetation—the fruits, the trees, entire forests—and then they rested. Then they created all the animals, including jaguars, deer, birds, and serpents. The gods were unhappy with their creations. The animals could not speak out the gods' names; they could not remember the stories of creation or honor them in worship. The gods were alone, with nothing to revere them. They first attempted to make humans by forming men from clay, but the men simply fell apart with the coming rain.

In their second attempt they tried to make men from the wood of trees, but that only created a race of voiceless, immovable beings. Again, humankind was destroyed. Finally, the gods utilized maize, which allowed them to make human flesh. Summoned forth by the gods, the fox, the coyote, the parrot, and the crow brought ears of white and yellow maize to the deities, and from these the gods formed four perfect creations, the first true men. These first four men became the foundation of the four bloodlines of the K'iche' Maya. They honored and nourished the names of the gods (Hancock 1995, pp. 490–92).

But as quickly as the First Men achieved glory, the gods became jealous of them. They sneered at the First Men for their progress and success; they were becoming too godlike. The gods ended their reign. The Popol Vuh describes this transgression:

They were endowed with intelligence; they saw and instantly they could see far; they succeeded in seeing; they succeeded in knowing all that there is in the world. The things hidden in the distance they saw without first having to move. . . . Great was their wisdom; their sight reached to the forests, the rocks, the lakes, the mountains and the valleys. In truth, they were admirable men. . . . They were able to know all, and they examined the four corners, the four points of the arch of the sky, and the round face of the earth. (Hancock 1995, p. 156)

The gods' effort to neutralize those who challenged their supremacy was swift: "The Heart of Heaven blew mist into their eyes. . . . In this way all the wisdom and all the knowledge of the First Men together with their memory of their origin and their beginning, were destroyed" (Hancock 1995, pp. 490–92). One finds similar themes in the Old Testament and the Talmud: God destroying humans before they could challenge his supreme authority and rule.

EAST AND WEST: A CONNECTION OF CULTURES

The next important matter for discussion is the apparent connection between Eastern and Western cultures. This reality is ignored by the majority of mainstream scholars, even though the similarities are striking. Rather than evolving in isolation from one another, the cultures of East and West have long shared a close, intimate relationship with one another. An enormous body of evidence links ancient Mesoamericans with their counterparts in the Middle East. The New World, far from being an outpost of human civilization, was a bedlam of global trade and human interaction. Recent discoveries have confirmed this beyond a shadow of a doubt.

John L. Sorenson, an emeritus professor of anthropology at Brigham Young University, has studied extensively the similarities between Old and New World cultures, as well as probable contact between them in pre-Columbian times. He is the author of *An Ancient American Setting for the Book of Mormon* as well as many other books and articles on the Book of Mormon and archaeology. The Book of Mormon is often called "Another Testament of Jesus Christ." It is a group of scriptures translated by the prophet Joseph Smith from a series of gold plates inscribed with reformed Egyptian, an extinct form of writing. The angel Moroni led Smith there and imbued him with the power to translate the plates. These translations then became known as the Book of Mormon and became the basis of Mormon, better known as LDS (Latter-Day Saints) teachings and faith.

Robert M. Schoch noted in his book *Voyages of the Pyramid Builders* the list of parallels Sorenson had drawn between the Mesoamericans and Middle Easterners. First and foremost is a common knowledge and working practice of astronomy, a passion that both cultures pursued in earnest. This led to the building of massive observatories and meticulously maintained records of eclipses. Both cultures shared the practice of ritual sacrifice, and both cultures divided the afterlife into a paradise and a hell—two concepts that speak of a common origin (2004, p. 114).

Peru was a country that was not discussed by Sorenson. His archaeological inquiries mainly revolved around the Book of Mormon. The majority of scholars in the LDS community consider Central America to be the lands of the Book of Mormon. Thus, the reason for Peru's exclusion is obvious. However, Peru has some fascinating parallels with Middle Eastern culture and civilization. Schoch observes that the megalithic architecture of Sacsahuaman, near Cusco, Peru, "with its precisely fitted stones, reminds one of the smoothly fitted, white limestone casing that enclosed the Khufu Pyramid or the limestone and granite walls of the Valley and Sphinx temples" (2004, p. 115). Some of the old stone walls at Tiahuanaco in Bolivia show evidence of being repaired with stone bolts that resemble those used at Medinet Habu in Egypt. There are also similarities between the Kalasasaya Temple at Tiahuanaco that predates the Inca occupation and the Egyptian Temple of Seti at Abydos that dates to 1300 BCE. Both enormous structures were constructed on a lake with reeds and lotus flowers and were graced with gilt doors (p. 115).

The Aztec possessed a profound spiritual and mathematical wisdom. The bloody stain of human sacrifice was a necessary way to placate the sun god and to ensure his daily return. Without an offering of blood the world would be left in darkness. Those who were sacrificed often gave their lives willingly. These acts of sacrificial appeasement to the gods, however, could not protect them from a far more horrible, ignoble, and humiliating end (Sagan 1980, pp. 305–7).

The Aztecs' monumental architecture dwarfed the Europeans' wildest imaginings. Tenochtitlan must have been a sight to behold for the Spaniards looking upon it for the first time. Gleaming in the afternoon sun were shining pyramids, temples, and a variety of other structures linked to a vast road system unlike anything found in Europe. The Europeans had truly arrived in the land of the gods. Indeed, in the words of Hernán Cortés, Tenochtitlan was "one of the most beautiful cities in the world. . . . The people's activities and behavior are on almost as high a level as in Spain, and as well-organized and orderly. Considering that these people are barbarous, lacking knowledge of God and communication with other civilized nations, it is remarkable to see all that they have" (Sagan 1980, pp. 305–7).

This impression was soon to be corrupted, for within two years Cortés would annihilate the Aztec Empire and nearly blot it out of history entirely. The diligent efforts of modern historians and archaeologists to keep the memory alive were their only salvation (Sagan 1980, pp. 305–7).

CONCLUSIONS

After reviewing the religious and archaeological background of the ancient Mesoamerican civilizations, it is clear that despite their demise at the hands of the Spanish conquerors they were a force to be reckoned with. There is no doubt also that they bear strong similarities, in terms of architecture, religious beliefs, cultural traditions, and even genetics, with the peoples of the Old World. In my opinion it is unlikely that these two societies grew up in total isolation from all other peoples of the world. Ancient America was the crossroads of civilization, not an isolated outpost.

13
Atlantis and the Lost Cities of Mesopotamia

From [Babylon] to Aššur and (from) Susa, Agade, Ešnunna, Zamban, Me-Turnu, Der, as far as the region of Gutium, the sacred centers on the other side of the Tigris, whose sanctuaries had been abandoned for a long time, I returned the images of the gods, who had resided there, to their places and I let them dwell in eternal abodes. I gathered all their inhabitants and returned to them their dwellings. In addition, at the command of Marduk, the great lord, I settled in their habitations, in pleasing abodes, the gods of Sumer and Akkad, whom Nabonidus, to the anger of the lord of the gods, had brought into Babylon.

THE CYRUS CYLINDER,

CIRCA 538 BCE

SUMER AND THE BEGINNING OF HISTORY

The ancient Sumerian civilization was born in the third millennium BCE between the Tigris and Euphrates Rivers into a world rich in both culture and faith. The Sumerians gave us the rudiments of our popular flood myth, immortalized in today's scripture as the great deluge of Noah. But an ever older legend, which strikes a chord with our popular Atlantis story, is the Babylonian myth that their people arrived in the Mesopotamian realm after a long sea journey from some long forgotten and destroyed distant homeland (Schoch and MacNally 2003, p. 8).

Our earliest biblical traditions can be traced back to this Mesopotamian homeland. Initially, a people with only a rudimentary Stone Age culture and technology inhabited the region. Then, around five thousand years ago, something happened. This primitive culture was mysteriously transformed into what became the most advanced, sophisticated culture the world had ever known. What this "something" was remains, to this day, a total mystery.

Ancient Sumer was the parent culture to every Old World civilization that came after. They were neither Semitic nor Indo-European, and their language was agglutinative, a kind of Finno-Ugric tongue suggesting some Caucasian connection.

According to Frank Joseph, the Sumerians referred to themselves as the

> black-headed people. Their eyes were light, their complexion fair to tan, and their build short and slender. They were apparently related to the same stock as the Followers of Horus, the Guanche aboriginals of the Canary Islands, the pre-Celtic inhabitants of the British Isles, and the ancient Iberians, of which today's Basque population may be the lone surviving remnant. In other words they were part of the Atlantean race. (2004, p. 88)

ENUMA ELISH
(THE BABYLONIAN CREATION MYTH)

Both the Babylonians and the Assyrians had almost identical creation myths. In the Babylonian account Marduk assumed a prominent role. In the Assyrian epic the national god Assur replaces Marduk as the central figure. The following creation myths represent the general beliefs of both the Assyrian and Babylonian peoples.

At the beginning of time, before eternal creation, heaven and earth stood nameless, and the primordial waters mingled together in the immense blackness of space. From this primeval force of creation, three generations of gods were born. Among them were the gods Anu and Ea, who were the Babylonian version of the earlier Sumerian god Enki. Apsu, their formless ancestor, did not welcome the new gods and decided to murder them. But Ea, being smart and imaginative, cast a spell on Apsu to lower him into a deep sleep so that he could usurp him and seize absolute control of the watery realms himself. Ea's wife, Damkina, bore him a son, Marduk. Marduk was quite unlike any other. He was the god of the sun and of Babylon, a holy, virtuous deity, possessing the elements of a true hero: dynamic, energetic, and fierce, full of pride and distinction, and devoid of fear. This god-hero was willing to fight and die for the gods.

Marduk's presence incensed Tiamat, the dragonlike goddess who once existed as an entity of the deep but returned as a flesh-and-blood monster. Marduk mounted his chariot and rode toward Tiamat. Her companions scattered in fear, leaving her alone with the magnificent god-hero. He commanded a legion of monsters and heroes, headed by Marduk's son Kingu, who keeps the Tablets of Destiny. Marduk cut Tiamat in half. Her upper body became the sky and the vault of Heaven, along with the sun, stars, and planets. The lower half he fashioned into the Earth, and her eye sockets became the channels through which the Tigris and Euphrates flow. Marduk used the tail of the mighty Tiamat as a dam to keep the floodwaters from Apsu from drowning the lands of the Earth. Then he erected two great pillars to hold in place the Earth and sky. Kingu, in the chaos of battle, incited a revolt against his father. Marduk had his son executed. From a mixture of Kingu's blood and clay, Marduk formed the first race of humans.

Marduk possessed magical qualities and was often associated with, and even identified as, the Old Babylonian solar god Shamash. In common with Shamash he shared the qualities of impartiality, justice, and compassion. Also, because of his attack on Tiamat and the utilization of her slain body, he became personified as a warrior and dragon slayer.

ANCIENT MESOPOTAMIA: BIRTHPLACE OF SYMBOLISM AND MYTHOLOGY

The Mesopotamian, Hindu, and Mesoamerican traditions share several key dates for important religious and cultural events. As the late mythologist Joseph Campbell remarked, both the Hindu Kali Yuga, which represents our current age, and the present Mesoamerican age, or "suns," in Aztec terminology, began on dates coinciding with a Mesopotamian time line. Our current Kali Yuga cycle began on February 17, 3102 BCE. The Mayan date marking the beginning of the fifth cycle of creation matched the Yuga date by only eleven. When we interpret the dates 3102, 3109, and 3113 BCE in Mesopotamian terms, they align precisely with the dates for the invention of writing, mathematics, and astronomy, events Campbell describes as "the initiation of this whole remarkable effort to translate celestial mathematics into the ordering principle of life on earth" (Campbell and Abadie 1974, p. 149). This in itself is interesting, but there is evidence of additional correlations in other cultures. This, Campbell remarks, at least suggests some higher design.

In 289 BCE the Babylonian priest Berossus (as mentioned in previous chapters) wrote a history of humanity spanning some one hundred thousand years. Writing in Greek, Berossus claimed the time that elapsed between the crowning of the world's first earthly monarch and the great flood was 432,000 years. Although the scroll containing his work is now lost to us, much of Berossus's teachings have survived due to the efforts of his colleagues at that time, who recorded his thoughts and writings (Campbell and Abadie 1974, p. 148).

The Roman philosopher Seneca informs us that

Berossus states that everything takes place according to the course of the planets, and he maintains this so confidently that he determined the time for the conflagration of the world and for the flood. He asserts that the world will burn when all the planets that now move in different courses come together in the Crab, so that all stand in a straight line in the same sign, and that the future flood will take place when the conjunction occurs in Capricorn. For the former is the constellation of the summer solstice, the later of the winter solstice; they are the decisive signs of the zodiac, because the turning points of the year lie in them. (Campbell and Abadie 1974, p. 149)

As with Seneca, Berossus explains in his writings that the end of times will be presaged by many terrifying omens, many related to the movements of the planets and the constellations, and the orbit of the earth around the sun, a reality that, contrary to popular thought, was known to the ancient Hellenistic community. We see this same emphasis on astrological symbols and the zodiac in both the central Mayan and Hindu beliefs and in their cyclical path of birth, death, and rebirth.

Persian Gulf Oasis

In 2010 Jeffrey Rose, a mainstream archaeologist and researcher with the University of Birmingham in the United Kingdom, put forth a fascinating hypothesis. He suggested that before it was inundated by the Indian Ocean around eight thousand years ago, a landmass beneath the Persian Gulf once provided a dry "Persian Gulf Oasis" for early humans outside Africa. According to Rose it continued as a major settlement for early humans migrating out of the common homeland for one hundred thousand years (ScienceDaily 2010b).

In his article, which was first published in *Current Anthropology,*

Rose presents a "new and substantial cast of characters" in what he proposes is an entirely different evolutionary saga, starting thousands of years prior to all current models of migration (ScienceDaily 2010b). In recent years numerous archaeological sites belonging to early humans have been found along the shoreline of the Persian Gulf. The latest date back some 7,500 years ago (ScienceDaily 2010b).

Rose explains, "Where before there had been but a handful of scattered hunting camps, suddenly, over 60 new archaeological sites appear virtually overnight. These settlements boast well-built, permanent stone houses, long-distance trade networks, elaborately decorated pottery, domesticated animals, and even evidence for one of the oldest boats in the world" (ScienceDaily 2010b).

Some criticize Rose's hypothesis by asking how such sophisticated human settlements could emerge with no trace of precursor cultures in the archaeological record. Rose asserts that all the corresponding evidence is hundreds of feet beneath the waters of the Persian Gulf (ScienceDaily 2010b). He continues, "Perhaps it is no coincidence that the founding of such remarkably well-developed communities along the shoreline corresponds with the flooding of the Persian Gulf basin around 8,000 years ago. These new colonists may have come from the heart of the Gulf, displaced by rising water levels that plunged the once fertile landscape beneath the waters of the Indian Ocean" (ScienceDaily 2010b). The exposed basin, which would have been the size of Great Britain, would have provided welcome refuge to the dry conditions of the surrounding areas. It would have enjoyed a temperate, relatively clement climate with fresh water running from the Tigris, Euphrates, Karun, and Wadi Baton Rivers, as well as natural springs (ScienceDaily 2010b).

A stone tool style, distinct from the East African tradition, was found at several archaeological sites in Yemen and Oman. That raises the possibility, Rose suggests, that primitive *Homo sapiens* were already well established throughout the southern Arabian Peninsula starting around 100,000 BCE, or earlier. This deviates from conventional wisdom, which holds that the first successful migration into Arabia took place between fifty thousand and seventy thousand years ago (ScienceDaily 2010b).

At that time the Near East was a harsh and arid landscape. In the north the ice age brought blistering cold weather throughout the year. This oasis was a godsend to the early humans who relied on its plentiful resources and abundant food and water supply to sustain them. Rose concludes by saying, "The presence of human groups in the oasis fundamentally alters our understanding of human emergence and cultural evolution in the ancient Near East" (ScienceDaily 2010b).

The Sumerian Flood Myth

Graham Hancock believes that Mesopotamia and Egypt were born from an earlier civilization in the Indian Ocean, which gave rise to the concept of Atlantis in that part of the world. According to Hancock, prior to 6000 BCE a system of ancient cities and settlements covered the land between the Mediterranean and the Persian Gulf. These were true "antediluvian" cities that were wiped out some 11,000 to 7000 BCE.

As an authority on lost civilizations, Hancock tackles the problem of the Great Flood as described in Genesis, the Babylonian Epic of Gilgamesh, and the earlier Sumerian version of the same story. The Sumerian flood myth predates the Babylonian Epic of Gilgamesh by many centuries but has often been confused as being the same ancient text. The Sumerian Noah, Ziusudra, is described as a "pious, god-fearing king," and because of this a nameless deity took pity on him. The god tells Ziusudra: "Take my word, give ear to my instructions: A flood will sweep over the cult centers. To destroy the seed of mankind, is the decision, the word of the assembly of gods" (2002, p. 25).

As Hancock notes, the next forty lines are missing from the original Sumerian flood story, which predates both the Epic of Gilgamesh and the biblical account by nearly two thousand years, but by the time the lines resume the flood has already begun.

> *All the windstorms, exceedingly powerful, attacked as*
>   *one,*
> *At the same time the flood swept over the land,*
> *And the huge boat tossed about the windstorms and the*
>   *great waters.* (2002, p. 26)

Similar to the story of Noah in the Bible, the maelstrom continued for seven days. But on the eighth day the storms subsided, and the rejuvenating rays of the sun broke through the once gray clouds. From the vessel's deck, mighty Ziusudra gazed upon the world now transformed. He offered the blood sacrifice of an ox and a sheep to the sun god (Hancock 2002, p. 27).

After this section of the story, there is another break in the text. Unfortunately, it is lost to us forever, but it most certainly told the location where Ziusudra and his mighty vessel of survivors made first landfall. As Hancock notes, at this point in the story Ziusudra stood before the entire pantheon of Sumerian gods, and in their gratitude for preserving the seed of humanity and life itself on Earth, they granted him immortality.

> *Life like a god they gave him;*
> *Breath eternal like a god they brought down for him,*
>   *Ziusundra the king.*
> *The preserver of the name of vegetation and the seed of*
>   *mankind.* (pp. 28–29)

Hancock looks to the rediscoveries of ancient cities to justify his claims. The principal cities described in the Book of Genesis were Erech (historical Uruk), Accad (historical Agade), Ur, Nippur, Kish, Lagash, Isin, and Larsa. These were not the earliest cities recorded in the region, however. The ancient Sumerian and Eblaite cuneiform texts, along with other credible sources, describe a number of cities that antedate those listed in the Bible. These sacred cities were Eridu, Badtibira, Larak, Sippar, and Shuruppak. These five cities were steeped in a rich tradition that, as Hancock notes, survived all the way to Christian times (p. 32).

Not far from the embattled city of Basra in southern Iraq are the buried ruins of Eridu. Between 1946 and 1949, Iraqi archaeologists excavated this vast prehistoric city. The first areas unearthed were dated to 4000 BCE, but as the excavation continued it yielded ever more ancient finds. There was a temple built to honor Enki, who was the patron god and creator of Eridu. Within the city Enki resided in the temple called Eengura (p. 72).

Enki was called Lord of the Earth. He is the son of An, the sky god, and Nammu, the immortal goddess of water and creation. Many scholars have assumed that he was the chief water god, similar to Poseidon, but in the Sumerian worldview the Earth rested on the ocean. Enki was also described as the great productive manager, linking the god to the importance of agriculture in early Mesopotamian society.

In addition to his throne in Eridu, Enki was thought to reside in the Apsu, the watery abyss beneath the Earth. *The Encyclopedia of Religion* relates a hymn in which Enki describes himself: "When I draw near unto heaven, the rains of abundance rain down; when I draw near to the earth, the early flood at its height comes into being; when I draw near unto the yellowing fields, grain piles are heaped at my command" (Eliade and Adams 1987, 5:455). The Sumerians imagined that below the Earth was a vast subterranean freshwater sea, which they called Abzu or Engur. This is somewhat linked to the older spiritual notion of the Apsu.

As the home of Enki, one of the major gods, Eridu had spiritual importance, and the city's inhabitants built immense temples and other constructions to honor him. Archaeologists excavated one structure in Eridu known as the ziggurat. It was uncovered in the center of the excavation site and dated to around 2030 BCE. Closer investigation revealed that it stood on top of a series of earlier structures. Under one of its corners, archaeologists unearthed the ruins of no less than seventeen temples, built one above the other in protohistoric times.

The buildings buried at the lowest level were the earliest and consisted of temples, with small rooms for worship and even altars. Eridu is by far one of the most ancient archaeological sites currently in modern-day Iraq. Without question it is one of the oldest of the five sacred cities extant before the Great Flood. The artifacts uncovered, including pottery shards, appeared religiously inspired and date to around 7000 to 5500 BCE. This makes Eridu the oldest city discovered in southern Iraq, rivaled only by some of the sites in modern-day Turkey (Hancock 2002, p. 76).

According to Frank Joseph:

The sacred mountain with its lofty stage-tower was memorialized in the Sumerian ziggurat. . . . Campbell writes of the ziggurat "towering" in five stages, in initiation of the holy mountain. Plato reports that the sacred numerals of Atlantis were five and six, representing male and female energies, respectively. To create a proper balance of spiritual energies, the Atlanteans incorporated these numbers in their monumental architecture, the same numerical symbolism at work in Sumer. But the decisive point here is that the pyramids and ziggurats were built entirely independently of each other. They were not the results of cross-cultural contacts. The step pyramid which was a style most resembling the ziggurat, developed from the mastaba, a free-standing tomb of a single story, whereas the ziggurat grew out of temples raised on platforms. In other words, both concepts sprang from a common inspiration that predated their own civilizations, but their methods of evolution were completely unrelated. (2004, p. 88)

The city of Sippar, dedicated to the sun god Utu, was mentioned by Babylonian priest and scholar Berossus as the place where the sacred knowledge of the antediluvian master race was hidden so that civilization could be renewed after the flood. Utu was also the god of justice and the patron of Ararma (Larsa). In both cities temples were erected in his honor. These imposing edifices were called Ebabbar. Utu's wife was Ninkurra. The supreme judge of the gods and men, Utu presided each day in various temples at specific places called "the place of Utu." He was greeted each morning by the sun as it arose on the horizon. He managed the dealings of common humans through his invisible, spiritual connection and also dealt with the presence of gods, demons, and other creatures of the underworld (Hancock 2002, p. 32).

The place-names of many of these cities and temples, along with the names of their patron gods, were also discovered. They were found along with references to both Babylonian and ancient Hebrew writings. These were recorded in the lost Tablets of Ebla, discovered in Syria in 1974, which told of a culture of immense antiquity and influence. In addition to providing a wealth of information about the Middle East, these records mention and confirm many of the biblical accounts. In early times there was a strong sense of continuity and interaction between cultures that was nearly forgotten in later epochs.

Another rediscovered lost city in present day Iraq was Shuruppak. Excavations revealed evidence of a massive flood—consisting of a significant layer of silt and deposits including bone and pottery fragments. Shuruppak was the home of Ansud, goddess of grain and daughter of

Ninshebargunu, the mistress of mottled barley. It was also the holy birthplace of Ziusudra, the Sumerian Noah who preserved the seed of humankind during the great torrents and storms that flooded and submerged his homeland. In Babylonian tradition the Noah of Shuruppak is Utnapishtim (Hancock 2002, pp. 24–25).

What these finds tell us is that there is without question a shared cultural heritage among not only Hebrews and Babylonians but also the entire Middle Eastern region.

CONCLUSIONS

According to the historical record, ancient Sumer is the oldest recorded civilization, but it is not the first. Prior to the current historic period there were many ages that came before, each highlighted by an advanced civilization and ending in total destruction. The cataclysm of 12,000 years ago, marking the end of the last ice age, wiped out the existing civilization, which paved the way for the emergence of yet another cycle and another advanced culture, this time in Sumer in Mesopotamia around 3500 BCE. Considering the wealth of data collected over the past century or so, it is clear that many new discoveries are awaiting us just around the corner.

14

The Lost Cities of Osiris and
the Mysterious Sphinx

*This Libyan prince, named Sheshonk (whom the Bible
called Shishak when he sacked Jerusalem), became the first
pharaoh of the Twenty-second Dynasty, and he used his
son's royal connection to breed a line of Pharaohs. In all,
eight Libyan pharaohs ruled for over 200 years.*

BOB BRIER,
DAILY LIFE OF THE ANCIENT EGYPTIANS, 1999

CHAMPOLLION AND THE REBIRTH
OF EGYPTIAN LANGUAGE AND KNOWLEDGE

In 1827 the French linguist Jean-François Champollion became the first
human being in almost two millennia to read the ancient hieroglyphic
inscriptions of Egypt. Traveling up the Nile and approaching the monuments of the seemingly "alien civilization," he recorded in his journal:

The evening of the 16th we finally arrived at Dendera. There was
magnificent moonlight and we were only an hour away from the
Temples: could we resist the temptation? I ask the coldest of you

mortals! To dine and leave immediately were the orders of the moment: alone and without guides, but armed to the teeth we crossed the fields. . . . The Temple appeared to us at last. . . . One could well measure it, but to give an idea of it would be impossible. It is the union of grace and majesty in the highest degree. We stayed there two hours in ecstasy, running through the huge rooms . . . and trying to read the exterior inscriptions in the moonlight. We did not return to the boat until three in the morning, only to return to the Temple at seven. . . . What had been magnificent in the moonlight was still so when the sunlight revealed to us all the details. . . . We in Europe are only dwarfs and no nation, ancient or modern, has conceived the art of architecture on such a sublime, great and imposing scale, as the ancient Egyptians. They ordered everything to be done for people who are a hundred feet high. (Sagan 1980, p. 293)

As Andrew Robinson noted in *Lost Languages: The Enigma of the World's Undeciphered Scripts,* the world of the pharaohs came to a climactic end with the conquest of Egypt by Alexander the Great just over two thousand years ago. This event heralded many changes. The Ptolemies, a Greek dynasty descended from one of Alexander's generals, came to rule over the country. Cleopatra descended from the Ptolemaic bloodline. Moreover, the newly conquered Egyptians now honored a Greek-Egyptian hybrid god called Serapis.

That civilization, which John Anthony West and Graham Hancock have written about, has long since vanished from memory. Both the Greeks and Romans admired the Egyptians for their antiquity and wisdom, but the Greco-Roman world was, in their opinion, superior to the lowly nature of the Egyptian race. Classical authors also made it clear, however, that the Egyptians must be credited with the invention of writing although Pliny the Elder maintained that cuneiform was the first written text. We shall soon see that neither were correct, and the invention of writing harkens back to a far more distant time in the history of humankind (Robinson 2002, p. 52).

The year was 1801. Jean-François Champollion was only an eleven-year-old boy when he was first introduced to the wonders of ancient Egyptian hieroglyphs. The prefect of the school system in Champollion's province was Joseph Fourier, and he had heard of this brilliant and imaginative child, his gifts for linguistics, mathematics, and history. Fourier invited the boy to come to his home for an interview. It was there that the scholastically minded youth stumbled upon something that would alter his life and change the world forever. In Fourier's home were artifacts that had been brought back from Napoleon's conquests of Egypt a few years before. Fourier told the young Champollion that no one could decipher the odd symbols found on the artifacts. Perhaps, Champollion thought, this could be something he himself would one day achieve.

In 1828, twenty-seven years after his original close encounter in Fourier's study room, Champollion's life ambition was finally realized. Until this time, there had been many contenders hoping to crack the code of the pharaohs. Thomas Young, an intelligent and scientifically minded scholar, was one of the more sterling individuals who attempted to rest his claim on history. But, as Andrew Robinson points out, only one man could accomplish this feat, and that was Champollion. He was much different from Young; he was cool, reflective, interested in ancient languages and their cultures and civilizations, almost from the perspective of a humanities professor rather than that of a mathematician.

Although Young contributed to the success of the decoding in that he could interpret part of the script, it was Champollion who was largely responsible for and credited with cracking the hierogylphs (Robinson 2002, pp. 61–62).

The key to understanding the ancient script was the Rosetta Stone. This ancient artifact was found by a French soldier working in the Nile Delta, at a place whose name in Arabic is Rashid, but following the British occupation of Egypt is known as Rosetta. The stone contained three separate inscriptions, with three separate forms of writing. The first two, Greek and Demotic, were already known. Champollion basically used the first two as a point of reference in comparing the scripts. Using an obelisk excavated at Philae that included the Greek name of Cleopatra, he compared letters in all three sections of the slab and identified the letters in both names, Cleopatra and Ptolemy. It was this comparison that eventually broke the code (Sagan 1980, p. 294).

Until Champollion, it was generally believed the Egyptian hieroglyphs were, as Carl Sagan put it, "murky" and "metaphorical," definitely pictographic and having some type of religious or mythological meaning. Now it was revealed that this was not true; the hieroglyphs represented letters and syllables, not ideas. Carl Sagan explained in *Cosmos:*

> Champollion, who was fluent in ancient Greek, read that the stone had been inscribed to commemorate the coronation of Ptolemy V Epiphanes, in the spring of the year 196 BCE. On this occasion the king released political prisoners, remitted taxes, endowed temples, forgave rebels, increased military preparedness and, in short, did all the things that modern rulers do when they wish to stay in office. (1980, p. 294)

We are thankful to Champollion for his miraculous skill and perseverance, which allow us now to speculate in areas that the early-nineteenth-century Egyptologists and linguists could never have thought possible.

A NEW VIEW OF EGYPT AND ATLANTIS

Today fresh figures of discovery—Graham Hancock, Robert Bauval, Robert M. Schoch, John Anthony West, Christopher Dunn, and others—have broken new ground. Other investigators, part of the old order, are slowly shifting to accommodate the emerging theories and methodologies of these new investigators. Mark Lehner, for instance, in his book *The Complete Pyramids,* made the following remark regarding Egypt's newest discoveries: "These mysterious facts hint that the history of the pyramids is not always as straightforward as Egyptologists may think" (1997, p. 3). Indeed, nothing regarding archaeology can now be taken entirely at face value. The past few decades have seen great transformation within the field. Göbekli Tepe in modern-day Turkey is the perfect example: a twelve-thousand-year-old temple that defies the accepted chronology of human origins. From ancient burial sites to anomalous structures, our long-held beliefs and assumptions are proved incorrect over and over again.

Dr. Lehner hit the nail on the head when he pointed out that modern Egyptologists have a lot to reconsider within their own branch of archaeology. Recent discoveries across the globe challenge all investigators to use greater scrutiny and originality when exploring ancient societies. This new mandate may well rewrite the book on modern scholarship.

In 3100 BCE, King Menes, history's first known pharaoh, ascended the throne of Egypt, unified the Upper and Lower Kingdoms, and established the First Dynasty. Around 320 BCE in the city of Heliopolis there lived a priest named Manetho. He spoke of a time long before the advent of King Menes. Manetho gave two main time periods that existed before Menes's rise to power. The first epoch lasted some 24,925 years, and it is called, in ancient sources, "the time of Ra," "the time of Horus," or "the time of Osiris." Immediately following was another great age. It lasted for 11,340 years and was marked by the rule of a divine race known as the Shemsu-hor, the "Companions," or "Followers of Horus" (Collins 2002, pp. 5–6). This period was known as the First Time.

In his first attempt at addressing Atlantis and the lost civilization issue, Graham Hancock made a rather brief mention of it in his biblical mystery book, *The Sign and the Seal.* The book addresses the origins, history, and current location of the Ark of the Covenant. Mr. Hancock and I had a few minutes to discuss his book in an October 2003 interview on *Archaeology TV,* the public-access TV program that ran five award-winning seasons. He speculated about a grand predecessor to the Egyptian civilization, perhaps a parent culture, or a forgotten society linked to it in some profound manner. In his book he writes, "I was sure that if Egypt had indeed received the gifts of civilization and science then some record of this momentous transaction would have been preserved. The deification of two great civilizers—Thoth and Osiris—was evidence of a kind: although presented as theology, the legends of these gods sounded to my ears much more like the echoes of long-forgotten events which had actually taken place." After investigating the mystery further he had the following revelation: "I did find such an account. It was the familiar story of the lost continent of Atlantis . . ." (Hancock 1992, pp. 319–20).

In *Lost Cities of Atlantis, Ancient Europe and the Mediterranean,* David Hatcher Childress mentions an ancient civilization known as the Osirian Empire. This primeval nation covered much of North Africa, the Mediterranean, and southern Europe. According to esoteric sources the Osirian Civilization was part of what modern archaeologists call predynastic Egypt. Far more advanced than conventional wisdom allows, the Osirians built the Sphinx, the pyramids, and many of Egypt's other glorious structures (1996, p. 26).

Two civilizations, the Rama Empire in India and classical Atlantis in the Atlantic Ocean, coexisted with the Osirian Empire. Moreover, there may have been an original mother continent in the Pacific known by some as Lemuria and by others as the lost continent of Mu. In *The Lost Continent of Mu,* James Churchward mentions that Egypt was settled from the lost continent of Mu via earlier settlements in Atlantis and the great proto-Mayan and Olmec cultures of the Americas (1926). This might contradict accounts that consider the Osirian Empire a thoroughly independent and separately evolved primeval society. Both of these ancient civilizations lived west of what is now Egypt.

THE STORY OF OSIRIS

The account of Osiris's auspicious rise to power, as described by the Greek historian Plutarch, has great relevance to the search for Atlantis and other lost civilizations (Childress 1996, p. 28). Osiris was born in Thebes, the offspring of Geb, the Earth god, and Nut, the sky goddess. Legend states that his arrival was presaged by a loud, mysterious voice proclaiming the coming of the "universal lord." Ra, the sun god, summoned his great-grandson, Osiris, to court and acknowledged him as the returning king and the one true heir. Geb relinquished his command and returned to the heavens, after which Osiris seized the reins of power over Egypt.

This account of Osiris being the first true king contradicts the historical record of the advent of King Menes. The whole idea of the Osirian Empire flies in the face of history's established time line. Regardless, the possibility of predynastic Egypt being part of a vast forgotten empire is compelling. This idea is directly connected with the Osiris myth (Childress 1996).

Osiris did become king. With his power now secure, he civilized the preexisting Paleolithic culture, which included the uneducated serfs of the previous rulers, and introduced agriculture, law, the worship of the gods, and the associated rituals. He also built Egypt's first temples. After achieving his goals he turned his attention to the rest of the world, which he believed also needed guidance and protection. He left Isis in power and, with the help of Thoth, his grand vizier, and his lieutenants, Anubis and Upuaut, he set out to conquer Asia. Whether this was in reference to Asia Minor and Persia or an allusion to all of modern-day Asia is unknown (Childress 1996).

Upon his return he found that Isis had governed well, and his empire was powerful and economically prosperous. Seth, his brother, however, had been making plans. Seth set a snare for him and succeeded in murdering him. His [Osiris's] wife, Isis, a "great magician," managed to become pregnant by the dead Osiris. After burying his body, she takes refuge in the Delta; there, hidden in the papyrus thickets, she gives birth to a son, Horus. Grown up, Horus first makes the gods of the Ennead recognize his rights, and then he attacks his uncle. Horus succeeded in bringing his dead father back to life. It was at this moment that the reborn Osiris decided not to re-establish his reign. He instead left the world and retired to the Elysian Fields. (Eliade 1978, p. 97)

In the Elysian Fields he ruled as god of the underworld, but his significance in the lives of Egyptians would continue. "If it were not for the powerful mythology of Osiris," Graham Hancock writes, "and if this civilizing, scientific, law-making deity was not remembered in particular for having introduced domesticated crops into the Nile Valley in the remote and fabled epoch known as the First Time, it would probably not be a matter of any greatest concern that at some point between 13,000 BCE and 10,000 BCE Egypt enjoyed a period of what has been described as 'precocious' agricultural development—possibly the earliest agricultural revolution anywhere in the world identified with certainty by historians" (1995, p. 411).

THE GREAT SPHINX: THE KEY TO ATLANTIS

In *Serpent in the Sky* author John Anthony West nobly attempts to propose a solution to the Atlantis riddle using the Great Sphinx of Egypt as a key. He also uses his mentor Schwaller de Lubicz as the main focus of his argument. West says, "A realistic approach to the mystery suggests alternatives that are unacceptable to the orthodox mind. The first is that Egyptian civilization did not develop in situ but was brought to Egypt by hypothetical conquerors. The second alternative is that Egypt did not develop her civilization, but inherited it" (1979).

West also says about the Atlantis mystery:

> The implications of this alternative are obvious. If the coherent, complete and interrelated system of science, religion, art and philosophy of Egypt was not developed by the Egyptians but inherited (and perhaps reformulated and re-designed to suit their needs), that system came from a prior civilization possessing a high order of knowledge. In other words, this alternative brings up the old question of "Atlantis." (1979)

His main point? "Schwaller de Lubicz observed that the severe erosion of the body of the great Sphinx of Giza is due to the action of water, not of wind and sand. If this single fact of the water erosion of the Sphinx could be confirmed, it would in itself overthrow all accepted chronologies of this history of civilization." This, in effect, would make the time line of Atlantis possible (1979).

The Great Pyramids of Giza and the Sphinx are perhaps the most iconic images of ancient times, readily identified by almost everyone in the world. The variety of speculation regarding these structures is quite monumental. Some of the oldest legends concerning the Great Pyramid of Cheops mention hidden treasure, and this has motivated more than one fearless explorer to enter its depths in search of fame and fortune. Other speculations, while considered spurious by mainstream experts, share an element of truth. Conventional views hold that this half-human, half-lion image was built 5,500 years ago and was subject to sandblasting and rain erosion. As we shall see, this theory has been challenged by a number of scholars, especially an open-minded Boston University geologist by the name of Robert Schoch (Sagan 1980, p. 99).

The Great Pyramid of Cheops, towering 76 meters high and built with 2.3 million blocks of stone, is aligned with the cardinal directions of true north, south, east, and west, as Graham Hancock has often maintained. This has fueled speculation that it is some type of ancient astronomical monument, dedicated to the constellations Orion or Cygnus. Mavericks such as Erich von Däniken have even considered an extraterrestrial origin for it.

In ancient texts the Sphinx is known as Hamachis, and in later hieroglyphic inscriptions, Hor-em-Akhet. According to Brad and Sherry Steiger, authors of the book *Atlantis Rising:*

> The Akhet is an Egyptian hieroglyph in the image of two triangles, which represents where the sun rises and sets—an image that comes to life when looking out from the Sphinx to the pyramids of Cheops and Cephren at sunset on the summer solstice. As the Sun sets between the pyramids it highlights the image of two triangles (the pyramids) connected by a line (the earth). (2003, 2:268)

Although the Sphinx has a human head, this current configuration might actually have been carved thousands of years after its construction, during the Old Kingdom's rejuvenation efforts. Some experts speculate that the original head was that of lion, in accordance with the Age of Leo, which dates from 11,000 to 9000 BCE. This may or may not be the construction date. The current face of the Sphinx is of significant interest to scholars, alternative and mainstream alike. A spiraling beard is a feature common to most depictions of Egyptian pharaohs and is not spared on the disproportioned face of the Sphinx. In addition to the beard there is also a large headdress, symbol of pharaonic authority and divinity. The Sphinx of Greek mythology has the body of a lion, the wings of an eagle, and the head and breasts of a human female. It forever guarded the entry into Thebes (Steiger and Steiger 2003, 2:268).

Herbert Ricke of the Swiss Archaeological Institute made an intriguing discovery in 1967. He found a correlation between the Sphinx and the image of the Egyptian sun god Ra. Ricke presented his theory following the initial excavations of a temple found at the foot of the Sphinx. This primordial structure included several sanctuaries, each with its own series of niches meant to capture the rays of the sun during the summer and winter solstices. In addition, a colonnaded courtyard featuring some twenty-four pillars was discovered at the site. In Ricke's view there was a distinct symbolic connection between the Sphinx, the temple, and the worship of the sun (Steiger and Steiger 2003, 2:268–69).

Sun worship was a very powerful religious and cultural phenomenon in ancient Egypt. The sun god Ra was of paramount importance in the daily worship of the Egyptian people. Indeed, Akhenaten introduced a monotheistic cult that emphasized worship of Aten, "the sun disk." Some sources even claim that Christ and the writers of the Dead Sea Scrolls at Qumran were inspired by the ideal of sun worship (Steiger and Steiger 2003, 2:270).

The Old School of Egyptology is firmly entrenched in our modern educational system and in the mainstream media. Adherents to the traditional view maintain that the monuments of Giza were built during the Old Kingdom, beginning with the Fourth Dynasty, during the reign of Khafre from 2520 to 2494 BCE. Hancock and Bauval rightfully add in their book *The Message of the Sphinx* that this time line "is the orthodox historical view and readers will find it reported in all standard Egyptological text, in all encyclopedias, in archaeological journals and in popular scientific literature. In these same sources it has also been repeatedly stated as fact that the features of the Sphinx were carved to represent Khafre himself—in other words, its face is his face" (1996, p. 19). They further note: "This confidence was particularly apparent in an article in the prestigious *National Geographic* magazine which appeared in the US in April 1991" (p. 19). The following extract from that article was written by Mark Lehner.

Zahi Hawass, Director General of the Giza Pyramids, invited me to join his excavation [around the Sphinx] in 1978. During the next four years I led a project to map the Sphinx in detail for the first time. We produced front and side views with photogrammetry, a technique using stereoscopic photography. . . . Maps were digitized to make a 3-D wireframe model; some 2.6 million surface points were plotted to put "skin" on the skeleton view. We have constructed images of the Sphinx as it may have looked thousands of years ago. To create the face, I tried matching views of other sphinxes and pharaohs to our model. With the face of Khafre, the Sphinx came alive. . . . (p. 20)

Hancock and Bauval respond to this article with these words:

A close reading shows that all that Lehner did in order to "reconstruct" the face of the Sphinx was to prepare a computerized three-dimension wireframe skeleton on which he then superimposed the face of Khafre. This is admitted in the *National Geographic,* which reproduces a photograph of the diorite statue of Khafre above the following caption: "The author used this face for the computer reconstruction of the Sphinx." (p. 20)

Hancock and Bauval conclude that these facial features on the Sphinx "are no more likely to be those of Khafre than they are to be those of a number of other Pharaohs—Thutmosis IV, for example, or Amenhotep, or Ramesses II (who is last known, as Lehner admits, to have 'extensively reworked' the monuments at around 1279 BC" (p. 20).

In *Voyages of the Pyramid Builders,* Boston University geologist Dr. Robert Schoch speculates on the age of the Great Pyramid and the Sphinx. Schoch concludes that both are considerably older than generally believed. Indeed, West invited Schoch to investigate the presence of rain erosion on the Sphinx and give his assessment. Schoch noticed that along the sides of the Sphinx there was a "rolling, undulating surface with deep vertical fissures, or tunnels which are wider at the top than the bottom" (2004). In Schoch's opinion this can only be the result of rain erosion. Of course, today there is very little precipitation along the parched and dry Sahara, certainly not enough to cause such a miraculous transformation. It therefore means that the Sphinx actually dates back to an earlier time when Egypt's climate was far different. Based on additional research by seismologist Thomas L. Dobecki on the weathered rock surrounding the Sphinx, Schoch posits a date of at least 7000 BCE. This would displace any notion of the Sphinx being carved for Khafre, because this time frame precedes his reign by millennia. These dates are Schoch's own conservative, academic view, but he admits the Sphinx could be far older, as many continue to believe.

In an interview on History Channel's *Digging for the Truth*, Zahi Hawass proclaims that Schoch is wrong (Caroli 2008). In counterpoint, in a contribution for Doug Kenyon's anthology *Forbidden History*, Schoch identifies Hawass as one of his longtime detractors, "one of his most ardent 'opponents,'" as Schoch puts it (Schoch 2004). In this same article, Schoch reviews his current findings and outlines them point by point. He prefaces this discussion by saying, "The manuscript for *Voices of the Rocks* was completed in August 1998. Since that time I have learned of two independent geological studies of the Great Sphinx and its age. These studies go a long way toward both supporting my analysis and conclusions and rebutting the inadequate counterarguments of the critics" (Kenyon 2005, p. 95).

The first study to set out to confirm or deny Schoch's findings was undertaken by another geologist, David Coxill. Dr. Coxill reviews Schoch's work in an article titled "The Riddle of the Sphinx," appearing in *Inscription: Journal of Ancient Egypt*. In it Coxill confirms Schoch's analysis concerning the weathering and rain erosion. He also makes clear that current explanations to the contrary are wrong, and more in-depth study is needed. Coxill says, "This [the data analysis he covers in the preceding portions of his paper] implies that the Sphinx is at least 5,000 years old and pre-dates Dynastic times" (Kenyon 2005, p. 96).

Another geologist, Colin Reader, also examined Schoch's findings and said the following:

In my opinion, the only mechanism that can fully explain this increase in intensity is the action of rainfall runoff discharging into the Sphinx enclosure from the higher plateau in the north and west. . . . However, large quarries worked during the reign of Khufu [as noted above, a predecessor of Khafre, the "traditional" builder of the Sphinx] located immediately up-slope, will have prevented any significant run-off reaching the Sphinx. (Kenyon 2005, pp. 95–96)

Reader concludes:

When considered in terms of the hydrology of the site, the distribution and degradation within the Sphinx enclosure indicates that the excavation of the Sphinx pre-dates Khufu's early fourth dynasty development at Giza. (Kenyon 2005, pp. 95–96)

Schoch then makes a few more remarks regarding his argument.

In my opinion, the nature and degree of weathering and erosion degradation on the Sphinx and in the Sphinx enclosure is much different from what would be expected if the Sphinx had not been carved until 2800 BCE, or even 3000 BCE. Also, mudbrick mastabas on the Saqqara plateau dated to circa 2800 BCE. . . . I do not find dating the Sphinx on the basis of "the known use of stone in ancient Egyptian architecture" convincing. I would point out that massive stonework constructions were being carried out millennia earlier than circa 2800 BCE, in other parts of the Mediterranean (for instance, at Jericho, in Palestine). Even in Egypt, it is now acknowledged that megalithic structures were being erected at Nabta (west of Abu Simbel in Upper Egypt by the fifth millennium BCE) and the predynastic "Libyan palette" (circa 3100–3000 BCE), now housed in the Cairo Museum, records fortified cities (which may well have included architectural stonework) along the western edge of the Nile delta at a very early date. (Kenyon 2005, p. 98)

Schoch writes in *Pyramid Quest,* "If the Sphinx dates to a time before that which conventional Egyptology assigns it, what of the pyramids themselves? How sure can we be that they were actually built by Khufu, Khafre, and Menkaure?" This question was answered by one of the ringmasters of alternative archaeology, Erich von Däniken. "In the Bodleian Library at Oxford," he writes, "there is a manuscript in which the Coptic author Mas-Udi asserts that the Egyptian King Surid had the great pyramid built. Oddly enough, this Surid ruled in Egypt before the Flood. And this wise King Surid ordered his priests to write down the sum total of their wisdom and conceal the writings inside the pyramid. So, according to the Coptic tradition, the pyramids were built before the Flood" (Schoch and MacNally 2005).

Indeed, the Greek historian Herodotus, according to Däniken, confirms this time line in Book II of his *Histories.* Herodotus was shown by the priests of Thebes 341 colossal statues that had stood in Thebes for 11,340 years, in line with the original chronology given earlier in this chapter. Schoch continues, "Many of the Giza samples from the 1980s study are much older than the pharaohs who supposedly commissioned the monuments. If we take the radio carbon-14 dating at face value, the charcoal-tainted mortar at the top end of the margin of error in the upper course of the Great Pyramid was put into place over 1,400 years before Khufu became pharaoh" (Schoch 2005, p. 16).

Schoch concludes, "The older samples at the top do make sense, however, if we assume that the Giza Pyramid was built, rebuilt, and rebuilt yet again in stages, there is no doubt the Giza Plateau was a holy site whose importance reached back to a time well before the Fourth Dynasty, possibly even before the sculpting of the Great Sphinx" (2005, p. 16).

CONCLUSIONS

It can be concluded from this chapter that the Sphinx—and for that matter, the pyramids—represent an order of civilization stretching back some 30,000 years to the Osirian Empire. Despite the rantings of Zahi Hawass and Mark Lehner, Robert Schoch's initial assessment of the Sphinx is, in fact, congruent with all of the available evidence. There should be no surprise that Schoch's views are met with disdain by the establishment, for are not all great thinkers met with resistence and controversy before their theories become validated?

John Anthony West's view of an ancient Egypt derived from a kind of Pythagorean-based ideal is clearly original, and he will no doubt be remembered as one of archaeology's great thinkers. It seems befitting that an ancient and far more sophisticated culture preceded Dynastic Egypt and that many of the structures of this past civilization are depicted in the country's surviving monuments. The legends and myths of the ancient Egyptian gods were based on the exploits of the Osirian kings and the histories of their many kingdoms.

There is no doubt that the Egyptian religion and way of life, its culture and architecture, has become better known in the past twenty years thanks to the efforts of individuals such as Schoch, Hancock, and West.

15

Mythical China

LAND OF THE DRAGON

*No victory of arms, or tyranny of alien finance, can
long suppress a nation so rich in resources and vitality.
The invader will lose funds or patience before the loins
of China will lose virility; within a century China will
have absorbed and civilized her conquerors, and will have
learned all the techniques of what transiently bears the
name of modern industry; roads and communications will
give her unity, economy and thrift will give her funds, and
a strong government will give her order and peace.*

WILL AND ARIEL DURANT,
THE STORY OF CIVILIZATION, BOOK 1,
OUR ORIENTAL HERITAGE, 1935

FOUNDATION MYTHS AND EARLY HISTORY

China is the source of numerous creation myths, some more obscure
than others. None of these early accounts, however, are part of an
official canon. There is the universal motif of a primeval world, with
mountains or pillars to hold up the sky. This stage of creation is quite

often portrayed as the protoworld before a Chinese hero or god-emperor begins to shape it into its more recognizable form. Another myth relates how the universe was formed from condensed vapor, billions of years in the past, an idea very similar to the scientific reality of star formation and cosmic evolution. Another myth proposes that the world began from something like a chicken's egg, which was then separated into heaven and earth. One of the least remembered yet uniquely fascinating myths shows how the goddess Woman Gua formed the entire universe and everything in it through the energies generated by her seventy transformations (Rosenberg 1994, pp. 356–58).

In *World Mythology: An Anthology of the Great Myths and Epics,* Donna Rosenberg writes in a preface to Chinese creation myths:

> Scholars believe that the Chinese myths that have come down to us are not as old and authentic as the myths from other ancient cultures. The principle reason is that in 213 BCE, the first emperor of China burned all books that were not about medicine, prophecy, or farming. During the great Han dynasty (206 BCE–220 CE), the emperors instituted the teachings of Confucius as the state religion and banned religions that involved nature worship. Many of the old myths that had been passed down orally were recorded anew during this period, but Han scholars revised them to reflect their own attitudes and the political and religious climate of their time. (1994, p. 359)

In the story of Pan-Ku we see the classic motif of the primordial egg that contained the whole universe. Inside the cosmic egg was a state of utter chaos. Prior to the existence of a heaven and earth, there was only a single formless reality. There were no stars, sun, or moon, and all was suffocated by a seemingly eternal darkness. Within this blackness and void the first being emerged: Pan-Ku, or Pangu. It was at this moment that Pan-Ku decided to make order out of chaos and establish the Earth and the known universe. His first task was to break through the world egg. After this initial act, Pan-Ku separated the sky from the Earth. The lighter part of the egg, or yang, became the heavens, while the heavier elements, the yin, coalesced to become the Earth. Pan-Ku decided that in order for life to emerge and then evolve upon the Earth, he had to keep the sky in its place, thus preventing it from crashing into our planet and extinguishing any hope at life (Rosenberg 1994, pp. 360–63).

For eighteen thousand years the process of creation continued unabated. Pan-Ku worked feverishly to keep the sky from falling upon the young planet. This process stretched Pan-Ku's arms, legs, and body, making him ever taller as he pushed with all of his might to stop the falling firmament. Finally, his efforts succeeded and the great mantle of heaven began to move farther from the Earth. He died, and when he did his body gave shape to the universe. His head composed the eastern mountains, and his feet, the western mountains (Rosenberg 1994, p. 364).

Pan-Ku's hair formed the constellations, his eyes the sun and the moon, and his breath the eternal winds of Earth. His blood became the oceans and rivers; his bones the rocks, mountains, and minerals; and the hair of his body formed all living things (Rosenberg 1994, p. 364). A surprising parallel can be found in the mythology of the Norse and Germanic peoples. In the Teutonic creation myth the three divine brothers, Odin, Vili, and Ve, ambush, kill, and dismember the frost giant Ymir. They then fashion the world from his lifeless body. Thus nature was formed.* Donald A. MacKenzie retells the story.

When Ymer was dead, the gods took counsel among themselves, and set forth to frame the world. They laid the body of the clay-giant on

---

*This common mythological theme, the slaughtering of a living being and then the creation of the world out of its lifeless body, has often been used to explain and justify the act of blood sacrifice. In societies in which this is not a common practice, its helps show the continuity and cycles of nature.

the mill, and the maids ground it. The stones were smeared with blood, and the dark flesh came out as mould. Thus was earth produced, and the gods shaped it to their desire. From Ymer's bones were made the rocks and the mountains; his teeth and jaws were broken asunder, and as they went round at their labour the giant maids flung the fragments hither and thither, and these are the pebbles and boulders. The ice-cold blood of the giant became the waters of the vast engulfing sea. (1985, pp. 5–6)

After nature had been formed in this way, another deity, Nu Kua, then made the first humans out of clay from the banks of the Yellow River, much as the god of the Judeo-Christian tradition had also done in the Genesis account. Just as Yahweh breathed life into Adam in the Garden of Eden, so did Nu Kua, or Nugua, breathe life into the ancestors of the Chinese. But unlike the Hebrew god, Nu Kua impregnated some with yang, the element that represents masculinity and aggression. Others who were to become women she impregnated with yin, an element that represents meekness and submission. Now the universe was created, and for the first time it was populated by men and women. Creation was complete (Cotterell and Storm 2004, p. 179).

THE GARDEN OF EDEN IN THE GOBI DESERT?

Since the seventeenth century people have searched for the Garden of Eden, and many times it seemed as though the myth and the quest were more important than the discovery itself. Indeed, part of the reason Columbus sought a faster route to India was to locate the Garden of Eden, which he believed was in East Asia. When he arrived in the New World, believing he was in Asia and not an entirely new location, he began looking for humanity's mythical homeland. He was convinced he had discovered it. The exotic flora, fruits, and vegetation; the abundant wildlife; the warm sun and clement breezes; and the sapphire blue waters of the Caribbean merely added to his conviction. He died believing he had found it.

Today there is a rather popular myth concerning the location of the Garden of Eden, one that also answers some persistent questions concerning the lineages of the Old Testament. The legend explains that before 3145 BCE, the Tarim Basin, now an empty, desert region in western China, was not parched and dry but rather sustained a freshwater inland sea. This legend also proposes that the Gobi Desert was in fact a rich, fertile land on the shores of the immense body of water. Resting on the southern edge of the sea were the Kun Lun mountains (Childress 1987).

According to the explorer and publisher David Hatcher Childress, "The Pamir Plateau on the western side of the lake is said by some biblical historians to have been the original garden of Eden" (Childress 1987). In Genesis 4:10 we read, "A lake also sprang up in Eden to supply the Garden with waters from which it divided and became four rivers." These four rivers were the Pison, the Gihon, the Hiddekel, and the Euphrates. Because the last river was named "Euphrates," biblical historians and archaeologists have often searched for the mythic garden primarily in the Middle East. The identity of the true Euphrates was the river Syr Daria in central Asia. Its original name was the Jaxartes River, and it flows into the Aral Sea. The other two rivers, the Pison and the Hiddekel were proposed to be, respectively, the Indus River and the Tarim River. Finally, the "River Gihon" has also been identified. According to the native peoples of the region, the Oxus River was often called the Dgihun or Gihon (Childress 1987).

Childress is also quick to point out that the central Asia of our own time was quite different six millennia ago. The southern steppes of Siberia were part of an inland sea, as were the Caspian and Aral steppes. Mammoth and saber-toothed cats roamed northern Siberia. "Interestingly," Childress adds, "Heberman and Capt believe the early

Hebrews originally migrated from the Pamir Plateau to Ur in Sumeria around 3100 BCE. Later the biblical progenitor Abraham migrated with his wife Sarah and their clan into the Arabian Peninsula" (1987).

CHINA AND THE STORY OF ATLANTIS

In China ancient myths tell of lost islands and extraordinary lands far across the sea, which were ruled by divine emperors. These other "worlds" were described as paradise on Earth, where death and disease did not exist, and a visitor could learn the secrets of eternal life. The names of these other worlds were Pheng-Lai, Fang-Chang, and Ying-Chou. There was also the long-remembered land of Rutas, or Mu. In China people recalled that the land of Tien-Mu was a mountainous realm on the other side of the Pacific Ocean. Frank Joseph further clarifies that while most of the motherland was low, near sea level, at least some of its territory in the western archipelagos was mountainous. In *Chou-li*, an ancient Chinese tome of rites, Rutas-Mu is identified as Chien-Mu. In this land time and space were irrelevant. Various other titles were attributed to the motherland in ancient China. Among these was Peng Sha, a land where magic and wizardry were common place. It became dominated by sorcerers who achieved levitation. According to Frank Joseph, "Peng Sha was ruled by Mu Kung, king of the gods, who dwelled in a golden palace beside the Lake of Gems" (2006, pp. 119–23).

China's first historical emperor, Chih-huang-ti (crowned in 221 BCE), was not content with his Chinese empire. He successfully modernized the country and consolidated his power. He now controlled everything, including the life and death of his subjects. However, he desperately sought the aforementioned mystical lands and wanted to unlock their secrets. His ancestors had sought these lands for generations, perhaps as long as modern humans have longed to find the ruins of Atlantis.

Chih-huang-ti assembled a fleet ("most likely sailing rafts") and commissioned Hsu Fu to captain the voyage (Joseph 2006, p. 120). Hsu Fu set out with the fleet, and when they returned, he claimed that three islands had indeed been discovered, but the seafarers had been interrupted from their endeavors when they were thrown off course by strong winds. During this course of events, Hsu Fu beheld a brass-colored guardian who was also a dragon. Hsu Fu claimed that the dragon told him to return with a larger fleet and more provisions. If Hsu Fu did this, the dragon would give him the drug of immortality for his emperor, Chih-huang-ti. In Frank Joseph's account the emperor "set three thousand young men and girls at Hsu Fu's disposal, gave him (ample supplies of) the seeds of five grains, and artisans of every sort, after which (his fleet again) set sail. Hsu Fu (must have) found some calm and fertile plain, with broad forests and rich marshes, where he made himself king—at any rate, he never came back to China" (pp. 120–24).

CHINA IN THE NEOLITHIC PERIOD (6000–2200 BCE)

For centuries Chinese historians have traced the origins of their culture back to the Shang Dynasty. Although based on an actual early Chinese civilization, it also existed as a time of myth and legend between 1700 and 1100 BCE. But now, with the unearthing of a whole new series of Neolithic discoveries that date from 6000 to 2200 BCE, Chinese archaeologists suggest that the extent of the Chinese New Stone Age territory was far more immense than previously thought.

In 1935 archaeologists uncovered the first evidence of the Hongshan culture, dating to between 4000 and 3000 BCE. Some of the buildings included murals and artifacts, which were both religious and secular in nature. This ancient realm was bound by the eastern Mongolian Plateau. It covered all of the present-day Liaoning Province in northeastern China. This find sparked renewed interest in archaeology and resulted in a series of theories and speculations concerning "the nature of Neolithic worship" (Dien 1999).

There is no doubt that these discoveries are helping Chinese archaeologists develop a deeper understanding of China's distant past. Why is archaeology so important to the People's Republic? As Cambridge University scholar Victor Purcell points out, the mandate of the People's Republic of China is to build a new society and purge the country of the last vestiges of feudalism. Allocating so much money to dig up the remnants of that past culture is strange indeed.

However, it serves a number of crucial purposes. "Archaeology fosters a pride in the past and a sense of self-identification, while demonstrating the indigenous name of Chinese culture. It provides grounds for celebrating what is said to be the genius of the common people, the anonymous creators of the artifacts they uncover. The discoveries, finally, serve to validate Marxist doctrines of historical development" (Ogden 2006, p. 96). This Marxian idea describes a general shift from early matrilineal communal clans to patrilineal property-owning families, and from this point onward we see a progression from slavery and feudalism all the way through to capitalism, ending in revolution and a socialist rebirth of society. Indeed, for the first time in China's history as a modern nation, the Chinese as a people are learning about the overall reality of their Neolithic heritage (p. 96).

The Chinese press authorities have recently announced the discovery of a prehistoric city in China's Southwest Sichuan Province. It dates to about 2300 BCE and is one of the oldest archaeological sites of the type found in the country. This discovery provides strong evidence in favor of theories that suggest that the upper reaches of the Yangtze River and the Chengdu Plain were one of the major centers of early Chinese civilization. The ancient citadel of Yandian stretches seven hundred meters from north to south and five hundred meters from east to west, ABC Online reports. Chen Jian, one of the chief archaeologists in charge of the Chengdu City excavation and the relics' preservation team, told ABC Online that it is "next to a river at an elevation of three meters above the river bank" (Chouinard 2003, p. 94).

In Jian's view this proved that the early city planners of China were mindful of floods. ABC Online reports, "Archaeologists unearthed a number of pieces of inscribed pottery, polished stone axes, chisels and spears at the site. They also found chips of human skulls on the city wall but were unable to explain how they got there" (Chouinard 2003, p. 94). Perhaps they were displaying the skulls of prisoners or human sacrifices as the Aztec and Maya had.

THE FEATHERED SERPENT

Graham Hancock recently stated that one of the prevailing myths of ancient cultures, especially in the Americas, is the depiction of a plumed serpent, or feathered snake. In many cultures this eerie image is often interpreted as being that of a dragon. In the New World this creature was associated with the birth of civilization, and it often took on a Caucasoid human form. In other parts of the world it takes on various other identities. Hancock believes that this iconic symbol is the key to the identity of this lost civilization in China (Chouinard 2003, p. 101) in that archaeologists working in Inner Mongolia recently discovered two Neolithic stone sculptures with this motif, which date back five thousand years.

The first sculpture has the frightening visage of a snake. It is green and 4.2 centimeters long. It shows characteristics of other animals as well, prompting many Chinese scientists to speculate that it is a dragon, which is an ancient Chinese symbol and folk figure. Chinese dragons do not have the violent and ominous connotation that so many European dragons have. The Chinese view them as possessing divine power and as one of the creators of Earth. This echoes the idea of a plumed serpent being the benefactor of the Americas. Two possibilities could account for this. First, the Chinese visited the New World and brought the myth of the dragon with them. Second, an even older civilization planted the image in both cultures at some time in the distant past (Chouinard 2003, p. 112).

The second sculpture is of a human face, 8.3 centimeters high, and is made of a red stone. Its meaning is ambiguous, and thus it sheds no light on the other idol. It is also somewhat grotesque in its proportions. It has huge eyes, arched eyebrows, a thin mouth, and a triangular nose. Given a hole on its right forehead, apparently this object was hung up, perhaps as an effigy in a religious ceremony. The difference in appearance of this image as contrasted with that of a modern Chinese man or woman of today could be due to an artistic interpretation or a representation of an earlier racial form that no longer exists (Chouinard 2003, p. 113).

The idea that China and pre-Columbian America share striking similarities is not new to readers of such magazines as *Ancient American* and *Atlantis Rising*. Leonard Nimoy's TV show *In Search Of. . .* stressed the connection during the late 1970s. In fact, it has almost become a cliché of modern diffusionism, and there is a stupendous amount of evidence that supports such claims. I will not attempt to prove or disprove them here. In my own analysis I came to the conclusion that the New World, far from being an isolated island, was the crossroads of world civilization and the central core of a global society that only now is emerging gradually from the darkness of our distant past.

CONCLUSIONS

The Chinese culture is the oldest culture on this planet. China itself has endured as a society and empire for more than six thousand years. Sarah Palin called the United States the last great hope for humankind; however, I disagree. I think there is much we can learn from the older civilizations of mankind, and, in China's case, I think it is time to learn from their ancient history, understand what made them successful as a nation then and now, and apply what we have learned to our current Western culture.

16

Investigating
the Eastern Atlantis

We knew the world would not be the same. A few people laughed, a few people cried, most people were silent. I remembered the line from the Hindu scripture, the Bhagavad-Gita. Vishnu is trying to persuade the Prince that he should do his duty and to impress him takes on his multi-armed form and says, "Now I am become Death, the destroyer of worlds." I suppose we all thought that, one way or another.

J. ROBERT OPPENHEIMER,
QUOTED FROM THE BHAGAVAD-GITA, JULY 16, 1945

The Bhagavad-Gita is the most systematic statement of spiritual evolution of endowing value to mankind. It is one of the most clear and comprehensive summaries of perennial philosophy ever revealed; hence its enduring value is subject not only to India but to all of humanity.

ALDOUS HUXLEY,
INTRODUCTION TO THE BHAGAVAD-GITA, 1944

THE DISCOVERY OF A SECRET MAP

In 1907 the Hungarian/British archaeologist Sir Aurel Stein was exploring western China near the town of Tun-huang, not far from one of the sites of the famed Silk Road. On his trek across this mountainous region he came upon a place called the "Cave of a Thousand Buddhas." Here he stumbled upon a miraculous archaeological find, an ancient sanctuary consisting of several hundred caves and grottos carved into sandstone cliffs. Concealed in the monumental structure was an ancient library with old manuscripts dating back, according to the resident monks, tens of thousands of years. There were books written in Sanskrit, Tibetan, Runic, Turkic, and Central Asian Brahmi—even Chinese (Childress 1987).

In *Lost Cities of China, Central Asia and India,* David Hatcher Childress notes that some of these writings were in an unknown language. It is possible that these ancient manuscripts were from the Rama Empire or one of the lost cities of the Gobi. Tucked away in one of these marvelous tomes were fragments of a map, and drawn on the center of the disintegrating parchment was an image. Stein had never seen anything like it before. It depicted a mysterious lost continent in the Pacific Ocean! This forgotten homeland, the monks told him, was destroyed almost a million years ago. James Churchward would later give this land the name of Mu (Childress 1987).

The lost continent of Mu, according to Churchward, was an Atlantis-size landmass in the Pacific Ocean with a population of millions. It was enveloped by the tempestuous South Seas more than twenty thousand years ago. This chronology roughly corresponds to the date given for the destruction of Atlantis. The demise of Mu, or Lemuria, and its western counterpart, Atlantis, may have been precipitated by the same global catastrophe.

Today all that remains of the once vast continent of Mu are its mountains, the peaks of which are still visible today. These include the Pacific islands of Hawaii, Fiji, and Tahiti, among others (Schoch 2004, p. 239).

In 1931 the American Rosicrucian Wishar Cerve put forth his own Lemurian ideas in *Lost Continent of the Pacific*. In his version the Lemurians possessed a rather small, round protrusion on their upper foreheads. This extra organ was linked to their telepathic capabilities and psychic gifts. This allowed them to view realities in the fourth dimension. Lemuria obviously no longer exists, and, to explain this fact, Cerve suggested earthquakes as the main catalyst for the submergence of the western half of the continent. After this catastrophe other segments of the continent broke off, forming Java, Sumatra, Australia, New Zealand, and parts of California (Steiger and Steiger 2003, 2:247–48).

Rumors of a lost continent in the Pacific or Indian Ocean begain circulating in occult circles in 1864. A French archaeologist named Charles-Etienne Brasseur became very interested in ancient Mayan hieroglyphs and was fascinated by the fact that by the time the Spanish arrived in the 1500s, the ruins were empty and silent, with no clue as to where their original inhabitants had gone or why. After his initial encounters with Mayan architecture and writing, Brasseur traveled to Spain to examine Mayan artifacts that had been taken back by Spanish conquerors in the 1500s and then nearly forgotten. Among the relics he found a guide to deciphering the Mayan code (Steiger and Steiger 2003, 2:247).

In one of the manuscripts, Brasseur found information describing a great continent in the Pacific, another variation of the Mu story, from which the Maya and other American civilizations descended. It described the common lineage of these people. In addition to the peoples of Oceania and the Pacific, the inhabitants of East Asia and India can also trace their heritage back to Lemuria, or Mu, the world's oldest culture (Steiger and Steiger 2003, 2:247).

Later archaeologists and linguists attempted to use Brasseur's guide to decipher the Mayan script anew and to learn more about the mysterious lost continent Brasseur claimed to have discovered. However, no further decoding was made by using his guide, the glyphs remained an enigma for another century, and there was no further evidence of Brasseur's lost world (Steiger and Steiger 2003, 2:247).

CHURCHWARD, THE NAGAS, AND THE INDUS-SARASVATI CIVILIZATION

Perhaps one of the most well-known names associated with Mu is Colonel James Churchward, a British officer stationed in India more than a century ago who we have mentioned previously in the pages of this book. As we know, he claimed to have acquired sacred clay tablets from a Hindu priest, who magically imbued him with the ability to decipher and read the ancient script engraved upon them. Churchward asserted that this ancient script was the product of the Naacals, an ancient white race that, according to the *Ramayana,* entered India some seventy thousand to thirty thousand years ago. This would coincide with Churchward's estimation for the destruction of Lemuria, or Mu. The Naacals left the "land of their birth in the east," which was the motherland, or classic Mu, as Churchward called it. (The Naacals are also known as the Nagas.) The *Ramayana* also identified Mu as the Empire of the Sun, responsible for bringing Bronze Age technology to China long before archaeologists have theorized (Steiger and Steiger 2003, 2:247).

Recently, side-to-side sonar has revealed the pattern of a series of sunken structures in the Gulf of Cambay off the southwest coast of India. Dredging has revealed potshards, stone and metal implements, weapons, and religious idols and other artifacts. These items were ultimately dated to 9500 BCE, old enough to be the historical Atlantis and coinciding with the idea that Vedic culture originated with a previously unidentified civilization.

The possibility of a lost Indian civilization, one that predates the Indus Valley culture, calls into question our currently accepted, existing chronology. The location and antiquity of this site suggest that this unnamed South Asian culture preceded the well-known Sumerian and Egyptian civilizations. French archaeologist Jean-François Jarrige says, "Everything ever written about civilization before five years ago is wrong" (Hancock and Faiia 2002, p. 117).

THE LOST CIVILIZATION BEFORE AND AFTER RAMA

Traditional theories hold that the Indus Valley Civilization employed a system of city-states that flourished in South Asia—from Baluchistan in the west to the Ghaggar-Hakra River in the east—some four thousand to six thousand years ago. However, new evidence suggests that the archaic roots of the Indus Valley Civilization go back not thousands of years, but tens of thousands of years. At the dawn of the twentieth century virtually nothing was known about this "cradle of human civilization," whose monuments had been dismantled to build fortifications and Buddhist stupas.

Childress notes that before the 1920s European scholars generally believed that Indian and Hindu culture bore little intrinsic value and was the possible product of Alexander the Great's expedition to the Indian subcontinent in 327 BCE. The discovery of the two main Indus cities of Harappa and Mohenjo-Daro changed those sentiments forever. This was but a prelude to unearthing many additional cities built with the same gridlike design. Among them were Kot Diji, Kalibanga, and Lothal, the port of Gujarat. Lothal was discovered forty-five years ago, and experts believe there are many more sites to be excavated. The discovery of the Indus Valley Civilization forced archaeologists to reconsider past misconceptions and push back the origins of Indian civilization to an earlier time.

In *Lost Cities of China, Central Asia and India,* David Hatcher Childress recalls:

As I walked through the dusty, deserted city streets of Harappa, a city [that] once contained possibly forty thousand people. I thought of its origins. Archaeologists really have no idea who its builders were, but attempts to date the ruins, which they ascribe to the "Indus Valley Civilization," an admittedly pre-Aryan culture, have come up with something like 2500 BCE and maybe older. According to ancient Indian epics and esoteric doctrine, Harappa and Mohenjo-Daro were two of the Seven Rishi Cities of the Rama Empire. (1987, p. 259)

All of northern India and Pakistan were once part of Krishna's powerful kingdom, with his northern capital of Dwarka as the primary focal point. The city of Mathura, another major city of Krishna's empire, is perhaps the oldest city in India. Its origin can be dated to at least 1800 BCE, but many sources suggest that this is only a conservative estimate and that it may be much older. Mathura was probably one of the Seven Rishi Cities of the Rama Empire. However, unlike the other cities, now abandoned and devastated, much of Mathura remains intact.

Not far from this location is yet another Rama site, the city of Ayodhya, Rama's former capital. Childress points out that *Ramayana* says, "Rama ruled the earth one age of the world ago. An age in Hindu Yuga is generally said to be 6,000 years, and the poet-philosopher Valmiki was generally thought to have written the Ramayana about 2,000 BCE, therefore would be at least 8,000 years old. Dr. Kunwarial Jam Vyas of India believes that the ancient Rama Empire dates back 31,000 BCE" (1987).

Childress identified three main high civilizations at the time of the Rama Empire. First, of course, Rama, then Atlantis, and finally the Osirian Civilization, which, according to esoteric doctrine, existed in the Mediterranean basin and North Africa. The Osirian Civilization was destroyed when the Mediterranean, formerly a dry plain, began to fill up with water. Childress says there are more than 250 known sunken cities in the Mediterranean. "The sinking of Atlantis," Childress writes, "has been dated at 8,500 BCE by Plato, and the civilization existed for thousands of years before that" (1987).

Childress then describes what was going on during this violent period before the final Catacylsmic Age. "Ancient Indian epics describe a war between the Rama and Atlantis, in which Atlantis attempted to invade the Rama Empire, which stretched from the Indus Valley across northern India. The *Mahabharata* epics speak of the war and of the weapons used: great fireballs that could destroy a whole city. Kapilla's Glance, which could burn fifty thousand men to ashes in seconds, and flying spears that could ruin whole "cities full of forts" (1987).

The original inhabitants of the Rama Empire were settlers from "the Motherland to the east" through Burma and across into India (Childress 1987). This new empire, ruled by a group of priest-kings known as the Nagas (mentioned previously), began to extend all over northern India and brought under its yoke the cities of Harappa, Mohenjo-Daro, and Kot Diji, now in Pakistan, and Lothal, Kalibanga, Mathura, as well as other key cities such as Benares and Pataliputra (1987).

The Rama Empire was marked by many prosperous metropolises and many capitals that in Hindu texts were known as the Seven Rishi Cities, a name derived from the Sanskrit word meaning "master" or "great teacher." (*Rishi* is a Sanskrit word meaning "master" or "great teacher.") Childress describes the Rama Empire's continued confrontations with Atlantis, a situation applicable to the Cold War, with Atlantis representing the Soviet Union; the Osirian Empire, China; and the Rama Empire, the West (1987).

ALIENS IN ANCIENT INDIA?

The Vedic writings of India provide scholars with a window to a forgotten world. Many of the ancient Hindu texts speak not only of a lost Indian Atlantis but also of a strange, alien presence in the universe of which the Hindus and the Harappans before them were very much aware. Why not use an extraterrestrial rather than terrestrial explanation for the origins of the Indus Valley Civilization? In his monumental work *Chariots of the Gods,* Erich von Däniken proposes, among other things, that ancient aliens had a role in building and ruling ancient India.

Von Däniken references ancient Hindu texts that describe what appear to be nuclear-powered spacecraft flying over the Earth and engaging in aerial battles with other alien ships. These spacecraft are a hallmark of the ancient astronaut theories. With the advance of science in the nineteenth century and the growing popularity of such authors as Mary Shelley, Jules Verne, and H. G. Wells, the possibility of human-driven flight became prevalent in Western culture. This gave scholars the ability to revisit and reevaluate many old myths and legends, reinterpreting them through a modern or futuristic prism. N. Dutt, for example, describes this so-called Vimana in an 1891 English translation of the *Ramayana*. The story unfolds as follows: "At Rama's behest the magnificent chariot rose up to a mountain of cloud with a tremendous din" (Von Däniken 1968). Von Däniken comments: "We cannot help but notice that not only is a flying object mentioned again but also that the chronicler talks of a tremendous din" (1968). This description is truly incredible when comparing these descriptions with those of our own aircraft and spacecraft.

Von Däniken also points out that "we shall not be very surprised when we learn in the *Ramayana* that Vimana, i.e., flying machines, navigated at great heights with the aid of quicksilver and a great propulsive wind. The Vimanas could cover vast distances and could travel forward, upward and downward. Enviably, maneuverable space vehicles!" (1968).

Von Däniken champions the omnipresent reality of these extraterrestrial visitors throughout his book and mentions one passage in particular from the *Mahabharata*: "Bhima flew with his Vimana on an enormous ray which was as brilliant as the sun and made a noise like the thunder of a storm" (1968). In yet another instance he states:

> In the Samsaptakabadha a distinction is made between chariots that fly and those that cannot fly. The first book of the *Mahabharata* reveals intimate history of the unmarried Kunti, who not only received a visit from the sun god but also had a son by him, a son who is supposed to have been as radiant as the sun itself. As Kunti was afraid—even in those days—of falling into disgrace, she laid the child in a little basket and put it in a river. Adhirata, a worthy man of the Suta caste, fished basket and child out of the water, and brought up the infant. (1968)

According to Von Däniken this statement ties the discoveries made at the Harappan sites and the idea that there was indeed a civilization that predated Mesopotamia, Egypt, and the New World. He noted the unusual similarities between this tale and the story of Moses. He also draws parallels with Gilgamesh and Arjuna, the hero of the *Mahabharata,* since both myths speak of the cross-fertilization of humans with the gods. This epoch could have been more than just the age of Atlantis; it could have been the time in which we were visited by the gods and were taught the secrets of civilization and science (1968).

As Zecharia Sitchin has pointed out in his concept of the planet Niburu, the evolutionary changes we recognize through anthropology and archaeology came not all at once but rather in successive waves over a long period of time. According to him these cycles occurred when the race that seeded humankind felt that we needed more technology, more science, and more advancement, and they gave it to us. Such visions of godlike entities raising humans from our infancy and into evolutionary adulthood may contain a kernel of truth. Most likely, however, the gods were symbols representing our own existence and the memory of some protocivilization.

THE TRUE "CRADLE OF CIVILIZATION"

Graham Hancock firmly believes that eleven thousand years ago a sophisticated and highly evolved civilization existed in a location that was inundated by the massive floodwaters following the glacial melt-down of the last ice age. This civilization spanned several hundred kilo-meters along what is now the Arabian Sea. Vedic scripture describes a massive flood and tells how Manu and the Seven Sages sought refuge in the Himalayas. It is clear that because the Himalayas are the tallest peaks on the planet it would be unlikely that a flood could have over-swept them entirely. Graham Hancock hypothesizes that

> the Indus-Sarasvati civilization, the development of which archaeol-ogists have already traced back 9,000 years, has an earlier episode of hidden prehistory. It was founded by the survivors of a lost Indian coastal civilization destroyed by the great floods at the end of the Ice Age. Such floods occurred many times between 15,000 and 7,000 years ago, but a particularly bad episode is attested in high salinity levels in the Arabian Sea and the Bay of Bengal between 12,000 and 10,000 years ago. . . . The survivors who established the early villages practiced a "proto-Vedic" religion that they had brought with them from their inundated homeland and probably spoke an early form of Sanskrit.
>
> There were secular rulers but the real leadership of the new com-munities remained vested down the generations in the brotherhood of sages whose forefathers had escaped the deluge—the lineage of Vedic masters whose task it was to preserve and transmit a precious body of antediluvian knowledge. (Hancock and Faiia 2002, p. 113)

In the Near East, Egyptian scribes told of a forgotten epoch in the history of humanity. It was an age when the world was ruled by the gods. This era was succeeded by an age governed by powerful overseers, the companions of Horus. But it is only in the East, on the Indian subcontinent, that we catch a glimmer of the true "cradle of civilization." In India the Rama Empire reigned, according to myth, some fifty thousand years ago. In *Forbidden History*, David Lewis writes, "The world is full of mysteries. And given its mystical traditions, no place in the world remains more mysterious than India, a country and culture said to be rooted in primordial timelessness" (Kenyon 2005, p. 35).

In the Indian worldview history is divided into four great epochs or "world ages." These lasted for enormous lengths of time. These epochs are defined as the Krita Yuga, the Treta Yuga, the Dvapara Yuga, and the Kali Yuga. Each era represents a transforming cycle of birth, growth, realization, death, and then rebirth, as the process begins anew. The Krita Yuga is depicted as a golden age. The Treta Yuga saw the start of a decline in virtue. In the Dvapara Yuga there is an increase in lying and quarrelling, and truth is less regarded. Finally, there is the Kali Yuga, our own age, when humanity is wicked, destroys his fellow humans, and lives in total iniquity and dishonor.

As Graham Hancock points out, "In the West time is an arrow—we are born, we live, we die. But in India we die only to be reborn" (Hancock and Faiia 2002). Essentially, this Eastern religious belief goes beyond individual rebirth and encapsulates the notion of world history and civilization, the cosmic cycles to which both humans and the gods are a part.

CONCLUSIONS

If we conclude that China is by far the most ancient of the Old World civilizations of the historic period, then without question India's existence stretches far back into the pre-Cataclysmic world. The people of India will tell you that their civilization goes back tens of thousands of years to a forgotten prehistory ruled by Vimana and fantastic weapons of war. India's presence on the world stage has never diminished, even during the regretful colonial period in which the British Empire brutally suppressed and controlled the whole subcontinent for economic gain.

India remains a nation of contradictions—a nation built on peace but often eclipsed by war. It produced Ghandi, one of the greatest men of all time, and has produced its own nuclear warheads, which now threaten Pakistan. Despite its modernity, ancient India still calls to us with its sacred songs of spiritualism and mysticism, which can never be lost. It is this author's supposition that some day the people of India may rule the world.

17

Lemuria

THE LOST LEGACY

The statues were polysemic symbols utilized within a multi-dimensional social context, and were central to the functioning of a cult which centered upon ancestor worship, fertility and rites of passage.

J. ANNE VAN TILBURG AND GEORGIA LEE,
"SYMBOLIC STRATIGRAPHY ROCK ART AND
MEGALITHIC STATUES OF EASTER ISLAND," 1987

The native peoples of India, Sri Lanka, and the islands of the Adaman Sea off Malaysia believe that a landmass once existed in the Indian Ocean. Graham Hancock maintains that

India's coastlines were more extensive at the end of the last Ice Age than they are today and the shape of the subcontinent was strikingly different. There was a land-bridge connecting mainland India with Sri Lanka. . . . A lost continent called Sundaland, consisting of Malaysia, Indonesia, and the Philippines and what is now the waters surrounding them, stretched as far north as Japan, and included the islands off East Asia's coast. (2009)

Related notions come from the father of uniformitarianism and the theory of evolution by natural selection, Charles Darwin. The incredible similarities of the fauna in Madagascar, India, and South Africa prompted Darwin and others to speculate that a submerged landmass in the Indian Ocean once connected these separate continents and islands. English zoologist Philip L. Schlater coined the term *Lemuria,* named after the lemur, one of the common life-forms that seems to biologically connect the three regions (Steiger and Steiger 2003, 2:247–48).

The ice age continent known as Sula was another landmass that may have inspired the tales of Mu and Lemuria. It was formed by the merging of Australia, Tasmania, and New Guinea in 20,000 BCE, exposing the ocean floor and creating an enlarged landmass. In *The Lost Continent of Mu,* Churchward writes, "The American written records, which are many, tell us the land of Mu lay to the west of America. The Asiatic records all say Mu, the Motherland, lay in the east of Asia— 'towards the rising sun'" (1926).

Others have speculated that perhaps the sunken landmasses could be a logical explanation for the absence of early human fossils. This idea was proved wrong, however, by the now abundant collection of prehuman and hominid fossils that give a clear picture of our evolutionary heritage. As David Lewis reminds us in *India: 30,000 BCE,* even for those who reject the work done by alternative scholarship, it is generally believed that massive Lemurian-like continents such as Gondwanaland and Pangea "must have existed" 180 million to 200 million years ago.

UNDERSTANDING THE REALITY
OF ANCIENT LEMURIA

The lost continent of Lemuria, or Mu, perhaps was home to the world's oldest culture. David Hatcher Childress suggests that it was the original lost civilization, which began no later than seventy-eight thousand years ago and lasted as a living culture for some fifty-eight thousand years. Childress suggests that a radical pole shift followed by a crustal slip destroyed the entire continent. This is an alternative explanation to earthquakes or floods, for which no evidence currently exists (1987).

The name *Lemuria* has often been intentionally or accidentally linked with Atlantis. As Atlantologist Kenneth Caroli points out, the Theosophists gave the name Atlantis to various places cited in Hindu lore such as Atala, Sveta Dwipa, Sancha Dwipa, Ruta, and Daitya. They used Plato's literal date for the demise of the final island but multiplied it by one hundred for the golden age as well as mingled that with certain enormous Hindu cycles like the Maha Yugas and Manvantaras. They also used channeled information.

Madame Blavatsky used the term *Atlantean* more chronologically than geographically. She acknowledged submerged lands in the Atlantic, some of which might once have been inhabited. But her Ruta lay in the North Pacific and Daitya in the Indian Ocean. She was heavily influenced on the subject by the French writer Louis Jacolliot. His 1879 book on lost continents predates that by Donnelly, the founder of Atlantology and author of *Atlantis: The Antediluvian World,* by three years. Jacolliot's book, however, was never translated into English. After Jacolliot's book came out and he wrote an article about Lemuria in 1880, Blavatsky gave Lemuria a more fantastic dating and occult significance. These ideas later spilled over into the works of proto-Nazis such as Guido von List and Georg Lanz von Liebenfelds, an ex-Cistercian monk who anticipated the ideals of National Socialism.

After Blavatsky's death in 1891, Colonel Scott-Elliot picked up the mantle. He standardized the Theosophical Lemuria and Atlantis in his books in the 1890s to 1920s. But he garbled or altered much of what Blavatsky wrote and shifted Atlantis to the Atlantic where Ruta and Daitya represented the middle phase in the geological evolution of the lost continent. He also explicated the various root races and sub-races. Blavatsky had mentioned these ideas here and there but had not given a coherent account of them.

The history of Lemuria, or Mu, was supposedly contained in a number of sacred tablets that had allegedly originated on the continent of Mu. Colonel James Churchward claimed to have translated these tablets while in India in the late 1860s and 1870s, but his books were not published until the 1920s and 1930s. Unfortunately, no one else has ever seen these tablets, and he does not name the temple where he saw them much less the supposed priestly mentor he worked with on them. In fact, while he did live in Ceylon for a while in the 1870s, it has not been proved he was ever in India proper, and his military rank might not be authentic either. Churchward says he was stationed near the temple due to famine relief, and there *was* a massive famine in India at about that time. While he accepted the idea of an Atlantic Atlantis, he made it younger than and subordinate to his Mu in the Pacific. He had met Mayanist LePlongeon in New York and favored LePlongeon's "translations" of the sacred Mu tablets over the earlier ones by Charles-Etienne Brasseur (Caroli 2011, personal communication).

According to Frank Joseph, the origins of the holy tablets revealed to Churchward can be traced directly to "the Holy Brothers"—the Naacals—a priestly brotherhood sent from the Motherland to the colonies to teach the sacred writings, religion, and the sciences. These Naacals formed in each countries' colleges for the teaching of the priestcraft, its religion and science. The priesthoods that were formed in these colleges in turn taught the people. Thus, the tablets were part of the attempt to instill the secrets of Mu within the Hindu temple structure by the storing of the tablets" (2006, p. 136).

These sacred writings were accompanied by illustrations depicting symbols and other images that displayed the chief iconography of the motherland. In addition to the mysterious script itself, the tablets served as a key for a number of sacred symbols and code. Churchward expressed in his writings that the symbol "T," or *tau*, was one of the most sacred symbols to the ancient inhabitants of Mu. Churchward also believed that it was one of the few unique inventions that Muvians were able to spread to other cultures across the postcataclysmic world (Joseph 2006, p. 138).

Joseph also states that the reported lost civilization—mentioned by many cultures across the Pacific—was an "undersea homeland, the Polynesian rendition of the lost Motherland—Haiviki—deriving from the root *ha* for 'breath, hence, life,' in Hawaiian." He continues:

> Remarkably, a crucial connection is made here between the Pacific Realm of Mu and Middle America. A *T* is also the most selectively portrayed of all Mayan hieroglyphs, featured oversized and set apart among stonework at the more important ceremonial centers, such as Palenque in Guatemala and Copan in Honduras. It is pronounced "ik" and signifies breath, actually the breath of life. In this, the T glyph is remarkably close to Churchward's characterization of the symbol as it appeared in Mu, where it stood for the beginning of human life. That such diverse elements from the Marquesas, Hawaii, Mesoamerica, and Lemuria so perfectly complement each other testifies to the validity of their connection. (2006, pp. 138–39)

Lemuria in Traditional Sources

While no legends name the lost civilization of Lemuria directly, it is not an entirely modern invention. The lost Pacific continent as presented by Churchward and Blavatsky was inspired by a preexisting wealth of oral and written traditions. These sources speak to us of lost lands inhabited by sophisticated civilizations destroyed by catastrophic floods and other disasters. The native Easter Islanders spoke of a previous motherland known as Hiva, which was destroyed by a great flood. The Samoans also had a Lemurian myth concerning a place they called Bolutu. There the laws of the universe could be bent, which allowed individuals to walk through solid objects. As regards New Zealand, the inhabitants there knew of a long-sunken island called Hawaiki, which was peopled by an ancient

Caucasoid race. It was said to be a mountainous land far across the ocean, hinting to some association either with Easter Island or the New World.

The Ica Stones of Central America have what appear to be engraved maps of Lemuria on them. Furthermore, the Native American tribe known as the Hopi speaks of the great destruction of a faraway land across the ocean. Some people escaped from this disaster into the center of the Earth, while others escaped in boats, moving from island to island until reaching the homeland of the Hopi in the American Southwest.

In Oceania there is a Mu tradition going back one thousand years or even longer. When the Polynesians first colonized the Pacific, they discovered that the islands were inhabited long before they arrived. Frank Joseph points out that these indigenous people were divided into two distinct races. The first race was the Menehune, who were dwarfish and primitive. The second race was known as the Mu, "a numerous and powerful race from whom the present race of Hawaiians is descended" (2006, p. 167).

Because of the similarity of the name of the people to the lost continent, researchers have suggested that the two are linked. Both races, however, were closely related and even participated in a symbiotic relationship. The Menehune-Mu were remembered as shipbuilders and skilled mariners. They hailed from an ancient, near-forgotten homeland in the east named Helani. Kumulipo, the Hawaiian story of creation, described it as a "ravaged land lying in the deep, blue sea" (Joseph 2006, p. 167). Thus, the very waters that made it an empire destroyed this once prosperous island or continent. Frank Joseph further explains, "The catastrophe depicted in the chant of creation was at the center of the Hawaiian religious ceremonies, wherein the gods were prevailed upon with offerings at their shrines to prevent the recurrence of that Deluge that had drowned Helani" (2006, p. 167).

The Menehune, according to Stephen Oppenheimer, author of the book *Eden in the East,* were "a dark-skinned hunter-gatherer" society (Joseph 2006, p. 167). In contrast, the Mu were described as belonging to another genetic population entirely. They were described as "pale-skinned coastal fishermen invading from the sea" (p. 167). At the time of its destruction, according to the Naacals, Mu was home to sixty-five million inhabitants, most of them Caucasian, or archaic Caucasian (p. 150).

EASTER ISLAND: HOME TO ARCHAIC CAUCASOIDS

Some 4,000 kilometers southeast of Nan Madol with its canals and temples constructed of basalt logs and 3,782 kilometers from the wind-swept coast of Chile lies the enigma known as Easter Island. It is a place that has fascinated and perplexed visitors for more than two centuries. It is also one of the most geographically remote and culturally isolated places on Earth. This island's native inhabitants are of Polynesian ancestry, but centuries of isolation have allowed them to evolve separately into their own distinct race. Although there is evidence of contact between the islanders and foreign visitors, and varying types of ethnicity are exhibited within the native population, including Caucasian traits, their culture remains distinct.

Today this tiny speck of land in the middle of the South Pacific known as Easter Island is also called Rapa Nui in the native tongue, meaning "Land of the Bird Men."

The official records attribute the island's discovery to the Dutch vessel *Afrikaansche Galei,* under the command of Admiral Jacob Roggeveen. The discovery occurred on Easter Day, April 5, 1722, at 5 p.m. In commemoration of its day of discovery, Roggeveen dubbed this tiny speck of land Easter Island. The following day, after visiting the island, he attempted to describe its material culture.

Concerning the religion of these people, of this we could get no full knowledge because of the shortness of our stay, we merely observed that they set fires before some particularly high erected stone images. . . . These stone images at first caused us to be struck with astonishment, because we could not comprehend how it was possible that these people, who are devoid of heavy thick timber for making any machines, as well as strong ropes, nevertheless had been able to erect such images, which were fully thirty feet high and thick in proportion. (Flenley and Bahn 2003)

After coming ashore the Dutch sailors, together with their officers, spent a considerable amount of time touring the twenty-five-mile island, marveling at its monuments and writing down firsthand accounts of the gigantic figures and the peculiar writings used by the natives. They also had the opportunity to have sexual intercourse with a number of the native females, as tribute from the chieftains and the gods. The Dutch explorers reported that the islanders wore very little clothing and inhabited reed huts (Flenley and Bahn 2003).

One of the most obvious realities of the people present on the island was their mixed racial heritage. A large number of the native people appeared Caucasian, while others, fewer in number, had brown or red skin. There were many intermediary groups. The long-eared group was tall and fair-skinned with ruddy cheeks. They often had brown, red, or blond hair (Joseph 2006, p. 170).

This is but one of many out-of-place Caucasian groups that western European explorers would encounter as they ventured to the remote corners of the Earth.

First contact ended in gunfire and the killing of about a hundred or so Rapa Nui islanders. David Hatcher Childress explains that Roggeveen ordered his sailors to fire into a crowd of natives who were engaged in thievery and touching and toying with the ship and its technology, mainly out of curiosity (Childress 1988, p. 118).

Some scholars, such as Robert Langdon, claim that Roggeveen and his ship of Dutch explorers were not the first Europeans to set foot on the island. Langdon believes that sailors from a lost Spanish caravel, the *San*

Lesmes, which disappeared in 1526 and apparently ran aground in Tahiti, survived and intermarried with the Polynesian women. Langdon suggests that somehow these offspring made it to Easter Island and entered the gene pool, leaving behind traces of Basque genetic markers. This would seem incredibly complex and fanciful if not for the fact that Easter Islander DNA contains a genetic structure common within the Basque population of western Europe (Flenley and Bahn 2003). Visitors to the island have handed down useful accounts of the people, culture, language, and monuments of Rapa Nui's two thousand inhabitants. According to the French explorer Comte de La Perouse, during his visit in 1786 both the statues and people possessed a distinct European quality, which was unmistakable. Other visits were less constructive. For example, the Spanish expedition launched from Peru early in 1770 came back without any commentary or report whatsoever, and only managed to print a ship's log over a century afterward in 1908 (Flenley and Bahn 2003).

In 1774 the era of exploration and scientific investigation began in earnest. This date marked the visitation of Captain James Cook to Easter Island. He was considered the Great White God by the Pacific Islanders, as were Pizarro and Cortez by the American peoples. On June 13, 1772, Cook departed Plymouth together with two ships, the *Resolution* and the *Adventure.* It was Cook's intention to sail around the world, navigate the southernmost waters, cross the Antarctic Circle, and confirm the existence of the legendary southern continent of Antarctica. They reached Easter Island on March 1, 1774. The British remained on Easter Island for only four days, as they rested and replenished what supplies they could amid the barren landscape. In his log, Cook recorded, "We could hardly conceive how these islanders, wholly unacquainted with any mechanical power, could raise such stupendous figures, and afterwards place the large cylindrical stones upon their heads" (Joseph 2006, p. 54).

Clearly the bizarre nature of the island and its inhabitants baffled its European visitors. Katherine Routledge, an early-twentieth-century investigator of Easter Island, put it like this: "In Easter Island, the past is the present. It is impossible to escape from it. The inhabitants of today are less real than the men who have gone. The shadows of the departed builders still possess the land" (Joseph 2006, p. 54). The magnificent and colossal stone figures are 11 to 22 meters high and weigh as much as 45 tons. Erich von Däniken called them "robots which seem to be waiting solely to be set in motion again" (Von Däniken 1968, p. 111). Originally, the statues also wore hats, and they traditionally faced inland and not out toward the ever crashing waves.

Dr. Jared Diamond, author of the national bestseller *Guns, Germs, and Steel,* indicates what could have been the evolutionary outcome of the Polynesian monument-building efforts and explains why even more grand structures didn't arise before their devastating encounter with Europeans. He writes:

The largest products of Polynesia were the immense stone structures of a few islands—the famous giant statues of Easter Island, the tombs of Tongan chiefs, the ceremonial platforms of the Marquesas, and the temple of Hawaii and the Societies. This monumental Polynesian architecture was obviously evolving in the same direction as the pyramids of Egypt, Mesopotamia, Mexico and Peru. Naturally, Polynesia's structures are not on the scale of those pyramids, but that merely reflects the fact that Egyptian pharaohs could draw conscript labor from a much larger human population than could the chief of any Polynesian island. Even so, the Easter Islanders managed to erect 24-ton stone statues—no mean feat for an island with only seven thousand people, who had no power source other than their own muscles. (1998)

Diamond was not privy to the more alternative explanations of the monuments' origins, but his general conclusions from a mainstream standpoint are basically correct. It is also clear that had these societies been left to develop on their own, untouched by outside influence, they would have undoubtedly continued to evolve along the lines of the Maya, Aztec, and Old World cultures such as the Egyptians and Mesopotamians.

In *The Polynesians: Prehistory of an Island People,* Peter Bellwood says, "Easter Island society of the eighteenth century was not described as highly stratified, and was dominated by independent warring tribes who probably spent much of their time fighting over scarce resource" (1978, p. 113). Bellwood also mentions the valiant expeditions of the maverick Norwegian explorer Thor Heyerdahl.

Bellwood divided Easter Island prehistory into three main periods. During the Early Period, 400–1100 CE, the earliest of the stone platforms were erected, and during the Middle Period, 1100–1680 CE, these platforms were equipped with the gigantic stone statues that define the island and their inhabitants to this day. During the Late Period, 1680–1868 CE, there was a drastic and devastating decline in the island's environment and the health and stability of its population, prompting the discontinuation of their religion and its traditions. The period concluded with the arrival and domination of Christian missionaries, who further undermined the native beliefs and traditions (1978, pp. 114–15).

THE ANCIENT RACES OF NORTH AMERICA

Genetic evidence indicates that a significant population of archaic Caucasoid peoples inhabited North America for at least thirty thousand years. This colonization was not achieved by crossing Beringia from Siberia into Alaska. As Frank Joseph points out, these ancient Caucasians had a maritime capability that could take them across great expanses of open ocean to new lands and conquests. The findings at Kennewick and Windover Pond confirm these notions.

In July 2001 additional evidence was found suggesting that

Caucasians lived in North America more than fifteen thousand years ago. These findings were brought to light by an international team of researchers headed by the University of Michigan's Museum of Anthropology. They maintain that Native Americans living south of the Canada–U.S. border have a shared genetic and cultural heritage with an early Caucasian population.

There is also strong evidence indicating a genetic link between the indigenous population of the Pacific Northwest and the Caucasian race that inhabited Japan some fifteen thousand years ago. According to Joseph and *Forbes Magazine* editor Priscilla Meyer, "Already evidence is stacking up to support the ancient scenario of an enormous migration of peoples by boat across the South Pacific as early as 5,000 years ago. Nothing in the official story would allow for such a migration, but the genetic evidence is clear and unmistakable" (Joseph 2006 pp. 149–50).

It is clear that Native Americans of the Pacific Northwest, particularly along the coast, more closely resemble the Japanese than other American Indians. This may be due to a shared genetic heritage. The original inhabitants of Japan, first the Jomon and then their surviving remnants, the Ainu, belonged to an archaic form of Caucasians, who recalled a past event during which the sea engulfed the land and most of humankind was consumed by the roiling waters. Some humans survived by escaping to the safety of the mountains.

EASTER ISLAND'S RONGORONGO SCRIPT

The world has seen the discovery of many mysterious texts that history has left undecoded. The mystical script Rongorongo of Easter Island is the perfect example. Aside from the massive carved figures, their grotesquely enlarged eyes forever looking inland, Easter Islanders developed a unique form of hieroglyphic writing that remains their most enduring relic of native origin, inscribed on, among other things, wooden tablets, paddles, and ceremonial staffs. These strange inscriptions are carved into the sides of the stone images as well. Examples of Rongorongo are preserved on hundreds of wooden boards, now scattered in museum storerooms and on display throughout the world.

As Andrew Robinson notes in *Lost Languages: The Enigma of the World's Undeciphered Scripts*, other written languages also remain uncracked. These include Meriotic, Etruscan, Linear A, and proto-Elamite. In these, the writing systems are intelligible, while their representative languages are not. But with Rongorongo we have a script that does entirely the opposite. Its language is simply a form of Polynesian, but the script itself remains baffling (2002, p. 219). Robinson comments in the German weekly *Der Spiegel*.

> They were cannibals who could write, they celebrated sexual rituals and put up huge statues made of tuff—the inhabitants of Easter Island established a bizarre advanced civilization. Now an attempt has been made at deciphering their mysterious writing all on their own, known as Rongorongo—the only such case in all of Oceania. While missionaries learnt the language of Easter Islanders fairly quickly, all attempts at deciphering their writing have so far failed.

Thor Heyerdahl has long been considered the bane of the established archaeological community. Heyerdahl links Rongorongo to a number of South American scripts. Among them is a system of picture writing belonging to the Cuna Indians of Panama and northwest Columbia. This archaic script, used for recording songs, was painted on wooden tablets, not dissimilar to the process seen on Easter Island (Flenley and Bahn 2008). Heyerdahl also "pointed to primitive writing systems found among the early historic (post-Columbian) Aymara and Quechua tribes of the Titicaca area. Like the Indus Valley script already discussed, the Rongorongo inscriptions are highly sophisticated and show enormous provision for a people so supposedly primitive." The Easter Islanders' cryptic form of writing comprises a system of parallel lines, small, fingernail-size engravings "incised on battle staffs, drift-wood tablets, small wooden Birdmen, and other statuettes, pectorals, ceremonial paddles, even human skulls" (Flenley and Bahn 2003).

Heyerdahl went on to compare Rongorongo with another indecipherable script, that of the Indus Valley Civilization, which dates to 4000 BCE, with cities such as Mohenjo-daro and Harappa. These cities, as previously stated, were considered to be two of the many cities of the Rama Empire. The Indus Valley Civilization predates the emergence of the Easter Island culture by 3,500 years. Childress writes, "That Rongo-Rongo writing is similar, if not identical, to this ancient, indecipherable language, and for this reason is extraordinary" (1988, p. 288). The Mohenjo-Daro script has now been linked to ancient Dravidian, the truly native inhabitants of India prior to the Indo-Aryan invasions of the third millennium BCE. Dravidian is the language of the pre-Aryan population that had its own script, a written language often identified with the Indus Valley but was based further south on the Indian subcontinent. Vestiges of this once dominant linguistic tradition still exist in southern India in parts of Tamil speech (p. 288).

CONCLUSIONS

It is clear that given the mysteries of the Rongorongo script, the colossal statues of Easter Island, the mythical accounts of lost civilizations and forgotten races, the enigma of Lemuria will not be settled in the immediate future. The mysteries will continue on, and brave and determined minds will ask the necessary questions, and never be afraid of controversy.

The Prometheus Factor

If archaeology has taught us anything, it is that we are a powerful and resilient species. An undying passion has shaped the evolution of civilization since the first stirrings of human life to global domination. There is much to overcome, but there is still much to become. In Hamlet we read, "What a piece of work is man! How noble in reason! How infinite in faculty! In form and moving, how express and admirable! In action how like an angel! In apprehension how like a god!"

In Genesis 3:22 we read, "The Lord God said, 'Behold, that man has become one of us to know good and evil. Now, lest he put forth his hand and take also of the tree of life and eat and live for ever [let us] send him forth from the Garden of Eden.'" God, the higher authority, was fearful of humankind and the trouble it could make for him. God knew that humanity could rise forth and steal the throne of creation for himself. It was humans, not God, who had the adaptive qualities, the resilience, and the compulsion to move forward regardless of the situation. Humans have a nature that makes them unique and imbues them with greatness.

As the late Carl Sagan put it in the Pulitzer Prize–winning *Dragons of Eden,* two ultimate consequences of the taste of the fruit and the expulsion from paradise were the pain of childbirth and the advent of mortality. Sagan also points out, "One of the earliest consequences of the anticipatory skills that come with the evolution of the prefrontal lobes must have been the awareness of death" (1997, pp. 92–93). Thus, the stealing of the forbidden fruit symbolizes an evolutionary occurrence. He continues:

> The fall from Eden seems to be an appropriate metaphor for some of the major biological events in recent human evolution. This may account for its popularity. It is not so remarkable as to require us to believe in a kind of biological memory of ancient historical events, but it does seem to me close enough to risk at least raising the question. The only repository of such a biological memory is, of course, our genetic code. (pp. 95–96)

This can help explain something Carl Sagan might have been reluctant to suggest himself. This genetic memory is partly defective. For some inexplicable reason, the full memory of our past civilization, or golden age, has been lost, but we still retain our common symbols, myths, and instincts as our final link to that forgotten time. For instance, the presence of evolution can be seen in one Native American tradition at least: the Ottawa Indians, who inhabited the Great Lakes region of Michigan, Wisconsin, and Canada, believed in Michabon, "the great hare," who created human beings from animals. This idea of lower forms of life being transformed into the more advanced human beings sounds, at first, remarkably similar to the concept of evolution. Perhaps the myth is some form of racial memory.

But the loss of paradise is not something to be mourned. It had to happen that way. Eating the forbidden fruit allowed humans to break away from servitude under God and to gain cultural and evolutionary independence from nature and from God. There is no doubt that paradise awaits us again, but this time in our image, on our terms.

As Eugen Weber, professor of history and philosophy at UCLA, suggested, the patron saint of the human race is the Greek god

Prometheus. It was he that lit the spark of human culture and civilization when he stole fire from the gods, giving it to man, and from this essential act the world and cosmos changed forever. Mankind united for the very first time under the banner of evolution and cultural success. This is, of course, mythology but its premise is a fundamental insight in understanding the heroic human past.

And upon this note I leave you a quote from Wordsworth.

> *I see what was, and is, and will abide;*
> *Still glides the Stream, and shall forever glide;*
> *The Form remains, the Function never dies;*
> *While we, the brave, the mighty, and the wise,*
> *We Men, who in our morn of youth defied*
> *The elements, must vanish; — be it so!*
> *Enough, if something from our hands have power*
> *To live, and act, and serve the future hour;*
> *And if, as toward the silent tomb we go,*
> *Through love, through hope, and faith's transcendent*
> *   dower,*
> *We feel that we are greater than we know.*

Bibliography

Alexander, Robert E. 2005. "The Velikovsky affair: case history of iactrogenic behavior in physical science." In *The Iatrogenic Handbook: A Critical Look at Research and Practice in the Helping Professions,* edited by Robert F. Morgan. Fresno, Calif.: Morgan Foundation Publishers.

Andrews, Peter. 1974. *Christmas in Germany.* Chicago: World Book Encyclopedia.

Anthony, David W. 2007. *The Horse, the Wheel, and Language: How Bronze-Age Riders from the Eurasian Steppes Shaped the Modern World.* Princeton, N.J.: Princeton University Press.

Archaeology TV. 2003. "The Windover Mystery." VHS. Director: Toni Van Pelt. Clearwater, Fla.: Public Access, Pat Chouinard Productions.

Auel, Jean M. 1980. *The Clan of the Cave Bear.* New York: Crown.

Bailey III, John H. 2003. "The Secrets of Burrow's Cave." *Ancient American,* 23–29. (Article dated April 2003; accessed October 9, 2010.)

Bansal, Sunita Pant, trans. 2009. *Mahabharata.* New Delhi: Om Books International.

Barber, Elizabeth Wayland. 1999. *The Mummies of Ürümchi.* London: Pan Books.

Baumer, Christoph. 2000. *Southern Silk Road: In the Footsteps of Sir Aurel Stein and Sven Hedin.* Bangkok: White Orchid Books.

BBC News. 1999. "Neanderthals 'mated with modern humans.'" http://news .bbc.co.uk/2/hi/science/nature/323657.stm. (Article dated April 21, 1999; accessed September 9, 2010.)

———. 2000. "Ancient temple found under Lake Titicaca." http://news.bbc .co.uk/2/hi/americas/892616.stm. (Article dated August 23, 2000; accessed March 20, 2011.)

BBC. 2002. *The Lost Pyramids of Caral* (television special). Transcript available at www.bbc.co.uk/science/horizon/2001/caraltrans.shtml. (Show dated January 31, 2002; accessed March 18, 2002.)

Beckwith, Christopher I. 2009. *Empires of the Silk Road: A History of Central Eurasia from the Bronze Age to the Present*. Princeton, N.J.: Princeton University Press.

Bellwood, Peter S. 1978. *The Polynesians: Prehistory of an Island People*. London: Thames and Hudson.

Bergman, Folke. 1935. "Newly discovered graves in the Lop-nor Desert." *Geografiska Annaler*. 17:44–61.

Bierlein, J. F. 1994. *Parallel Myths*. New York: Ballantine Books.

Blavatsky, H. P., E. Preston, and Christmas Humphreys. 1966. *Secret Doctrine*. London U.K.: Theosophical Pub. House.

Bower, Bruce. 2010. "Ancient Mongolian tomb holds skeleton of western man." *Discovery News*. http://news.discovery.com/archaeology/mongolian-tomb-western-skeleton.html. (Article dated February 3, 2010; accessed October 10, 2010.)

———. 2010. "Go north, young hominid, and brave the chilly winter weather: stone tools in New England hint at early arrival of human relatives." *Science News*. Please go to http://findarticles.com and search on "Go north, young hominid." (Article dated July 31, 2010; accessed February 29, 2012.)

Bruce, F. F. 1947. *The Hittites and the Old Testament*. London: Tyndale Press.

Burrows, Russell, and Fred Rydholm. 1991. *The Mystery Cave of Many Faces: First in a Series on the Saga of Burrow's Cave*. Marquette, Mich.: Superior Heartland.

Campbell, Joseph. 1949. *The Hero with a Thousand Faces*. Princeton, N.J.: Princeton University Press.

———. 1959. *The Masks of God: Primitive Mythology*. New York: Viking Press.

Campbell, Joseph, and M. J. Abadie. 1974. *The Mythic Image*. Princeton, N.J.: Princeton University Press.

Caroli, Kenneth. 2008. Personal communication.

———. 2011. Personal communication.

Ceram, C. W. 1956. *The Secret of the Hittites; The Discovery of an Ancient Empire*. New York: Knopf.

Childress, David Hatcher. 1986. *Lost Cities and Ancient Mysteries of South America*. Stelle, Ill.: Adventures Unlimited Press.

———. 1987. *Lost Cities of China, Central Asia, and India*. Stelle, Ill.: Adventures Unlimited Press.

———. 1988. *Lost Cities of Ancient Lemuria and the Pacific*. Stelle, Ill.: Adventures Unlimited Press.

———. 1992. *Lost Cities of North and Central America*. Stelle, Ill.: Adventures Unlimited Press.

———. 1995 *Extraterrestrial Archaeology: Incredible Proof We Are Not Alone.* Kempton, Ill.: Adventures Unlimited Press, 1995.

———. 1996. *Lost Cities of Atlantis, Ancient Europe and the Mediterranean.* Stelle, Ill.: Adventures Unlimited Press.

———. 1999. *Extraterrestrial Archaeology.* Kempton, Ill.: Adventures Unlimited Press.

China Daily. 2003. "Archaeologists rewrite history." Also available at www .china.org.cn/english/2003/Jun/66806.htm. (Article dated June 12, 2003; accessed September 12, 2010.)

Chouinard, Patrick. 2003. *A Legacy of Gods and Empires: The Quest for Ancient Mysteries.* First edition. Clearwater, Fla.: Shadow Books.

———. 2008. *A Legacy of Gods and Empires: The Quest for Ancient Mysteries.* Second edition. Clearwater, Fla.: Vanir House Publishing.

Churchward, James. 1926. *The Lost Continent of Mu: The Motherland of Man.* New York: W. E. Rudge.

Clotworthy, Robert. 2011. *Ancient Aliens. Season Two.* A & E Television Networks.

Collins, Andrew. 2002. *Gods of Eden: Egypt's Lost Legacy and the Genesis of Civilization.* Rochester, Vt.: Bear and Co.

———. 2010. *The Cygnus Mystery: Unlocking the Ancient Secret of Life's Origins in the Cosmos.* n.l.: Watkins Pub., Ltd.

Coppens, Philip. 2009a. "Göbekli Tepe, the world's oldest temple." *Nexus Magazine* 16, no. 4. Also available at www.philipcoppens.com/gobekli. html. (Article dated June–July 2009 accessed March 2011.)

———. 2009b. "White masters in the deserts of China?" *New Dawn Magazine* 10, no. 12. Also available at www.philipcoppens.com/tarim_mummies. html. (Article dated January–February 2009 accessed March 2011.)

———. 2010. "The wanderers of the fourth world." www.philipcoppens.com/ hopi.html. (Accessed March 4, 2011.)

Cotterell, Arthur, and Rachel Storm. 2004. *The Encyclopedia of World Mythology.* London: Lorenz.

Cremo, Michael A. 2003. *Human Devolution: A Vedic Alternative to Darwin's Theory.* Los Angeles: Bhaktivedanta Book Pub.

Cremo, Michael A., and Richard L. Thompson. 1993. *Forbidden Archaeology: The Hidden History of the Human Race.* San Diego: Bhaktivedanta Institute.

Cunliffe, Barry W. 1997. *The Ancient Celts.* Oxford: Oxford University Press.

Curry, A. 2008. "Göbekli Tepe: The World's First Temple?" *Smithsonian* 39, no. 8: 54–60. (Article dated November 2008.)

Darnton, John. *Neanderthal.* 1996. New York: Random House.

Davidson, Hilda Roderick Ellis. 1990. *Gods and Myths of Northern Europe.* Harmondsworth, UK: Penguin Books.

———. 1993. *The Lost Beliefs of Northern Europe.* London: Routledge.

———. 2007. *Myths and Symbols in Pagan Europe: Early Scandinavian and Celtic Religions.* Princeton, N.J.: Recording for the Blind and Dyslexic.

Davis-Kimball, Jeannine, with Mona Behan. 2002. *Warrior Women: An Archaeologist's Search for History's Hidden Heroines.* New York: Warner Books.

De Santillana, Giorgio, and Hertha von Dechend. 1969. *Hamlet's Mill: An Essay on Myth and the Frame of Time.* Boston: Gambit.

Deavin, Mark. 1997. "The Aryans: culture bearers to China." *National Vanguard Magazine.* (Article dated March–April 1997.)

Diamond, Jared M. 1998. *Guns, Germs, and Steel: The Fates of Human Societies.* New York: W. W. Norton and Co.

———. 2005. *Collapse: How Societies Choose to Fail or Succeed.* New York: Viking.

Dien, A. E. 1999. "Images of dynasty: China's golden age of archaeology." *Archaeology* 52 (2): 58–69.

Discovery Programme. 2002. *Discovery Programme Reports 6.* Dublin: Royal Irish Academy/Discovery Programme.

Donnelly, Ignatius. 1971. *Atlantis: The Antediluvian World.* New York: Harper. First published in 1882.

Eliade, Mircea. 1978. *A History of Religious Ideas.* Chicago: University of Chicago Press.

Eliade, Mircea, and Charles J. Adams, eds. 1987. *The Encyclopedia of Religion.* New York: Macmillan.

Eliade, Mircea, and Willard R. Trask. 1984. *From Gautama Buddha to the Triumph of Christianity.* Chicago: University of Chicago Press.

Ellis, Peter Berresford. 1999. *The Chronicles of the Celts: New Tellings of Their Myths and Legends.* New York: Carroll and Graf.

Flenley, John, and Paul G. Bahn. 2003. *The Enigmas of Easter Island: Island on the Edge.* Oxford: Oxford University Press.

Freud, Sigmud. 1939. *Moses and Monotheism.* New York: Vintage Books.

Gallegos, F. 2009. "Beyond History: Alternative Historical Perspectives." San Jose State University: Research Paper.

Gaster, Theodor Herzl. 1952. *The Oldest Stories in the World*. New York: Viking.

———. 1969. *Myth, Legend and Custom in the Old Testament: A Comparative Study with Chapters from Sir James G. Frazer's Folklore in the Old Testament* (vol. 1). New York: HarperCollins, 1969

Gimbutas, Marija. 1982. *The Goddesses and Gods of Old Europe, 6500–3500 BC, Myths and Cult Images*. Berkeley: University of California.

Gimbutas, Marija, and Colin Renfrew. 1990. "Review of archaeology and language: the puzzle of Indo-European origins." *American Historical Review* 95, no. 1 (1990): 125–27.

Gnostic Liberation Front. 2003. www.gnosticliberationfront.com/story_of_hans_hoerbiger.htm.

Godwin, Joscelyn. 1993. *Arktos: The Polar Myth in Science, Symbolism, and Nazi Survival*. Grand Rapids, Mich.: Phanes Press.

Gomez, Gina. 2010. "Humans and Neanderthals interbred, suggest scientists." *Thaindian News*. www.thaindian.com/newsportal/sci-tech/humans-and-neanderthals-interbred-suggest-scientists_100360119.html. (Article dated May 7, 2010; accessed February 29, 2012.)

Goodrick-Clarke, Nicholas. 1992. *The Occult Roots of Nazism: Secret Aryan Cults and Their Influence on Nazi Ideology: The Ariosophists of Austria and Germany, 1890–1935*. New York: New York University Press.

Gore, Rick. 2002. "National Geographic research and exploration new find." *National Geographic*. (Article dated August 2002.)

Gowlett, J. A. J. 2006. "The early settlement of Northern Europe: fire history in the context of climate change and the social brain." *C. R. Palevol* 5 (2006): 299–310.

Grant, Madison. 1936. *The Passing of the Great Race; or, the Racial Basis of European History*. Fourth revised edition. New York: Charles Scribner's Sons. First published in 1916.

Gribbin, John R., and Mary Gribbin. 1996. *Fire on Earth: Doomsday, Dinosaurs, and Humankind*. New York: St. Martin's Press.

Grimm, Jacob. 1882. *Teutonic Mythology*. London: George Bell and Sons.

Guerber, H. A. 1895. *Myths of the Northern Lands*. New York: American Book Company.

Gugliotta, Guy. 2001. "Peru May Harbor Americas' First City." *The Washington Post*. www.latinamericanstudies.org/peru/caral.htm. (Article dated April 27, 2001; accessed April 29, 2001.)

Gurney, Oliver Robert. 1952. *The Hittites*. Harmondsworth, UK: Penguin.

Haddon, Alfred C. 1911. *The Wanderings of Peoples.* Cambridge, UK: University Press.

Hancock, Graham. 1992. *The Sign and the Seal: The Quest for the Lost Ark of the Covenant.* New York: Crown.

———. 1995. *Fingerprints of the Gods.* New York: Crown.

———. 1998. *The Mars Mystery: The Secret Connection between Earth and the Red Planet.* New York: Crown.

———. 2002. *Underworld: The Mysterious Origins of Civilization.* New York: Crown.

Hancock, Graham, and Robert Bauval. 1996. *The Message of the Sphinx: A Quest for the Hidden Legacy of Mankind.* New York: Three Rivers Press.

Hancock, Graham, and Santha Faiia. 2002. *Underworld: The Mysterious Origins of Civilization.* New York: Crown.

Hapgood, Charles H. 1979. *Maps of the Ancient Sea Kings.* New York: Dutton.

Heine-Geldern, Robert. 1964. "Comments on Gimbutas the Indo-Europeans: archaeological problems." *American Anthropologist* 66, no. 4: 889–93. (Article dated August 1964.)

Hemphill, Brian E., and J. P. Mallory. "Horse-mounted invaders from the Russo-Kazakh steppe or agricultural colonists from western central Asia? A craniometric investigation of the Bronze Age settlement of Xinjiang." *American Journal of Physical Anthropology* 125: 199ff.

Hoagland, Richard C. 1987. *The Monuments of Mars: A City on the Edge of Forever.* Berkeley: North Atlantic Books.

Hoerbiger, Hans, and Philip Fauth. 1925. *Glazial-Kosmogonie: eine neue Entwicklungsgeschichte des Weltalls und des Sonnensystems auf Grund der Erkenntnis des Widerstreites eines kosmischen Neptunismus mit einem ebenso universellen Plutonismus.* Leipzig: R. Voigtlanders.

Johanson, Donald C., et al. 1994. *In Search of Human Origins.* Boston: WGBH Educational Foundation.

Jones, Prudence, and Nigel Pennick. 1997. *A History of Pagan Europe.* London: Routledge.

Joseph, Frank. 2003. *The Lost Treasure of King Juba: The Evidence of Africans in America before Columbus.* Rochester, Vt.: Bear and Co.

———. 2004 (a). *Survivors of Atlantis: Their Impact on the World.* Rochester, Vt.: Bear and Co.

———. 2004 (b). *The Destruction of Atlantis: Compelling Evidence of the Sudden Fall of the Legendary Civilization.* Rochester, Vt.: Bear and Co.

———. 2005. "Japan's Underwater Ruins." In *Forbidden History: Prehistoric Technologies, Extraterrestrial Intervention, and the Suppressed Origins of Civilization,* edited by J. Douglas Kenyon. Rochester Vt.: Bear and Company.

———. 2006. *The Lost Civilization of Lemuria: The Rise and Fall of the World's Oldest Culture.* Rochester, Vt.: Bear and Co.

———. 2010. *Atlantis and 2012: The Science of the Lost Civilization and the Prophecies of the Maya.* Rochester, Vt.: Bear and Co.

Joseph, Frank, and Zecharia Sitchin. 2006. *Discovering the Mysteries of Ancient America: Lost History and Legends, Unearthed and Explored.* Franklin Lakes, N.J.: New Page Books.

Jowett, Benjamin, and John Harward, trans. 1952. *The Dialogues of Plato.* Great Books of the Western World 7. Chicago: W. Benton. Originally published in 1871.

Jueneman, Frederic B. 1987. "Atlantis unfounded." *Research and Development* 25. (Article dated February 1987.)

Kaiser, Jr., Walter C., and Duane Garrett. 2005. *NIV Archaeological Study Bible: An Illustrated Walk through Biblical History and Culture.* Grand Rapids, Mich.: Zondervan.

Katsonopoulou, D. 2002. "Helike and her territory in the light of new discoveries." In *Gli Achei e l'identita etnica degli Achei d'occidente,* edited by E. Greco, *Tekmeria* 3: 205–16.

Katsonopoulou, D. 1999. "Mycenaean Helike." In *Meletemata: Studies in Aegean Archaeology Presented to M. Wiener as He Enters his 65th Year, Aegaeum* 20: 409–13.

Kenyon, J. Douglas. 2005. *Forbidden History: Prehistoric Technologies, Extraterrestrial Intervention, and the Suppressed Origins of Civilization.* Rochester, Vt.: Bear and Co.

Kenyon, Doug, and John F. Michell. 1999. *English Sacred Sites: The Atlantis Connection.* Los Angeles: Lightworks Audio and Video.

King, David. 2005. *Finding Atlantis: A True Story of Genius, Madness, and an Extraordinary Quest for a Lost World.* New York: Harmony Books.

Knight, Christopher, and Robert Lomas. 2001. *Uriel's Machine: Uncovering the Secrets of Stonehenge, Noah's Flood, and the Dawn of Civilization.* Gloucester, Mass.: Fair Winds Press.

Lalueza-Fox, C., H. Römpler, D. Caramelli, et al. 2007. "A melanocortin 1 receptor allele suggests varying pigmentation among Neanderthals." *Science* 318:1453–55.

Larsen, Clark Spencer. "Bioarchaeology: the lives and lifestyles of past people." *Journal of Archaeological Research* 10, no. 2: 119–66. (Article dated June 2002.)

Lehner, Mark. 1997. *The Complete Pyramids*. New York: Thames and Hudson.

Levy, Joel. 2007. *The Atlas of Atlantis and Other Lost Civilizations: Discover the History and Wisdom of Atlantis, Lemuria, Mu and Other Ancient Civilizations*. London: Godsfield.

Li, Shuicheng. "A discussion of Sino-Western cultural contact and exchange in the second millennium BC based on recent archeological discoveries." *Sino-Platonic Papers* 97. (Article dated December 1999.)

Light, Nathan. 1999a. "Hidden Discourses of Race: Imagining Europeans in China." Presented at the Association for Asian Studies Conference, Boston.

———. 1999b. "Tabloid archaeology: is television trivializing science?" *Discovering Archaeology* 98–101. (Article dated March–April 1999.)

Liu, Xinru. 2001. "Migration and settlement of the Yuezhi-Kushan: interaction and interdependence of nomadic and sedentary societies." *Journal of World History* 12, no. 2: 261–92.

Mackenzie, Donald A. 1985. *German Myths and Legends*. New York: Avenel Books.

Maenchen-Helfen, Otto J. *The World of the Huns: Studies in Their History and Culture*. Berkeley: 1973.

MacManus, Seumas. 1944. *The Story of the Irish Race: A Popular History of Ireland*. New York: Devin-Adairco.

Magli, Giulio. 2009. *Mysteries and Discoveries of Archaeoastronomy: From Giza to Easter Island*. New York: Copernicus Books.

Mallory, J. P., and Victor H. Mair. 2000. *The Tarim Mummies: Ancient China and the Mystery of the Earliest Peoples from the West*. London: Thames and Hudson.

"Mars and Beyond." *Disneyland*. December 4, 1957. Television program.

May, Wayne N. *The Michigan Artifacts and the Burrows Cave*. Lecture presented in Wellsville, Utah, January 27, 2007.

Mierow, Charles Christopher, trans. 1915. *The Gothic History of Jordanes: In English with an Introduction and a Commentary*. Princeton, N.J.: Princeton University Press.

Mission to Mars. Directed by Brian De Palma. Burbank, Calif.: Touchstone Home Video, 2000.

National Space Science Data Center. 2005. "Comet Shoemaker-Levy 9 Collision with Jupiter." http://nssdc.gsfc.nasa.gov/planetary/comet.html. (Article dated February 2005; accessed August 26, 2008.)

Newman, Francis William. 1853. *A History of the Hebrew Monarchy: From the Administration of Samuel to the Babylonish Captivity.* London: John Chapman.

NOVA. 1997. "In Search of Human Origins." Television program first aired June 17, 1997.

———. 1998. "The Mysterious Mummies of China." Boston: WGBH. Television program first aired January 20, 1998. Transcript available at www.pbs.org/wgbh/nova/transcripts/2502chinamum.html.

———. 2000. "Mystery of the First Americans." Boston: WGBH. Television program first aired February 15, 2000. Transcript available at www.pbs.org/wgbh/nova/transcripts/2705first.html.

Ogden, Suzanne. 2006. *China.* Guilford, Conn.: McGraw Hill/Dushkin.

Pettyjohn, F. S. 2001. "The Caucasian 'Mummy People' of Alaska." *Ancient American* 6 (39). (Article dated June 2001.)

Ringle, William M., Tomas Gallareta Negron, and George J. Bey III. 1998. "The return of Quetzalcoatl: evidence for the spread of a world religion during the Epiclassic Period." *Ancient Mesoamerica* 9 (2).

Robinson, Andrew. 2002. *Lost Languages: The Enigma of the World's Undeciphered Scripts.* New York: McGraw-Hill.

Rolleston, Thomas. 1998. *Myths and Legends of the Celtic Race.* London: Senate. First published in 1911.

Rosenberg, Alfred. 1982. *Myth of the Twentieth Century: An Evaluation of the Spiritual-Intellectual Confrontations of Our Age.* Costa Mesa, Calif.: Noontide Press. First published in 1930.

Rosenberg, Donna. 1994. *World Mythology: An Anthology of the Great Myths and Epics.* Lincolnwood, Ill.: NTC.

Rydberg, Viktor. 2007. *Teutonic Mythology,* vol. 1. Eastbourne, U.K.: Gardners Books.

Sagan, Carl. 1980 *Cosmos.* New York: Random House

———. 1997. *The Dragons of Eden: Speculations on the Evolution of Human Intelligence.* New York: Random House.

Sayce, A. H. 1888. *The Hittites: The Story of a Forgotten Empire.* London: Religious Tract Society.

Schoch, Robert M. 1999. "La pirámide de Yonaguni: recuerdo de Mu?" *Más Allá de la Ciencia* 123:20–25.

Schoch, Robert M., and Robert Aquinas McNally. 2004. *Voyages of the Pyramid Builders: The True Origins of the Pyramids, From Lost Egypt to Ancient America.* New York: Jeremy P. Tarcher/Putnam.

———. 2005. *Pyramid Quest: Secrets of the Great Pyramid and the Dawn of Civilization.* New York: Jeremy P. Tarcher/Penguin.

Schurr, Theodore G. 2001. "Tracking genes across the globe: a review of *Genes, Peoples, and Languages,* by Luigi Luca Cavalli-Sforza." *American Scientist* 89 (1). (Article dated January–February 2001.)

Science Daily. 2006. "Researchers find evidence of the earliest writing in the New World." www.sciencedaily.com/releases/2006/09/060914154552.htm. (Article dated September 14, 2006; accessed March 28, 2011.)

———. 2008. "Earliest known Hebrew text in proto-Canaanite script discovered in area where 'David slew Goliath.'" www.sciencedaily.com/releases/2008/11/081103091035.htm. (Article dated November 3, 2008; accessed March 28, 2011.)

———. 2009. "World's oldest submerged town dates back 5,000 years." www.sciencedaily.com/releases/2009/10/091016101809.htm. (Article dated October 16, 2009; accessed March 15, 2011.)

———. 2010a. "Dig discovers ancient Britons were earliest North Europeans." www.sciencedaily.com/releases/2010/07/100707193825.htm. (Article dated July 7, 2010; accessed February 9, 2011.)

———. 2010b. "Lost civilization under Persian Gulf?" www.sciencedaily.com/releases/2010/12/101208151609.htm. (Article dated December 8, 2010; accessed March 20, 2011.)

———. 2010c. "Oldest written document ever found in Jerusalem discovered." www.sciencedaily.com/releases/2010/07/100712102816.htm. (Article dated July 12, 2010; accessed March 28, 2011.)

———. 2011a. "Atlantis found? Film highlights professor's efforts to locate fabled lost city." www.sciencedaily.com/releases/2011/03/110312135018.htm. (Article dated March 12, 2011; accessed March 27, 2011.)

———. 2011b. "First skyscraper was a monument to intimidation: how Jericho's 11,000-year-old 'cosmic' tower came into being." www.sciencedaily.com/releases/2011/02/110217125.htm. (Article dated February 17, 2011.)

Scott-Elliot, W. 1968. *The Story of Atlantis and the Lost Lemuria.* London: Theosophical Publishing House.

Scrutton, Robert. 1977. *The Other Atlantis.* St. Helier, Jersey Island: Neville Spearman.

———. 1978. *Secrets of Lost Atland.* St. Helier, Jersey Island: Spearman.

Shirer, William L. 2008. *The Rise and Fall of the Third Reich: A History of Nazi Germany.* Campbell, Calif.: Paw Prints. First published in 1960.

Shklovskii, I. S., and Carl Sagan. 1966. *Intelligent Life in the Universe.* New York: Holaenday.

Siefker, Phyllis. 1997. *Santa Claus, Last of the Wild Men: The Origins and Evolution of Saint Nicholas, Spanning 50,000 Years.* Jefferson, N.C.: McFarland.

Sitchin, Zecharia. 1976. *The 12th Planet.* New York: Stein and Day.

Smith, Michael Ernest. 1996. *The Aztecs.* Malden, Mass.: Blackwell.

Sophia Echo. 2007. "Europe's Oldest Writing Style Found in Bulgaria." www .sophiaecho.com. (Accessed November 1, 2008.)

Spanuth, Jurgen. 1980. *Atlantis of the North.* New York: Van Nostrand Reinhold.

Steiger, Brad, and Sherry Hansen Steiger. 2003. *The Gale Encyclopedia of the Unusual and Unexplained.* 3 vols. Detroit, Mich.: Thomson/Gale.

Sturluson, Snorri, and Lee Milton Hollander. 1964. *Heimskringla: History of the Kings of Norway.* Austin, Tex.: University of Texas Press. First written in approximately 1230.

Tao, Shui. "Relation between human existence and environment viewing from the distribution of prehistoric archaeological sites in the Three Gorges Reservoir region of the Yangtze River, China. *Chinese Science Bulletin,* vol. 53, supplement 1 (2008)

Thornton C. P., and T. G. Schurr. 2004. "Prehistoric 'Europeans' in Xinjiang? A case for multiple interpretations." In *The Interplay of Past Present: Papers from a Session held at the 9th Annual EAA Meeting in St. Petersburg 2003,* ed. H Bolin, pp. 85–98. Södertörn Archaeoligcal Studies, no 1, Stockholm, Sweden.

UFO TV. 2005.*Technologies of the gods the case for pre-historic high technology.* Venice, Calif.: UFO TV.

Viegas, Jennifer. 2010. "New written language of ancient Scotland discovered." DiscoveryNews. http://news.discovery.com/history/ancient-scotland-written-language.html. March 21, 2010. (Article dated March 21, 2010.)

Von Däniken, Erich von. 1968. *Chariots of the Gods? Unsolved Mysteries of the Past.* New York: Putnam.

———. 2010. *Twilight of the Gods: The Mayan Calendar and the Return of the Extraterrestrials.* Pompton Plains, N.J.: New Page Books.

Wells, H. G. 1976. *An Outline of History: Being a Plain History of Life and Mankind.* St. Clair Shores, Mich.: Scholarly Press.

Wells, H. G. 1898. *The War of the Worlds.* London: Heinemann.

———. 1920. *The Outline of History: Being a Plain History of Life and Mankind.* New York: The MacMillan Co.

West, John Anthony. 1979. *Serpent in the Sky: The High Wisdom of Ancient Egypt*. New York: Harper and Row.

Whitehouse, David. 1999. "'Earliest Writing' Found." BBC News. http://news .bbc.co.uk/2/hi/science/nature/334517.htm. (Article dated May 4, 1999; accessed July 7, 2002.)

Wikipedia. 2010. "Tarim Mummies." http://en.wikipedia.org/wiki/Tarim_ Mummies. (Accessed April 20, 2010.)

———. 2011. "Bonfire of the Vanities." http://en.wikipedia.org/wiki/Bonfire_ of_the_Vanities. (Accessed March 9, 2011.)

Wilford, John Noble. 1999. "Who Began Writing? Many Questions, Few Answers." *New York Times*. (Article dated April 6, 1999.)

Wilkins, Harold T. 1952. *Secret Cities of Old South America: Atlantis Unveiled*. New York: Library Publishers.

———. 1956. *Mysteries of Ancient South America*. New York: Citadel, 1956.

———. 1998. *Secret Cities of Old South America*. Kempton, Ill.: Adventures Unlimited Press.

Williams, Joseph J., trans. 1886. *Vendidad*. n.p.: Bombay.

Wilson, Colin. 2006. *Atlantis and the Kingdom of the Neanderthals: 100,000 Years of Lost History*. Rochester, Vt.: Bear and Co.

Winn, Shan M. M. 1981. *Pre-writing in Southeastern Europe: The Sign System of the Vinča Culture, ca. 4000 B.C.* Calgary, AB: Western Publishers.

Xie Chengzhi, Li Chunxiang, Cui Yinqui, et al. 2007. "Mitochondrial DNA analysis of ancient Sampula population in Xinjiang." *Progress in Natural Science* 17 (8): 927–33.

Yu, Taishan. 2003. *A Comprehensive History of Western Regions*. 2nd ed. Zhengzhou, China: Zhongzhou Guji Press.

Zicree, Marc Scott. 1989. *The Twilight Zone Companion*. New York: Bantam Books.

Index